What Is the
LITERAL SENSE?

What Is the
LITERAL SENSE?

Considering the Hermeneutic of John Lightfoot

JACE R. BROADHURST

☙PICKWICK *Publications* • Eugene, Oregon

WHAT IS THE LITERAL SENSE?
Considering the Hermeneutic of John Lightfoot

Copyright © 2012 Jace R. Broadhurst. All rights reserved. Except for brief quotations in critical publications or reviews, no part of this book may be reproduced in any manner without prior written permission from the publisher. Write: Permissions, Wipf and Stock Publishers, 199 W. 8th Ave., Suite 3, Eugene, OR 97401.

Pickwick Publications
An Imprint of Wipf and Stock Publishers
199 W. 8th Ave., Suite 3
Eugene, OR 97401

www.wipfandstock.com

ISBN 13: 978-1-61097-406-6

Cataloguing-in-Publication data:

Broadhurst, Jace R.

    What is the literal sense? : considering the hermeneutic of John Lightfoot / Jace R. Broadhurst, with a foreword by Carl R. Trueman.

    xiv + 226 p. ; 23 cm. Includes bibliographical references and indexes.

    ISBN 13: 978-1-61097-406-6

    1. Lightfoot, John, 1602–1675. 2. Bible—Hermeneutics. I. Trueman, Carl R. II. Title.

BS2335 B736 2012

Manufactured in the U.S.A.

For Jaclynnette,
who will only read this one page

Contents

Foreword by Carl R. Trueman / ix
Preface / xi
List of Abbreviations / xiii

1 Who Cares about Pre-critical Exegesis and John Lightfoot? / 1
2 Lightfoot's Presupposition of Dual Authorship and Its Implications for *Sensus Literalis* / 19
3 Lightfoot's Use of Logic, Reason, and the Scholastic Method / 48
4 Lightfoot's Critical and Linguistic Approach / 69
5 Lightfoot's Use of Chronology and a Historical Approach / 111
6 Lightfoot's Understanding of Community and Authority / 129
7 Lightfoot's Figurative and Christological Approach / 160
8 Summary of Findings / 196

Bibliography / 201
Author Index / 213
Subject Index / 217
Scripture Index / 222

Foreword

Theologians do theology best when they do it in dialogue with the past. For all of the technical advances in various branches of theological study, it remains the case that there are few, if any, completely new questions which theologians today have to address. As long as this is the case, the theological past will remain perennially relevant for the theological present.

In this study of the great seventeenth-century Hebraist, John Lightfoot, Jace Broadhurst offers insights into that most Protestant of questions: the doctrine of Scripture. Lightfoot was one of the greatest linguists of his generation; he was also a Protestant theologian of some note, being one of the divines at the Westminster Assembly. Convened in 1643, the Assembly was originally intended as a means by which the Church of England might be brought to a more thorough Reformation in the wake of the Laudian policies of Charles I. In fact, it was to develop into a much more far-reaching and radical body, producing among other things a Confession of Faith and two Catechisms, which have become the standard of Presbyterian faith and life around the world.

That Lightfoot was one of the Westminster divines tells us much about his churchmanship, his intellectual accomplishments, and his pastoral concerns. Yet his greatest contributions were probably not made on the floor of the Assembly but rather in his voluminous writings on Scripture. Here, he wrestled with many of the issues that still concern the church today: matters of textual criticism, scriptural perspicuity, and the nature of that most contentious of notions—the literal sense.

Historians of exegesis know that the literal sense has been a constant concern for Christian theologians since the patristic era. Anyone who spends time looking at the different exegetical approaches of, say, an Origen and a John Chrysostom will know that questions of allegory, typology, and literalism have been hardy perennials for the church.

From the twelfth century onwards in the West, these matters became increasingly pressing; finally, in the Reformation the issue of the literal sense combined with questions of perspicuity and sufficiency to become a major part of the Protestant protest against Rome and then to fuel debates within the variegated ranks of Protestantism itself.

It is in this context that this fine work by Jace Broadhurst should be understood. By focusing on one brilliant but neglected figure, Jace provides fascinating insights into the intellectual dynamics of a crucial debate as it played out in the seventeenth century; but he also does more than that. Given the significance of the Westminster Standards for later church history, he also helps us to understand why Protestant understanding of Scripture developed the way it did and thereby gives us an excellent way of understanding the background to some contemporary hermeneutical debates.

This is a significant and helpful work, not only in the growing field of studies of early modern exegesis but also in the current context of reappropriation of seventeenth-century theology in a modern context. It is a pleasure to recommend it to a wider readership.

Carl R. Trueman
Westminster Theological Seminary, PA
February 2012

Preface

It's been a while, but you don't quickly forget one of your conservative, evangelical church elders accusing you of heresy. You know it's going to be a good week when you are called out in front of more than fifty people for questioning some theological sacred cow. The leading accusation: I wasn't taking the text in its "literal sense." The problem, as I tried to explain to him and many others over the next few months, is found in the phrase "literal sense." It simply has no inherent meaning. Although the terminology might be slightly anachronistic, the debate over *sensus literalis* began long before the Bible was finished and has continued to rage to the present time. We could easily ask, "what is the literal sense of the 'literal sense?'"

This book seeks to make available a moment in the historical dialogue; a moment after medievalism and before historical criticism. The goals are simple and humble: to introduce postmodern exegetes to a man both entrenched in his era and far beyond it. John Lightfoot was a master and while most modern exegetes would disapprove of many of his interpretations (myself included), his methods have principles we dare not ignore. In order to make my argument that Lightfoot is indeed a *via media* between Judaism and Protestant Orthodoxy I have riddled the manuscript with (what some might call tedious) examples. This is intended for Puritan scholars and readers of historical exegesis. For those who received this as a gift or plan to relax on a picnic blanket for some casual reading, please feel free to skip to final paragraphs for conclusions.

There are several people worthy of my appreciation. First, I must say a word of appreciation to all my fine teachers at Reformed Theological Seminary and Westminster Theological Seminary. Each of them contributed to what is before you. A special thanks to those who fostered my love for hermeneutics and the Old Testament: Richard Pratt, Mike Glodo, Mike Beates, Bruce Waltke, Peter Enns, and Doug

Green (my second reader). I also want to thank Carl Trueman who willingly became my supervisor when Pete was unable and pushed me through to the end. Derek Cooper also had helpful advice that I incorporated throughout.

Besides my teachers, all researchers know the benefit of librarians who are out for your good. For most of the writing my librarian at Westminster was Emily Sirinides who went far beyond what was expected in getting me books and articles as well as looking the other way when I was eating a sub in the library. My appreciation also goes to Grace, Marsha, and Karla who were always very helpful and to the dissertation editor who spent so much time with this—Leslie Altena.

My family is not to be left out. My parents always encouraged me to go forward and my wife and three boys sacrificed much in the long process to get this to print. While none of them will likely read this book, just knowing they are on my side is more than enough.

Abbreviations

AUSS	*Andrews University Seminary Studies*
Autol.	*Ad Autolycum*
b. Ketub.	*Ketubbot*
b. Kid.	*Kiddushin*
b. Šabb.	*Sabbat*
b. Ta'an.	*Ta'anit*
b. Yebam.	*Yebamot*
b. Yoma	*Yoma (= Kippurim)*
BSac	*Bibliotheca Sacra*
Cels.	*Against Celsus*
CH	*Church History*
CTJ	*Calvin Theological Journal*
De Oeconom.	*De oeconomia foderum Dei cum hominibus*
Epist.	*Epistulae*
Exod. Rab.	*Exodus Rabbah*
Faust.	*Contra Faustum Manichaeum*
Haer.	*Against Heresies*
Int	*Interpretation*
JRH	*Journal of Religious History*
Leg.	*Legatio pro Christianis*
Lev. Rab	*Leviticus Rabbah*
LXX	Septuagint
m. Meg	*Megillah*
m Yad.	*Yadaim*
Moral.	*Expositio in Librum Job, sive Moralium*

MT	Masoretic Text
Obs. Sac.	*Sacrarum Observationum Libri Sex*
ODJR	*Oxford Dictionary of Jewish Religion*
PG	*Patrologia Graeca,* edited by J. P. Migne. Paris, 1857–66
PL	*Patrologia Latina,* edited by J. P. Migne. Paris, 1844–55
Pesiq. Rab. Kah.	*Pesiqta de Rab Kahana*
Philologia Sac.	*Philologia Sacra*
Praescr.	*De Praescripione haereticorum*
Princ.	*First Principles*
PRRD	Richard Muller, *Post Reformation Reformed Dogmatics: The Rise and Development of Reformed Orthodoxy, ca. 1520 to ca. 1725*
SOS Rabbah.	*Rabbah Song of Songs*
ThTo	*Theology Today*
WTJ	*Westminster Theological Journal*

1

Who Cares about Pre-Critical Exegesis and John Lightfoot?

INTRODUCTION

JOHN LIGHTFOOT'S USE OF Jewish sources as a key to understanding the Scripture has had significant impact on the Christian history of interpretation. This is widely recognized. What is not so widely recognized is the degree to which these Jewish sources, along with Lightfoot's Protestant heritage, shaped his understanding of *sensus literalis*. Like most Christian interpreters, this seventeenth-century Hebraist and Westminster Divine claimed that one could plainly understand the Bible as a witness to God and his Christ. But, to say that one can "plainly" understand the Bible is actually to say very little because the *sensus literalis*, or the plain sense, differs from interpreter to interpreter. In order to understand John Lightfoot's plain sense and so establish his general hermeneutic, we must first examine his presuppositions and then his exegetical principles.

Because of the relative lack of interest in the time of Protestant Orthodoxy, a case must first be made for the significance of this historical era. Only then will we show why more work on John Lightfoot himself is helpful. Finally, we will conclude by presenting the organizational structure for the project.

THE NEED FOR PRE-CRITICAL STUDY

Living in a post-critical world, one might question the significance of even studying pre-critical exegesis. Scholarly work in the field of Puritan hermeneutics is relatively lacking, and yet, through it, we can learn a lot that will directly contribute to modern hermeneutics.

Very Little Work Has Been Done

Every academic discipline should have a proper understanding of its intellectual heritage. While works of intellectual history saturate the field of hermeneutics, it appears that the research is relatively deficient in the area of pre-critical Puritan hermeneutics. Richard Muller, Professor of Historical Theology at Calvin Theological Seminary, is one of the few experts in this area. In *After Calvin: Studies in the Development of a Theological Tradition*, he says: "The history of biblical interpretation is, moreover, a comparatively new field: it is really only in the last twenty years that we have seen examinations of the biblical interpretation of sixteenth and seventeenth centuries that do justice, historically and contextually, to the exegesis of the era—and the study of the seventeenth century still lags behind."[1] This is not to say that there are no books on Puritans and their hermeneutical principles. In fact, the world seems well aware of the general hermeneutical principles of the Puritans. Thomas Lea's simple article, "The Hermeneutics of the Puritans," is a great example, with several generic points made and then supported by various Puritan quotations.[2] J. I. Packer and Leland Ryken have also contributed popular guides through Puritanism in their books *The Quest for Godliness*[3] and *Worldly Saints: The Puritans as They Really Were* respectively.[4] As helpful as these brief surveys are, one can hardly expect them to do justice to Puritan hermeneutics. In the last three decades, a number of more scholarly contributions have appeared,[5] but there is still a very real lacuna in

---

1. Muller, *After Calvin*, 41.

2. Lea, "The Hermeneutics of the Puritans," 271–84.

3. Packer, *The Quest for Godliness*. This is published in England as *Among God's Giants: The Puritan Vision of the Christian Life*.

4. Ryken, *Worldly Saints: The Puritans as they Really Were*. See also Miller and Johnson, *The Puritans*. Daniel Neal's *The History of the Puritans* although quite dated, is still helpful in its general assessments.

5. See Cohen's "Two Biblical Models of Conversion: An Example of Puritan Hermeneutics," 182–96; Howson, "The Puritan Hermeneutic of John Owen," 351–76; Feinberg, "Thomas Goodwin's Scriptural Hermeneutics and the Dissolution of Puritan Unity," 32–49; Davis, "Exegetical Traditions of Puritan Typology," 11–50; Gane, "Exegetical Methods of Some Puritan Preachers," 21–36; Coughenour, "The Shape and Vehicle of Puritan Hermeneutics," 23–34.

pre-critical historical exegetical studies, one that extends through most of the seventeenth century. Richard Muller bemoans the "sad state of study and indeed, of the intellectually imperialistic way in which seventeenth-century biblical interpretation has been neglected and even dismissed."[6] This neglect is due to what some perceive to be the Puritan's *a priori* thinking, which some consider untenable for today's more-sophisticated exegesis.[7]

This relative disregard of Puritan hermeneutics is disturbing in light of the brilliant exegesis of the period. Henry Ainsworth was "one of the most able and prolific of the Puritan exegetes of the seventeenth century," writing a "most learned commentary on the five books of Moses, by which he appears to have been a great master of oriental languages and of Jewish Antiquities."[8] Perhaps only Andrew Willet was greater in regard to his mastery of the Pentateuch.[9] Neither these predecessors to Lightfoot, nor many others of this time have had their methods of biblical interpretation adequately explored. In essence, the present study attempts to begin to fill the gap.

Significance of Pre-Critical Exegetical Research

It is more than the lack of adequate research in this area, however, that compels this study. The subject of Puritan hermeneutics is significant because many of the church confessions used today came out of this period. The last half of the sixteenth and the first half of the seventeenth century boast of a great number of Reformed confessional works. These include the *Gallican Confession* (1559), *Scots Confession* (1560), *Belgic Confession* (1561), *Thirty-Nine Articles of the Church of England* (1563), *Heidelberg Catechism* (1563), *Second Helvetic Confession* (1566), *Consensus Ministrii Bremensis Ecclesiae* (1595), *Confession of the Reformed churches in*

---

6. Muller, *After Calvin*, 156.

7. This despite Gadamer's generally accepted idea that the interpreting reader contributes to the process of understanding. Much can be said here regarding the belief (often expressed by Hegel) that since our present age is the most highly evolved it is also the best vantage point from which to survey past ideas. Little is said regarding the impossibility of doing anything else. See Skinner, "Meaning and Understanding in the History of Ideas," 52.

8. Neal, *The History of the Puritans; or, Protestant Nonconformists; from the Reformation in 1517 to the Revolution in 1688*, 41–42, quoted in Muller, *After Calvin*, 156.

9. Muller, *After Calvin*, 156.

4   WHAT IS THE LITERAL SENSE?

Germany (1607), *Irish Articles of Religion* (1615), *Canons of Dordt* (1619), *Declaratio thoruniensis* (1645), and perhaps the most significant ones for our purposes: the *Westminster Confession* (1647) and the *Formula Consensus Helvetica* (1675). It is not that these statements of faith made significant leaps in understanding, for they did not. Still, while none of these confessions added much to the doctrine of Scripture already accepted by the Reformers, they did include nuances and elaborations that are important today. The *Second Helvetic Confession* emphasized the sacramental connection of the preached word to the written word, an idea that continues up to the present in many Reformed churches. This confession elaborates on some things, such as the relationship between tradition and Scripture and the issue of the clarity and sufficiency of the Bible in things necessary to salvation.[10] Some confessions were written specifically to combat what was seen as heresy to the "orthodox" world. For instance, the *Formula Consensus Helvetica* was written to defend against the heresies of Amyraldism and the school of Saumur, which "departed from the rigid orthodoxy then prevailing in the Lutheran and Reformed Churches on three points—the verbal inspiration of the Scriptures, the particular predestination, and the imputation of Adam's sin."[11] These confessions had a significant impact on the church of later years, confirming that this is indeed a significant time and is worthy of study.

While it is certainly true that this period of Protestant Orthodoxy largely emphasized dogmatics, it is unfair to suggest that hermeneutics

---

10. For tradition and Scripture, see Zanchius, *De religione Christiana fides*, I.xii–xiv, in *Operum theologicorum*, 8 vols. (Geneva, 1617). He says that the church traditions help in the interpretation of Scripture but it is not a rule and does not replace exegesis. For "Clarity and Sufficiency" see *Irish Articles*, I, in Schaff, *The Creeds of Christendom* III, 5–6.

11. *Helvetic Consensus Formula* in Schaff, *Creeds*, I: 479. For more on the rejection of verbal inspiration see Louis Cappel, "*Arcanum Punctationis Revelatum*," an addition to his *Commentarii et notæ criticæ in Vetus Testamentum* (Amstelodami: Ex Typographia P. & J. Blaeu, 1689) and *Vindiciæ Arcani Punctationis Revelatum*, which were published in 1669 as an appendix on his commentary. On hypothetical universalism see Amyraut, *Traité de la Prédestination* (also in Latin), and Saumur, 1634; *Echantillon de la doctrine de Calvin sur la Prédestination*, 1637; *De la justification*, 1638; *De providentia Dei in malo*, 1638; *Defensio doctrinæ Calvini de absoluto reprobationis decreto*, 1641; *Dissertationes theol. quatuor*, 1645; *Exercitatio de gratia universali*, 1646; *Disputatio de libero hominis arbitrio*, 1647; *Sermons sur divers textes de la Ste. Écriture*, 1653; *Irenicum sive de ratione pacis in religionis negotio inter Evangelicos*, 1662. On the rejection of federalism see Josua Placeus, *De statu hominis lapsi ante gratiam*, 1640; *De imputatione primi peccati Adami*, 1655, in his two volume *Opera omnia*, Franeker, 1699, Aubencit, 1702.

was insignificant in any way.¹² Muller aptly summarizes the significance of hermeneutics in his article:

> Rather, moreover, than producing on a single form (i.e., a dogmatic one) of exegetical work, the Protestant orthodoxy must be recognized as producing highly varied and diverse exegetical works and commentaries, ranging from text-critical essays, to textual annotations, theological annotations, linguistic commentaries based on the study of cognate languages and Judaica, doctrinal and homiletical commentaries, and, indeed all manner of permutations and combinations of these several types of effort.¹³

While intellectual histories continue to emphasize Puritan dogmatics, they seldom consider the pre-critical exegesis that was so closely tied to it.¹⁴ This may even create the impression that hermeneutics and dogmatics are unrelated, but this is hardly the case.¹⁵ During the period of Protestant Orthodoxy, no formal or informal distinctions existed between historically conceived biblical theology and contemporary dogmatics.¹⁶ This distinction came much later under Gabler. Muller suggests it is "impor-

---

12. Protestant Orthodoxy is synonymous with Protestant Scholasticism and is a phase of orthodoxy that characterized both Lutheran and Reformed theology in the period following the sixteenth-century Reformation and before the period of Rationalism (from about 1560–1700). The terms Protestant Orthodox or Protestant Scholastic will be used interchangeably with the more specialized Reformed Orthodox or Reformed Scholastic.

13. Muller, "Calvin and the 'Calvinists': Assessing Continuities and Discontinuities between the Reformation and Orthodoxy," 133.

14. Muller, "The Problem of Protestant Scholasticism," 63. "This linguistic and exegetical ability, moreover, was far more closely tied to the dogmatic task by the scholastic orthodox of the seventeenth century than it has been since that time. Discussions of the era have often missed this point, inasmuch as they have paid even less attention to the so called 'pre-critical' exegesis of the era than they have to the dogmatic theology itself." Muller is certainly correct in this assessment, but dogmatics more than exegesis did seem to be of greater concern to the scholastic authors. Muller himself seems to say this in chapter 2 ("The Doctrine of Scripture in its Protestant Development") in *PRRD* 2:63–150.

15. "Weeme's studies combine the interest in Judaica characteristic of the age and a strongly textual approach to exegesis and interpretation with a clear interest in the movement from exegesis to doctrinal formulation." Muller, *PRRD*, 2:1128. See also John Weemse, *The Christian Synagogue*.

16. This is a generally agreed on point and although I have adopted Muller's phraseology here (and it applies perfectly), it might be good to inform the reader that the context of his point is a discussion of Cocceius' federalism. Muller, *PRRD*, 2:122. Cf. Muller, *PRRD*, 2:454–55.

tant to recognize both the hermeneutical interest of dogmatics and the dogmatic nature of Protestant hermeneutics."[17] Because of their close relationship, the current scholarship on this era strangely and unfortunately continues to emphasize the one over the other.[18]

Protestant Orthodoxy is the offspring of the Reformation and an immediate predecessor to critical approaches.[19] It is, therefore, the lynchpin connecting the Reformers to the more modern rationalistic philosophies that followed in the eighteenth century. The Reformation era, despite the Reformer's insistence on what we now call the grammatical-historical method, was still a time of spiritual and theological hermeneutics.[20] Scholastics accepted and defended the Reformer's ideas of *analogia fidei*, but were beginning to take critical steps as well. Increasingly logical approaches (the need for historical and empirical evidences) to exegesis and interpretation made linguistic studies prevalent, which resulted largely in the recognition of an ever-changing text.[21] Debates ensued regarding the inspiration and date of the vowel points in the MT. It was also during this period of "high orthodoxy" that scholars began to recognize oriental study more and moved it to the forefront of their exegesis. For example, Bishop Brian Walton's *London Polyglott Bible*, with its lexical companion, was "the most technically advanced textual study and apparatus of its time, never superseded *in toto*," and his critical preface influenced the biblical critical movement.[22] Louis Cappel began to show inconsistencies in Mosaic Pentateuchal authorship (without denying it), and his critical historical argumentation led him to question the inspiration of the Hebrew Text.[23] Benedictus de Spinoza was excommunicated when he rejected both Mosaic authorship and a literal Bible in favor of allegorical

---

17. Muller, *PRRD*, 2:111.

18. Some, like John Hayes in *Old Testament Theology*, 19–23, try to find a link between the Reformation and Gabler in seventeenth-century thinkers such as Cocceius, but this is plainly anachronistic. Muller, *PRRD* 2:121.

19. The terms "Orthodoxy" and "Scholasticism" are often used interchangeably although strictly, this should not be the case. As will become evident in chapter 4, one implies doctrine and the other, method.

20. Muller, *PRRD*, 2:144–45.

21. Chapters 4 and 5 discuss this further in relation to the idea that it may actually be a high view of Scripture that led to linguistic emphases.

22. Muller, *PRRD*, 2:132.

23. Ibid., 400–401. He was most noted for conjectural emendations and retranslations. See also *PRRD*, 2:131–6.

teachings about the nature of God and he is known now as the father of biblical criticism.[24] Protestant Orthodoxy was a period of transition between the theology of the Reformers and the higher-critical methods of Rationalism.

This was indeed a significant era in church history. The new existence of confessions, which continue to be recited, as well as the advent of a new way of critical thinking should prevent one from ignoring Puritan hermeneutics and, especially, exegesis.[25]

THE NEED FOR WORK ON JOHN LIGHTFOOT

Some in the past have suggested that divines of this pre-critical era have little to offer a modern scholar. This is simply not the case. John Lightfoot, like many of his contemporaries, has had significant impact on modern thinking. Again, we will look first at the relative lack of research on Lightfoot and then raise the issue of his significance.

Previous Research in the Field

While several Lightfoot biographies and introductions exist, there is significant deficiency in regard to his interpretational methodology and from where it derived. John Rogers Pitman edited *The Whole Works of the Rev. John Lightfoot, D.D.* in 1825 and claims to have gathered all relevant content on John Lightfoot up to that time.[26] It included everything published for Lightfoot by George Bright and John Strype in the

---

24. Muller, *PRRD*, 2:139–40. Frederic W. Farrar mentions this excommunication in *History of Interpretation*, 383.

25. I am using exegesis as a subcategory under hermeneutics. The larger hermeneutics would include all things that contribute to a particular understanding and exegesis more specifically concerns the methodology.

26. Pitman, ed. *The Whole Works of the Rev. John Lightfoot D.D.* 13 vols. All subsequent references to Lightfoot are from these volumes. In order to facilitate both being able to find the reference in the future and also knowing with a quick glance the variety of books and articles he published, I have chosen to consistently include the authors name, the book or article within the multi-volume *Works*, the volume number, and the page as follows:

Lightfoot, *Horae Hebraicae et Talmudicae*, 12:36.

Pitman's work is over 180 years old and can no longer claim to be exhaustive. Still the newly found letters and works have not proven to be relevant to my hermeneutical study. For these other works see Van Dixhoorn, "Reforming the Reformation: Theological Debate at the Westminster Assembly 1643–1652" Appendix A, Lightfoot's Journal. PhD Thesis.

seventeenth century as well as additional works and letters. Each of these three gentlemen wrote excellent introductions to his life, but perhaps the best known and exhaustive is Pitman's "Preface to the Octavo Edition."[27] John Strype's work, while unsystematic in its treatment, is perhaps the most beneficial for our purposes, owing to Strype's own understanding of Judaica and its impact on hermeneutics. We are also privileged to have approximately one hundred personal letters to and from Lightfoot, which allow us a more candid glimpse at his personal life.[28] His journal regarding the proceedings of the assembly of Divines from 1643–44, is also extremely helpful.[29] Still, none of these authors attempts to do more than regurgitate Lightfoot's actual words and conclusions. This is also true of the few modern dictionary entries and monographs on his life, work, and thoughts.[30] The literature about Lightfoot includes very little interaction with his exegesis or hermeneutic overall and very little analysis regarding his influence by others.

Chaim Schertz's 1977 dissertation entitled "Christian Hebraism in 17th Century England as Reflected in the Works of John Lightfoot" is the only full-length work on Lightfoot that attempts to interact with his hermeneutics. Schertz says, "With few exceptions no comprehensive study has been undertaken to discover how pro[f]ound was [the seventeenth-century English Divines'] understanding of the Hebrew Scriptures."[31] Schertz's work is the first, and it is a worthwhile contribu-

---

27. Lightfoot, 1:v–cvi. George Bright's work was entitled "Some Account of the Life of the Reverend and Most Learned John Lightfoot, D.D." (also called "Authors Life" in the original English Folio edition) and John Strype's was entitled "An Appendix or Collection of Some More Memorials of the Life of the Excellent Dr. John Lightfoot." These can be found respectively in Lightfoot, 1:43–62 (English Folio edition 1:1–9) and Lightfoot, 1:63–124.

28. Most letters can be found in Lightfoot, *Works*, 13:345–487. Other letters are scattered throughout. See vol. 1, 378–424 for "a Battle with a Wasp's Nest" written for a wide readership but written as a letter to Dr. Heming.

29. Lightfoot, *Journal of the Assembly of Divines*, 13:1–344.

30. Newton E. Key, "John Lightfoot," *Oxford Dictionary of National Biography*, 33:753–56; Thomas Hamilton, "John Lightfoot," *Dictionary of National Biography* 11:1108–10; *Biographia Britannica, or the Lives of the Most Eminent Persons who have Flourished in Great Britain and Ireland*, s.v. "Life of Lightfoot," 5:2931–36; R. A. Muller, *Historical Handbook of Major Biblical Interpreters*, 208–12; D. M. Welton, *John Lightfoot the English Hebraist*.

31. Chaim E. Schertz, "Christian Hebraism in 17th Century England as Reflected in the Works of John Lightfoot," 2–3.

Who Cares about Pre-Critical Exegesis and John Lightfoot? 9

tion and excellent foundation for the present work. His goal is simply to discover the profundity of Lightfoot's understanding of the Hebrew Scriptures, to what extent he knew the vast Jewish literature devoted to the interpretation and preservation of those Scriptures, and to what effect rabbinic learning had upon his theology and religious institutions.[32]

Despite his valuable work, more needs to be considered. First, while the final third of Schertz's dissertation is devoted to Lightfoot's understanding of texts, his themes and quotations are almost exclusively procured from Lightfoot's *Horae* and his *Harmony of the Four Evangelists*. Schertz seldom pulls from Lightfoot's works on the Hebrew Scriptures. Second, Schertz's own heritage makes it no small irony that he "does little to engage in Lightfoot's thought, seeking rather to highlight negative uses of Jewish literature in Lightfoot's writings."[33] While scholars should attempt to correct these minor weaknesses, a third reason makes this continued work on Lightfoot significant: it was not Schertz's intention to interact significantly with his biblical exegesis and hermeneutical ideas. Despite Schertz's foray into Lightfoot's understanding of Hebrew Scripture, Schertz's thesis is certainly more a work of intellectual history and not biblical scholarship, as he strongly stresses.[34] Quite simply, he is concerned with the history of Lightfoot, while this present work is more focused on his hermeneutics and exegesis. Thirty-five years after Schertz's contribution, the need for hermeneutical inquiry into Lightfoot's life remains.

Significance of John Lightfoot

William Fraser Mitchell, whose work on English pulpit oratory in the seventeenth century is well known, considers Lightfoot an extreme Presbyterian and therefore deems his work inconsequential.[35] This is unfortunate and can hardly be defended when we consider Lightfoot's achievement. After briefly introducing Lightfoot and his place in history we will look at his legacy as condensed into three main, interconnected

32. Ibid.

33. Van Dixhoorn, "Reforming the Reformation," xiii. Schertz's Jewish heritage makes him somewhat at odds with Lightfoot since the latter had many unpleasant things to say regarding the Jews.

34. Schertz, "Christian Hebraism," 13–14.

35. Fraser Mitchell, *English Pulpit Oratory from Andrewes to Tillotson*, 257.

areas: his vast oriental learning, his interaction in most of the theological controversies of his day, and his work in the Westminster Assembly.

John Lightfoot was born to Puritan parents on March 29, 1602, in Staffordshire, England.[36] Little is known of his childhood other than his elementary education, but he began his studies at Christ College, Cambridge at fifteen years of age. He was a master at Greek and Latin but had all but forgotten his Hebrew at the time of his ordination some years later. It was there at Norton under Hales that Lightfoot met and befriended Sir Rowland Cotton the wealthy and learned gentleman who would educate him in Hebrew. While Cotton had intentions to convert the Jews by translating the New Testament into Hebrew, Lightfoot had no such desires. In fact, the only reason Lightfoot learned Hebrew was because he served as Cotton's chaplain and he was embarrassed that Cotton was his better in the Old Testament language. Once he mastered Hebrew, he began to study the Talmud and other rabbinic writings and all of this despite having no real contact with Jews.

He did marry and raise six children, but his early married and fathering years were spent in his study at Sion College and later at his country residence in Stafforshire. From there he remained undisturbed in his work, stopping only to preach. From there also he published *Miscellanies*, his first book and his entrance into the academic elite. He went on to publish many valuable works and in 1643 was appointed master at St. Catherine's Hall and rector at Mundham, Herforshire. In 1652 he received his Doctor of Divinity and three years later was chosen as vice chancellor of the University at Cambridge. He remained there until he died of a cold in 1675.

John Lightfoot was one of the first English scholars to argue that writings such as the Talmud, Midrash, and later rabbinic commentaries, among other similar Jewish writings, greatly clarified the apostles' writing. There had certainly been gifted Hebraists before him: Nicholas of Lyra, for instance, over three centuries earlier had sought to amend the Hebrew text and used other techniques of what would later be called text criticism. Even Calvin and Luther were not ignorant of the Hebrew. And Lightfoot himself lived in a time of Hebrew studies. What distinguished him was not only his noted excellence in the text, but his desire to use

---

36. The following two paragraphs on Lightfoot's life are a synopsis of George Bright's "Some Account of the Life of the Reverend and Most Learned John Lightfoot, D.D." A good summary is also found in Schertz's "Christian Hebraism," 17–43.

Jewish commentaries to aid exegesis. And he did this not for missionary purposes (as his contemporaries did) but as the primary hermeneutical tools in his biblical studies. In fact, as we will later make more obvious, Lightfoot had little use and no hope for Jews as a people since they had, in his opinion, been cursed even before Jesus was crucified. He ignored Cromwell's meeting with Manasseh ben Israel in 1655 despite an overwhelming exuberance among his theological contemporaries. Even though delegates to this several-year long discussion included Drs. Cudworth, Owen, Whitecoat, and Godwin, as well as John Carroll and Henry Wilkensen, Lightfoot remained uninvolved. He would play no part in the readmission controversy, choosing rather to use the Jewish writings for their exegetical benefits alone.[37]

While he published many things early in his life, his crowning achievement and what he is most known for, is perhaps the greatest example of his "interpretation by Judaica": the *Horae Hebraicae et Talmudicae*. Edmund Castell, upon receiving a part of the *Horae*, remarked that it deserved "to be enrolled among the very next records to those of infallibility."[38] Johannes Buxtorff, himself, upon reading the *Horae*, says that he could not help but love, esteem, extol, and admire Lightfoot because of his skill, diligence, and accuracy in the Scriptures and Talmud.[39] Lightfoot was neither the first Christian Hebraist, nor even the first Christian Talmudist.[40] Still, his reputation in Judaica "is firmly

---

37. For brief comments on the readmission controversy and John Lightfoot see Schertz, "Christian Hebraism," 38–40. For a more exhaustive look at the motives for allowing Jews back into England see Cecil Roth, *A Life of Menasseh Ben Israel: Rabbi, Printer, and Diplomat*, 236–38.

38. Strype, "Appendix to Authors Life" in Lightfoot, 1:83.

39. Ibid., 85.

40. In fact, he was in good company. Rev. D. De Sola Pool has a very helpful article where he lists many Hebraists of the time. Some he includes are Governor Bradford (a *Mayflower* Pilgrim), William Brewster, John Cotton, Thomas Welde, Henry Dunster, Charles Chauncy, Michael Wigglesworth, Thomas Thacher, Increase and Cotton Mather, John Selden, John Spencer, and Francis Taylor. There were 181 men commissioned to attend the Westminster Assembly (although this number is in constant flux) and only three of these are mentioned in de Pool's article (understandably, since it is predominantly about *New* England Puritans). The three mentioned are the commoner John Selden and two divines—Francis Taylor and John Lightfoot. Still, it is true that despite the great Hebrew learning the progress was squelched by the limitation of books especially on the continent. When Lightfoot bequeathed his entire oriental library to Harvard he considerably enriched the possibilities of future Hebrew study. De Sola Pool, "Hebrew Learning among the Puritans of New England Prior to 1700," 31–83. For information regarding his

established and his unrivalled excellence has been acknowledged by scholars most competent to decide upon his merits."[41] He was, by far, the most revered and sought-after Gentile expert on Judaica.[42]

Because of his fluent grasp of the Hebrew language, it is said that he received from Gibbon the tribute that "by constant reading of the rabbis, he became almost a rabbi himself."[43] Texelius, in the preface to the edition of his works, says "omnium judicio, in antiquitatibus Judaeorum perrimandis praestitisse videtur, quod ante eum nemo.[44] "Dr. Adam Clark(e) considered Lightfoot to be the first of all English writers in biblical criticism as regards learning, judgment, and usefulness" and Daniel Neal says that he "was the most complete master of oriental learning of his age."[45]

It was Lightfoot's expertise in Hebraica that led him to be included in most of the theological controversies and accomplishments of his day, some of which have had considerable impact on modern hermeneutics. Bishop Walton was grateful for Lightfoot's agreement to work on the Polyglot project. In a letter to Lightfoot, Walton wrote: "and though you seem to doubt in the employment at a sense of inability, yet give me leave to impute that to your modesty, rather than to any want of abilities, of which you have given so sufficient and public testimony to the world, that it should be accounted a great obligation, if you shall please to contribute your assistance about the Samaritan version, or to say what you advise about any other part of that work."[46]

---

even earlier predecessors and their Hebraic knowledge read Schper, "Christian Hebraists in Sixteenth-Century England."

41. Pitman, "Preface to the Octavo Edition," Lightfoot, 1:xxxv.

42. Charles Taylor said he "showed considerable acquaintance with Talmud and Midrash, greater perhaps than any non-Jew has shown before the present day." Charles Taylor, "John Lightfoot," 84.

43. Stephen Neil and Tom Wright, *The Interpretation of the New Testament: 1861–1986*, 314.

44. Translation: "In my judgment, nobody excelled in the Antiquities of the Jews as much as he." Texelius, quoted in Pitman, "Preface to the Octavo Edition," Lightfoot, 1:xxxvi.

45. Hamilton, "Lightfoot, John," 1109. The original quote is not cited. However in another location Clark(e) says "By his deep researches into the Rabbinical writings, he has done more to illustrate the phraseology of the Sacred Writings, and to explain the various customs &c. alluded to, particularly in the New Testament, than any author before or since." Clark(e), *Bibliographical Dictionary*, 269. Neal, *History of the Puritans*, 2:255.

46. Brian Walton to Lightfoot, 2 Jan 1663/4, in *Letters to and From Dr. Lightfoot* in Lightfoot, 13:348.

Mr. Samuel Clark, who had a great hand in the Polyglot, praised Lightfoot's "eminent judiciousness" in giving him any credit and consistently conferred with him on works such as the Targum to Chronicles and the tractate *Berakot*.[47] Edmund Castell, the author of the Heptaglot Lexicon, spoke thus of Lightfoot's "worth and works": "so transcendent to the vulgar way of writing, all the learned world doth and ought highly to esteem."[48] Elsewhere, he writes, "all pretenders to the oriental tongues must confess their great obligation to you."[49] The Elder Buxtorff himself, in a letter to Castell, praises the diligence of Lightfoot's work in the *Horae* and hopes to use him as an interpreter.[50]

Lightfoot's work on the Polyglot, along with the "seventeen year drudgery" that resulted in the Heptaglot Lexicon and his help on Matthew Poole's *The Synopsis of the Critics*, has placed Lightfoot unwittingly within the newly emerging biblical critical worldview.[51] While this was true, he was also quite willing to voice his disagreement with some of his colleague's critical conclusions. For example, one specific difference Lightfoot had with Walton was "his late dating of the vowel pointing system in the Masoretic Text."[52] Lightfoot took up this debate in various parts of his writing, but all conclude in similar fashion to this: "From

47. Strype, "Appendix to Authors Life" in Lightfoot 1:87, 90. His questions of the targum concerned whether an obscure line in the Talmud did indeed designate Onkelos as the legitimate author.

48. Dr. E. Castell to Lightfoot, 22 Feb 1663/4; Lightfoot, 13:366. He closes letters with signatures like "The most religious honourer of your eminent worth and rare abilities." Lightfoot, *Letters to and from Dr. Lightfoot*, 13:370.

49. Castell to Lightfoot, 20 Aug 1669, in Lightfoot, 13:396.

50. Ex Horis ejus Talmudicis incepi illius doctrinam et diligentiam valde amare . . . Atque vir praestantissime, si occasion dabitur, mei erga ipsum affectus eris interpres; multum eum a me salver jubebis, et valere. Castell to Lightfoot, 16 Aug 1664, in Lightfoot, 13:372–73.

51. The "seventeen year drudgery" is mentioned in Edmund Castell, Letter 41 in Lightfoot, 13:392. Earlier, after only fifteen years of work on it, Castell said that he is "still sustained in the tormenting purgatory of this cruel undertaking." Castell to Lightfoot, 5 Aug 1667, in Lightfoot, 13:383. Lest one think that Lightfoot was a biblical critic, let me say that his disagreements with critics were rarely based on critical methods, but rather on his own presuppositions. It is also good to remember that "there is no clear or sudden division between "precritical" and "critical exegesis" and that the Protestant Orthodox themselves often contributed positively to the development of exegesis and hermeneutics, even when some of their results would eventually have a somewhat negative effect upon traditional dogmatics" (Muller, *PRRD*, 2:136).

52. Muller, *PRRD*, 2:134.

mine own satisfaction I am fully resolved, that the letters and vowels of the Hebrew were,—as the soul and body of a child,—knit together at their conception and beginning; and that they had both one author."[53] He was also quick to defend his view regarding the authorship of biblical books and historical validity of the New Testament.[54] While failing to mention people by name, he stood against Richard Simon's views on the book of Joshua's historical development by gradual collection of sources and the non-Mosaic authorship of a large part of the Pentateuch.[55]

As already mentioned, Lightfoot also played an influential role in the creation of what is certainly the greatest confessional document written during the age of Protestant scholasticism—the *Westminster Confession of Faith*.[56] The Confession is 350 years old, and this durability demands respect. Nevertheless, its longevity and its man-made character, make inquiries regarding its continued legitimacy justified. One way to initiate the question of legitimacy is to investigate the interpretive facilities of its various authors. We want to be careful on the one hand not to dismiss their influence through neglect, as Muller has warned; on the other hand, we must be careful not to give these authors undue reverence.[57]

As a considerably younger divine invited to the Westminster Assembly, Lightfoot was nevertheless outspoken in his contributions there. At the age of twenty-seven, Lightfoot had already published works such as his *Miscellanies*, which gave him a strong reputation and a well-heeded voice. Nevertheless, Lightfoot has noted in his journals and other writings his many disagreements with his colleagues. Lightfoot's Erastian view of church-state relations was almost unique among the divines with Thomas Coleman as the only other exception.[58] He opposed the

---

53. Lightfoot, *Miscellanies*, 4:50.

54. He was always conscious of the importance of proving the historical validity of the New Testament which only rabbinic learning could provide. Shertz, "Christian Hebraism," 5.

55. However, as we will see later, he did not agree that Joshua the man wrote the book of Joshua.

56. Muller, *PRRD*, 2:77. On whether this time is properly scholasticism see the dissenting view in McNeil, *The History and Character of Calvinism*, 325; Rogers and McKim, *Interpretation and Authority of Scripture*, 202–3, 218–23, and the affirmative view in Loonstra, "Scholasticism and Hermeneutics"; Muller, *PRRD*, 2:77; and Muller, *After Calvin*, 25–46.

57. Muller, *After Calvin*, 156.

58. The commoner John Selden and several parliamentary members were also Erastian.

otherwise unanimous decision regarding limited entrance to the holy sacrament, arguing rather that there should be general admission.[59] He disagreed with the consensus view of the 13th Article of Religion, which stated that works done before justification are not pleasing to God.[60] He also argued unsuccessfully that the Sabbath command did not include the words "before it come." At the same time, his arguments were more often convincing. Some opposed the use of all strange tongues in sermons, and Lightfoot was able to soften the language to what we now find: "against the unnecessary and unprofitable use of it."[61] He argued that the Directory of Prayer phrase "freeing us from antichristian darkness" was too low and convinced the assembly to add "and tyranny" to the end of it.[62] He convinced his colleagues that *dikaio* in Rom 5:9, 17–19 was correctly translated "righteousness" over against "just satisfaction."[63] Those at the Assembly respected him greatly.

Lightfoot's expertise in oriental learning and in critical and logical thought, as well as his renown as a Westminster Divine, justifies continued research on him. By examining his understanding of the Bible, we may gain insights into the hermeneutical milieu of the time, which may better help us answer questions regarding his continued influence.[64] For all of these reasons, I maintain, that a study on John Lightfoot should prove beneficial to modern hermeneutics and biblical research.

PARAMETERS OF THE STUDY

A primary contribution of this study will be the systematic organization of John Lightfoot's hermeneutic. However, with that comes the inherent danger of categorizing anything of the past in terms familiar to the modern world. Lightfoot's hermeneutic is pre-modern, and it is important that we realize that his society, like our own, "places unrecognized constraints upon our imaginations."[65] The study of Lightfoot's interpre-

59. Strype, "Appendix to Author's Life" in Lightfoot, 1:75–77.
60. Ibid., 80.
61. Ibid.
62. Ibid., 82; Pitman, "Preface to the Octavo Edition," Lightfoot, 1:xii–xiii.
63. Strype, "Appendix to Author's Life" in Lightfoot, 1:79.
64. The questions of importance for Lightfoot may not be truly perennial questions. However, sufficiently abstractly framed questions can still be relevant today. See Skinner's, "Meaning and Understanding in the History of Ideas," 52.
65. Skinner, "Meaning and Understanding in the History of Ideas," 53.

tational worldview is the best way to put limits on these constraints and to widen our allegedly "modern, more fully evolved" hermeneutic.[66] In order to accomplish this, we will look at Lightfoot in terms of his day and notice, therefore, not his essential sameness, but rather the essential variety of his commitments compared to those of today.[67]

While Lightfoot is not a modern day interpreter, it would be unwise to say that his insights have no application today, at least on some level. In fact, with the rise of theological exegesis, the recent trend is to make a move in our hermeneutical theory from methodological uniformity to a pre-critical multiformity.[68] The idea is that a study of Lightfoot's *sensus literalis* may inspire modern scholars not to castigate pre-modern hermeneutics but instead to allow it to be a part of postmodern hermeneutics.

Despite a book entitled *Rules for a Student of Holy Scriptures*, Lightfoot has written no explanation of his method of interpretation. This simply means that we are compelled to search out his commentaries and sermons for examples of his exegetical judgments. This will be most evident by looking at Lightfoot's exegesis in conjunction with that of his contemporaries. What he finds disagreeable and agreeable in their interpretation will lead us to a better understanding of his own method.

Since our goal is to discover how Lightfoot understands *sensus literalis*, it will be helpful, before launching into Lightfoot's view, to take a brief look in chapter 2 at the definition of this literal sense throughout history. While our emphasis is more hermeneutical than historical, this is a book on an individual's hermeneutic, and thus necessitates some interaction with the time period itself. Muller is justifiably frustrated with the "review of major theological writings that has persistently judged the [earlier] materials on the basis of nineteenth- and twentieth-century theological models, and that has all but ignored the context of the intellectual history

---

66. We want to avoid the criticism that we are blaming or praising Lightfoot according to how far he "may seem to have aspired to the condition of being ourselves." Ibid., 11.

67. Skinner, "Meaning and Understanding in the History of Ideas," 52.

68. See Steinmetz's "The Superiority of Pre-Critical Exegesis," 27–38; Fowl and Jones, "Practicing the Rule of Christ," 111–31. See also Steinmetz, Muller and Thompson, *Biblical Interpretation in the Era of the Reformation: Essays Presented to David C. Steinmetz in Honor of his Sixtieth Birthday*, where the authors propose a retrieval of premodern exegesis as essential to the recovery of Scripture as a Word addressed to the living and not just to the dead. See also Maddox, "Recovering the Riches of Premodern Exegesis," 18.

of the sixteenth and seventeenth centuries."[69] Carl Trueman also bemoans contemporary prejudice when he says, "while the whole notion of judging Reformed scholasticism by the criteria of twentieth-century theology of any variety, be it neoorthodoxy or conservative Calvinsim, is highly dubious, historical analysis of the relevant documents demonstrates that many of contemporary scholarship's dearest shibboleths are unsustainable in the light of the evidence."[70] What we are involved in is a hermeneutical study that has used the history of hermeneutics as the doorway into the subject. It will be contextual, but at the same time, will purpose to avoid the dangers Skinner mentions.

In this same chapter, we will seek to understand the driving presupposition of Lightfoot's exegesis: that the Bible is both completely divine and utterly human. It is from both of these characteristics, divine and human, that he derives his understanding of the clarity and obscurity of the text as well as the unity of the Old and New Testament. This presupposition and its resulting implications have tremendous bearing on Lightfoot's understanding of the literal sense.

After reviewing the background material that comprises the first section of this study, the second section, chapters 3 through 7, will emphasize Lightfoot's exegetical methods. Through examination of his commentaries and sermons, Lightfoot's most important rules for determining the literal sense become evident. They include 1) reading logically and reasonably, 2) reading slowly and carefully (even perhaps critically), 3) reading historically and chronologically, 4) reading ecclesiastically, and 5) reading christologically.

Chapter 3 will examine Lightfoot's use of reason and how this seems to include a *via media* between Christian and Jewish exegesis. He attempts to realize the best of both Judaism and Protestant Orthodoxy. Chapter 4 flows from this and emphasizes his careful and somewhat critical approach to the Bible. There is good reason to consider Lightfoot pre-critical in his exegesis, but, at the same time, to recognize that he is not afraid to question the status quo. He is heavily engaged in translation and commentary by both Jew and Christian and is asking many of the same questions that subsequent generations of critical scholars will ask. Chapter 5 will examine his third rule of reading historically and chrono-

69. Muller, *After Calvin*, 156.

70. Trueman, "John Owen's *Dissertation of Divine Justice*: An Exercise in Christocentric Scholasticism," 103.

logically. Lightfoot is convinced that the Bible gives a perfect record of events and their times. And, while the events and times are literal, he seems to include a form of typology that allows him to determine exact times and geographical locations for New Testament events by reading the Old Testament, and vice versa. Chapter 6 will consider, in more depth, his analogy of faith and to what degree he is attached to that analogy. Again, he seems to have great animosity towards the Jews, and his desire is never to criticize the Christian giants of the past; nevertheless, we find that Lightfoot walks a thin line. The church seems to retain authority for Lightfoot, but he is unafraid to approach things differently and even to come to separate conclusions. Since Lightfoot is impressive in his use of Jewish sources, chapter 7 must necessarily contrast this to his christological reading. It is his understanding of the *sensus literalis* that insists that the entire Bible is about Jesus, but he uses allegorical and typological methods to come to his conclusions.

CONCLUSION

It seems certain that while there is a disparity in examining pre-critical exegetes, it is, nevertheless, of great value. Not only is the study of pre-critical exegesis of importance, but a closer look at the presuppositions and exegetical methods of John Lightfoot are of equal significance. Lightfoot was both a man of his time and one who made great advances in hermeneutics. As we look at his beliefs and his advances we will see that Lightfoot consistently attempts to chart a middle course between Protestant Orthodoxy and Jewish learning.

2

Lightfoot's Presupposition of Dual Authorship and Its Implications for *Sensus Literalis*

INTRODUCTION

JOHN LIGHTFOOT BELIEVES THAT the meaning of Scripture is found in its literal sense. But throughout history, the fluidity of this *sensus literalis* had greatly diversified interpretations. Some defined it through the magisterium or a confession, while others limited it to what they could derive from a grammatico-historical approach. Still others understood "literal" to include allegory and moralism. In order to understand the *sensus literalis* of John Lightfoot, one must first understand his driving presupposition. It is this presupposition, that the Bible is simultaneously both divine and human, that influences everything else he does.

Dual authorship means, for Lightfoot, that the Bible is both clear and obscure. Its nature and ultimate intention is clearly understandable but its specifics require diligent study to understand. Furthermore, the Bible's authorship by men means that the books of the Bible all have unique purposes and require understanding of the time to properly glean from them. Yet, the Bible's divine authorship insists that Scripture tells one coherent story from the Old Testament to the New. Understanding these implications of dual authorship, that the Bible is clear and obscure, individual and cohesive, is essential if one wishes to discover what "literal sense" meant to Lightfoot. His rules of exegesis derive directly from this presupposition.

Because Lightfoot is a man of his time and the student of both Christianity and Judaism, it is helpful to examine these dual authorship implications in light of his community and his heritage. We will find that in both his presuppositions and his methodological rules, Lightfoot walks a line between Judaism and Christianity. His *sensus literalis* is, in a very real way, a *via media* approach to Scripture.

DUAL AUTHORSHIP

Historical Survey of Divine Authorship

Throughout history, the Jews and the church commonly assumed that the Bible was *both* divine *and* human. Tannaite Judaism's understanding of the nature of biblical authority seems to have been similar to that of early Christianity in that they both agreed that Scripture was the Word of God, the contents of the Bible were consistent and homogenous, and it contained no contradictions.[1] The Bible was the result of a divine author. When the early church tended towards allegorical interpretation, it did so largely because it considered the Bible to be from God, and God had to have a deeper message than what was on the surface. By reading the texts figuratively, Christian exegetes thought they were honoring the Old Testament texts for their mysterious, many-sided, and spiritual profundity.[2] Origen insisted that "the sacred books were not the works of men, but that they were composed and have come down to us as a result of the inspiration of the Holy Spirit."[3] Karlfried Froehlich says Origen believed that since God through his Spirit is the author of Scripture, one must expect all Scripture to have a spiritual sense, though not everything in it also has a bodily sense.[4] Without completely disregarding the literal sense, Origen did conclude that the Bible was only ultimately understandable through the spiritual or allegorical sense and only by those who were

---

1. There were certainly differences but they were the same in the sense suggested. It is important to remember that the Jews thought the Torah antedated humanity and was only later given to Moses. Therefore, they had a special place for Torah even though the rest of the Hebrew Bible was understood to be inspired. Robert D. Preus, "The View of the Bible Held by the Church: The Early Church through Luther," in Geisler, *Inerrancy*, 358.

2. Frei, "The 'Literal Reading' of Biblical Narrative in the Christian Tradition: Does It Stretch or Will It Break?," in *The Bible and the Narrative Tradition*, 40.

3. Origen, *Origen on First Principles*, 4.2.2, 272.

4. Froehlich, "'Always to Keep the Literal Sense in Holy Scripture Means to Kill One's Soul': The State of Biblical Hermeneutics at the Beginning of the Fifteenth Century," in *Literary Uses of Typology*, 22.

"enlightened" enough to grasp this sense.[5] Even the Antiochene *theoria*,[6] which opposed the Alexandrian allegorical extremes, was convinced of a higher sense beyond the literal, and this because it was divine.[7] Augustine also said the divine aspect of the text necessitated a figurative interpretation.[8] Aquinas accepted a two-fold interpretation of the Bible because it was the only book that was both human and divine. To him the literal sense was that which the author intended, and since God was the author, the literal sense had many meanings.[9] The Reformation divines popularly pioneered a single literal sense while, simultaneously, affirming the divine character of the Bible.[10]

Christians throughout history have also generally agreed that the Old Testament, while certainly divine, was the product of human hands. Basing their belief on Matt 1:22; 2:6, 17; 3:3; 4:14 (and others), the early church considered the human writers to be instruments of the Holy Spirit.[11] Preus says that "they were not suggesting that the human authors are unthinking, unwilling instruments, divested of consciousness or personality or *usus scribendi*.[12] God condescended by accommodating himself to the unique personalities, thought forms, and intellectual abilities of the human authors.

5. See his discussion in *Princ.* 4.

6. *Theoria* basically means a perception of the spiritual sense of Scripture. In its most general sense it is used by the Alexandrian School as well and is closely equivalent to allegory. The specific theoria used by the Antiochene School is defined by Julian of Aeclanum: "Theoria est autem (ut eruditis placuit) in brevibus plerumque aut formis aut caussis earum rerunm quae potiores sunt considerate perception." [*Theoria* is the perception of the future which a prophet enjoys through the medium of the present circumstances which he is describing; my translation.] See Raymond Edward Brown, "The *Sensus Plenior* of Sacred Scripture," chapter 2, especially pages 45–46.

7. Bromiley, "The Church Fathers and Holy Scripture," in *Scripture and Truth*, 214.

8. Augustine, *City of God*, 11.32; Augustine, *On Christian Doctrine*, 212.

9. *Summa Theologiae* Ia I, 10, quoted in Moo, "The Problem of Sensus Plenior," in *Hermeneutics, Authority and Canon*, 182 n14; see also Smalley, *The Study of the Bible in the Middle Ages*, 300.

10. Luther did approve of allegorical interpretation where theological sense can be derived from a text in no other way and Luther's radical christological reading of Scripture is arguably allegory by another name at many points. Flacius also approves of allegory in certain circumstances. See Moo, "The Problem of Sensus Plenior," 183.

11. Athenagoras, *Leg.* 7 [*PG* 6, 386]; Theophilus of Antioch, *Autol.* 2, 9.10 (*PG* 6, 1063); Jerome, *Epistulae.* 65, 7 [*PL* 22, 627]; Gregory the Great, *Moral., praef.* 1 (*PL* 75, 515), cited in Preus, "The View of the Bible Held by the Church," 363 n18.

12. Preus, "The View of the Bible Held by the Church," 363.

While virtually everyone believed the Old Testament to be human, few wrote on this subject in comparison to that of its divine authorship. In fact, because of their profound commitment to its divinity, many early and medieval church fathers tended to ignore the human aspects. The divinity of the Scriptures was not obvious and therefore needed an argument, but the fact that the Bible was written by man was self-evident and difficult to deny and therefore required little defense. Writing about the early church's view of Scripture, Moises Silva says it was regarded as having been written by "real-life historical individuals rather than appearing from nowhere," and "it was written in human languages rather than in some unknown angelic tongue."[13] Because of these obvious human traits, the church did not have to come up with an apologetic regarding its humanity.[14]

Still, the early and medieval church defended the Bible's humanity, both implicitly and explicitly. Since Origen and many other early scholars were so concerned with textual and philological details, one can assume that they understood the text as human. What is more, Origen was explicit regarding his rejection of ecstasy as part of inspiration.[15] Later, even Augustine, who used the word "dictate," spoke of human intention and human selectivity being involved in what the authors wrote.[16] They generally assumed the text's humanity. It is fair to say that Christian scholars have generally understood that the Bible is both divine and human.

Lightfoot's Understanding of Dual Authorship

Lightfoot holds firmly to both the divinity and humanity of the Scripture. Throughout his writings, he speaks of both the human author and the divine one.[17] Because it is this basic presupposition from which all of Lightfoot's "rules" derive, it is important to understand to what degree Lightfoot thought each of the authors was involved.

---

13. Silva, *Has the Church Misread the Bible?*, 40.
14. Ibid., 40.
15. Origen, *Cels.*, 7, 3.
16. Polman, *The Word of God according to St. Augustine*, 47–51. Augustine uses both *dictare* and *suggerere*. While this could cause confusion, Augustine seems to use these words interchangeably.
17. The Holy Ghost reckoneth the time of this . . . Lightfoot, *Harmony of the Old Testament*, 2:213.

Unfortunately, Lightfoot does not seek to answer the authorship question explicitly. He does, however, give a few hints regarding his understanding of inspiration. On a few occasions, he speaks of the pen of the Holy Spirit. For example, in an exposition of 1 Kgs 15:14, he says: "A human chronicler is not able to say, 'Such a one's heart was perfect with God;' because he is not able to discern, what the heart is. He writes the story of a man's actions; he cannot write the story of his heart, because he cannot know it. But he that held the pen, and wrote these sacred chronicles, the Holy Ghost, saw the carriage of all actions, saw the secret frame and temper of all hearts . . . and he could not but give right judgment."[18]

Apparently, the Holy Ghost holds the pen. Lightfoot's longest treatise on the divinity of Scripture is found in his sermon on 2 Sam 19:29. In this text, he encounters numerous difficulties and this allows him a platform to exhort his readers to study the Scriptures diligently. The reason difficulties exist, after all, is that the author is challenging us to more intense study. And the author is first and foremost the Holy Ghost. "The Holy Ghost hath purposely penned the Scriptures so as to challenge all serious study of them. Else, what think you is the meaning of that, 'He that readeth, let him understand?'"[19] Later in this sermon, he waxes eloquent regarding the authorship by the Spirit:

> It became the Holy Ghost, the penner of Scripture, to write in a majesty, that the wits and wisdom of all the men in the world should bow before it . . . If the Holy Ghost wrote the scriptures, we must needs conclude, that he wrote them like the Holy Ghost, in a divine majesty. Nor is it enough that we give to the Scriptures, if we should think only they were written for the benefit of men, if we do not think and consider also, that they were written in the demonstration of God. And however a blasphemous Jesuit durst be so daring as to take the Bible in his hand, and to say, "thou Spirit, that, the Protestants say, breathest in the Scriptures, I defy thee"; yet we have better learned the Scriptures, and cannot but tremble at such blasphemy: but are no whit moved, by the boldness and confidence of it, the less to own and maintain, that the Holy Ghost, that gave the Scriptures, breatheth in the Scriptures

---

18. Lightfoot, *Meditations upon Some Abstruser Points of Divinity and Explanations of Divers Difficult Places of Holy Scripture*, 5:376.

19. Lightfoot, *Sermons*, "Difficulties of Scripture," 7:208.

in majesty and power; in power, to convert souls,—and in majesty, to confound confidence in man's own wisdom.[20]

It appears that divine authorship means that the Holy Spirit penned the Scriptures. But Lightfoot could not have meant for his comments on penmanship to be taken so rigidly. After all, he mentions a human chronicler in his discussion on the passage in Kings. Furthermore, Lightfoot also speaks of dictation—at least the Pauline epistles are *dictated* from God to Paul: "Peter tells us, that there are divers things in Paul's Epistles hard to be understood [2 Pet 3:15–16]; and why did the Holy Ghost dictate them so hard by Paul? And why did not Peter explain them, who had the same Spirit?"[21]

In that earlier mentioned exposition of 1 Kgs 15:14 where Asa's heart is said to be perfect he says: "That his heart was so, is confirmed by the mouth of two witnesses, the Book of Kings and Chronicles; and the Mouth of the Holy Ghost hath spoken it twice over, here and there; and his word is truth, and no falsehood in it."[22] The two witnesses are two books of the Old Testament and Lightfoot considers these biblical witnesses to be the same thing as the mouth of God himself. If God dictates with his mouth what he wants a human to write and reveal, then he cannot also pen what he wants revealed.

Neither literal speaking nor writing is what Lightfoot has in mind when discussing the divine authorship of the Bible. Rather, he has in mind a synergistic relationship that results in a fully authorized text. He insisted, of course, that authors of Scripture did write, but they simply could not write on their own. What they write must absolutely come from above for one to grant it full authority as canonical Scripture. In his *Harmony of the New Testament* he says that "inspired men may be considered under a double notion; viz. those that were inspired with prophecy, or to be prophets and to preach,—and those that were inspired to be penmen of divine write, which was higher."[23] The human authors do not write on their own; rather, God inspires them for the task. Lightfoot believes the book of Luke supports this in the first few verses of his Gospel. Luke says

---

20. Ibid., 212.

21. Ibid., 208.

22. Lightfoot, *Meditations upon Some Abstruser Points of Divinity and Explanations of Divers Difficult Places of Holy Scripture*, 5:378.

23. Lightfoot, *Harmony of the New Testament*, 3:334.

that whereas there are plenty of good writings on the life of Jesus, most are written only by human authorities. Books authored solely by humans are those undertaken without the "injunction of the Holy Ghost."[24] Lightfoot believes that Luke insisted that these Gospels and books mentioned in the Old Testament, such as the books of Jasher, of Gad, of Iddo, of the wars of the Lord, etc., were only the works of men and were "neither as altogether disapproved, nor yet approved above human."[25] Luke's Gospel was different, and this is clear for Lightfoot from Luke 1:3. The explanation is found in the word ἄνωθεν in the phrase ἔδοξεν κἀμοὶ παρηκολουθηκότι ἄνωθεν πᾶσιν ἀκριβῶς. This word is most often translated as "beginning" or "first," but Lightfoot says it is best translated as "from above."[26] "And, thus taken, it showeth Luke's inspiration from heaven, and standeth in opposition to the many gospels mentioned ver. 1;—which were written from the mouths and dictating of men, ver. 2; but his intelligence for what he writeth, was 'from above.'"[27] Scripture, therefore, is divine or "from above," and that which is from above is Scripture, and other books do not have the kind of approval given to these which are authored by injunction of the Spirit. But what is the injunction of the Spirit? If, as seems apparent, Luke actually pens the information, then how do the Holy Spirit and the human author work together? Does the human author hear, either in an ecstatic or consciously controlled state, exactly what he should put on paper and then do so without respect to personality or intellect? While Lightfoot never explicitly deals with these questions, he certainly believes that the human author is relevant to the inspiration process.

Lightfoot's sermon on Exod 20:5 entitled "A Jealous God" seems to suggest that God supersedes the human author. Here he speaks of the "Holy Ghost's story" and the "explanation of the Holy Ghost." But even more telling are his numerous statements about the style of the Holy Ghost. He closes his discussion saying, "These and other things of the

---

24. Lightfoot, *Harmony of the Four Evangelists*, 4:114.

25. Ibid.

26. Interestingly, while Lightfoot uses a;nwqen to make his point in Luke 1:3, it is not apparent that John 3:3 (where Jesus tells Nicodemus that he must be born "from above") is relevant. This despite an extended discussion on the significance of ἄνωθεν being translated "from above" and a 54-page commentary on the first fourteen verses of John. Lightfoot seems to be more interested in the context of John 3 then in using this to make any argument about Scripture. Lightfoot, *The Harmony of the Four Evangelists*, 5:1–54.

27. Lightfoot, *Harmony of the Four Evangelists*, 4:115.

like nature, may be observed in the very style and dialect the Holy Ghost useth in Scripture."[28] In a sermon on 2 Sam 19:29, he again mentions the "style and strength" of the Holy Spirit's writing.[29] But Lightfoot does not mean to imply here that the Holy Spirit has a unique non-human style. In fact, in this passage the style and dialect have more to do with the content than they do with writing techniques. The Holy Spirit works through the person, who remains a thinking and feeling vessel:

> So that the Spirit of God inspired certain persons, whom he pleased, to be the revealers of his will, till he had imparted and committed to writing what he thought fit to reveal under the Old Testament; and when he had completed that, the Holy Ghost departed, and such inspirations ceased. And when the gospel was to come in, then the Spirit was restored again, and bestowed upon several persons for the revealing farther of the mind of God, and completing the work he had to do for the settling of the gospel and penning of the New Testament.[30]

For Lightfoot, the Holy Spirit used people in the "penning of the New Testament," and he believes that the process did not ignore the personality and intellect of the human author. In the previously quoted comments about Luke's Gospel, he says that Luke is setting out to do something different from everyone else; that is, Luke has a plan. The apostles and evangelists, by divine skill, were to understand the "sense and marrow" of the words of the language of the Old Testament prophets and "plainly and fully unfold their mysteries in apt and lively and choice words, according to the mind of God."[31] If they were to be careful to use the right words to reveal God's mind, then it follows that they were to choose the words, and therefore God did not supersede their intellect.

IMPLICATIONS OF DUAL AUTHORSHIP

The assumption that the Bible is both human and divine introduces many additional questions. Who decides which content is to be included? How is it to be arranged? How is it to be worded? Is it written by the Holy Spirit or the human author? Is the Holy Spirit ever at odds with the human au-

---

28. Lightfoot, *Sermons*, "A Jealous God," 7:357.
29. Lightfoot, *Sermons*, "Difficulties of Scripture," 7:212.
30. Lightfoot, *Harmony of the New Testament*, 3:371.
31. Lightfoot, *Horae*, 12:540.

thor? Did the human author ever write anything that the Holy Spirit did not approve, and did the Holy Spirit ever mean something by the words that the human author would not have understood?

One can determine Lightfoot's answers to these questions in large part from the rules of interpretation that he chooses to follow. For instance, he insists that one read the Bible critically because it is divine, and there are many things to be found therein that seem to surpass the human author's abilities. On the other hand, one must read critically because God has chosen to use mankind and write mainly using the conventions of mankind. If man is the author, then expertise in the language and grammar of the author is essential.

Lightfoot's rules and their relationship to the dual authorship of Scripture are a main concern of this work, but one can understand his rules best when seen through the implications of his presupposition: the Bible is both clear and obscure and both divided and unified.

Clarity and Obscurity

James Callahan says that in the first fifteen hundred years of Christian history, few addressed the clarity and obscurity questions apart from the discussion of the meaning of Scripture and the admission that Scripture is obscure. The obscurity of Scripture is more of an assumption than a conscientious assertion, at least until the modern era.[32] It should certainly be admitted that the medieval church considered the Bible to be fundamentally obscure and that it was not until the Reformation that a decidedly different hermeneutic evolved emphasizing the clarity of Scripture.[33] That being said, it is important not to exaggerate the positions of the medieval church as opposed to those of the Reformation. After all, perspicuity and obscurity were not completely antithetical. All understood that the Bible was both obscure and clear albeit in different respects.

Clarity and Obscurity in the History of Interpretation

The medieval church had well established the belief that the Bible was obscure. Augustine had admitted obscurities in the sacred text when he suggested that these were to stimulate our appetite. Rome had argued sufficiently that there are so many dark and difficult places in the text that

---

32. Callahan, *The Clarity of Scripture*, 17.
33. Silva, *Has the Church Misread the Bible?*, 63.

the untutored cannot understand it.³⁴ Musculus noted that there were many adversaries claiming that the Scriptures "are too obscure for us to gather any certain judgment out of them."³⁵ Commoners were not only unable to understand Scripture, they were unable even to read it and were therefore largely dependent on the recognized authority of the church.

On the other hand, the early and medieval church did not completely reject the clarity of Scripture. In his work on 2 Thessalonians, John Chrysostom says πάντα τὰ αναγκαῖα δηλα (all the things necessary are plain).³⁶ Origen said that virtually all Christians understand the fundamental doctrine of the spiritual significance of the law.³⁷ Augustine also said that almost nothing is dug out of those obscure passages which may not be found set forth in the plainest language elsewhere.³⁸ The Bible was, quite simply, both clear and obscure.

Over time, Rome's emphasis on magisterial authority contributed to an emphasis on the obscurity of Scripture. The Reformers, on the other hand, took it upon themselves to emphasize the perspicuity of the Scripture and considerably advanced previous similar arguments. Rejecting the view of the Sophists, and that of Erasmus, Luther said that the idea that everything is not plain is unproven. He called this notion of theirs mad and phantasmagoric.³⁹ But Luther himself did not ignore obscurities in Scripture. He admitted that Scripture was abstruse, but only because of our ignorance, and that these obscurities did not "hinder a knowledge of the subject matter of Scripture."⁴⁰ This subject matter, which turns out to be the fundamentals of the faith, is clear to all, although certain sections may be obscure and must be helped by more clear passages.

Luther and the other Reformers believed that individual interpretation was valid, and thus translations into the common language began. They tried to produce a definitive critically acceptable text of Scripture

---

34. Muller, *PRRD*, 2:323.

35. Musculus, *Loci Communes* xxv (*Commonplaces*, 358, cols 1–2), quoted in *PRRD*, 2:323.

36. This quote is cited by Farrar who also adds that "Scripture is perfectly perspicuous in those few and simple truths which suffice for salvation . . ." and also that "Scripture reveals distinctly all necessary truth." Farrar, *History of Interpretation*, 329.

37. Silva, *Has the Church Misread the Bible?*, 64.

38. Augustine, *On Christian Doctrine*, Book 2, chapter 6.8.

39. Rupp and Watson, eds., *Luther and Erasmus: Free Will and Salvation*, 110.

40. Ibid., 110–11.

based on the best of the extant codices and a definitive interpretation of the whole of Scripture by carefully comparing text with text and by interpreting the obscure passages in the light of related but clearly stated texts.[41] Flacius used a basic exegetical *analogia Scripturae* to interpret difficult or vague passages by means of clear passages dealing with the same subject.[42] Calvin insisted on the clarity of the grammatical meaning, and Musculus cited Chrysostom and Augustine saying obscure texts are always clarified elsewhere.[43] Vermigli said that one should determine that piece of Scripture that is hard and dark by another part that is more plain and easy.[44] Bullinger said that similar passages should be compared for mutual enlightenment; difficult and obscure passages should be interpreted by the simple and clear.[45] He further suggested that the way to keep the Scriptures sound and perfect was "to look to those places in Scripture first which state the Word of God 'so plainly . . . that they have no need of interpretation,' and to recognize that here the mind of God is revealed."[46]

There is little question that the Reformers believed, much like their Roman Catholic antagonists, that there were obscure passages. There was certainly a denouncing of Roman Catholic "obscurity," while at the same time there were specific methods for interpreting obscure passages.[47] What this means is that both the Reformers and the Roman Catholics referred to obscurity in different ways. Both agreed that the Holy Spirit was the author of Scripture, but this led to two different emphases.[48] The medieval church opted for magisterial authority since the Spirit was to be found in the church and, therefore, its leaders were specially privileged. The Reformers, on the other hand, believed Scripture alone was authoritative.[49]

41. Muller, *PRRD*, 2:117.
42. Ibid., 106.
43. Ibid., 119, 323–24.
44. Muller, *PRRD*, 2:459.
45. Bullinger, *Decades*, I.iii (p. 78), quoted in *PRRD*, 2:458.
46. Bullinger, *Decades* I.iii (pp. 74–75), quoted in *PRRD*, 2:457.
47. Muller, *PRRD*, 2:106.
48. Ryken, *Worldly Saints*, 141.
49. This is, perhaps, too simplistic. "Medieval exegetes were quite creative (and contradictory) in their use of the *quadriga*; and the reformers, though they believed Scripture to be authoritative, still (i) relied heavily on the early fathers and ecumenical creeds and (ii) differed extensively on different interpretation of Scripture (i.e., passages about the

The Protestant Orthodox inherited the emphasis on perspicuity, but unfortunately did not greatly advance the idea. Farrar considerably exaggerates this issue:

> The Reformation witnessed an immense advance; but in the epoch which succeeded it, the mediaeval subordination of Scriptural study to Papal authority was succeeded by another subordination of it, nominally to a so-called "Analogy of Scripture," really to the current Confessions of the various Churches. The whole Bible from Genesis downwards was forced to speak the language of the accepted formulae, and the "perspicuity of Scripture" was identified with the facility with which it could be forced into semblable [sic.] accordance with dogmatic systems. To this day men repeat the vague and extravagant assertions of seventeenth century divines, which furnish no assistance and solve no difficulty, and which can only be maintained in detail by an accumulation of special pleas.[50]

Farrar sees Protestant Orthodoxy and Roman Catholicism as equally flawed due to their extreme confessionalism. For him, the authority of the magisterium had been replaced with the authority of the Confessions and dogmatics.

It is true that the Reformers did not base their belief in clarity on a logical argument; rather, it appeared that clarity was an accepted dogmatic assumption. And while the Protestant Orthodox are generally known for supporting the Reformers' beliefs through cogent argumentation, this was less often the case in this situation. Muller says: "The attributes of Scripture noted by the orthodox are never elicited inductively or empirically by examination of the text either in whole or in part in order to determine whether, on rational or evidential grounds, it could be inferred to be authoritative, necessary, perfect, clear, sufficient for salvation, and so forth."[51] He continues: "these are dogmatic assertions resting both on the prior assumption of divine agency in the writing of Scripture and of the

---

Lord's Supper and various other parts)." Derek Cooper, Biblical Seminary, email message to author, March 5, 2010. Regardless of its simplicity and need for great nuance, the overall picture is accurate and sufficient to place Lightfoot in his appropriate context.

50. Farrar, *History of Interpretation*, 26–27 contra Muller, "Scholasticism and Reformed Orthodoxy in the Reformed Tradition: An Attempt at Definition," 20 who says that "they consistently refused to place confession above Scripture and constantly affirmed their confessions as expressions of the truth taught in Scripture."

51. Muller, *PRRD*, 2:299.

necessity of such a divine work for the offer and effecting of salvation."[52] Muller again states, "perspicuity is a doctrinal assumption, resting on the declaration of the inspiration, authority, and soteriological sufficiency of the biblical revelation."[53] While presuppositions of Scriptural authority were their basis, the Reformers and the medieval Catholic Church shared these presuppositions and so allowed them a common ground from which to engage.

When the rationalists began to attack this fundamental principle of perspicuity as contradictory to the obscurities in the text, the Protestant Orthodox did not consider it necessary to argue rationalistic standards of clarity. They simply claimed that "it does not represent a denial of difficulties of interpretation: rather these including the genuine and freely acknowledged obscurity of certain texts, are encountered in the context of the presupposition that whatever is needful for the preaching of the church and the teaching of its fundamental doctrines is somewhere stated clearly and plainly."[54]

At the same time, dissenters had to be refuted. Bert Loonstra writes: "An ecclesiastical and confessional theology had to be developed, which could meet the academic standards of univocity and logical consistency. The clarity of the Scripture had to be demonstrated by the systematic perspicuity of the dogmatical exposition, and in return, the truth content of dogmatics had to be justified by appeals to the Scripture."[55]

Calvin had argued for perspicuity based on humanistic views about rhetoric. If the author had something he wanted to impress on the reader, this would come from the authors mind (*e mene auctoris*) to the written page, and it was the interpreter's job to determine that author's intention.[56] The Protestant Orthodox understood clarity via logic, not rhetoric. They argued for clarity based on the nature of truth: that there is only one truth. The truth is not ambiguous, but univocal and logically consistent.[57]

While we have concluded that assumptions based on dogmatics were a significant, perhaps the most significant, factor contributing to

52. Ibid.
53. Ibid., 325.
54. Ibid.
55. Loonstra, "Scholasticism and Hermeneutics," 300.
56. Ibid., 301.
57. Ibid.

Protestant belief in clarity, we have also seen that these dogmatics were based strongly on logical consistency and the univocal nature of Scripture itself. In fact, the Scripture must be clear if, indeed, it is what it claims to be: the word of God.[58] The logic of the argument might appear circular, but "the basic premise, that Scripture is the Word of God, sufficient in all things necessary to salvation, was held by virtually all of the adversaries in the sixteenth- and seventeenth-century debate."[59]

Lightfoot's Understanding of Obscurity and Clarity in Scripture

It is an undeniable fact, Lightfoot believes, that the Bible is full of difficulties and in such a sense can be said to be obscure. He says explicitly, "the Scripture itself tells us, there are difficulties in it: and, if it did not so in words, yet we might easily find it in deed."[60] After all, if the Holy Spirit were the "penner" of Scripture, it would only be natural that he would "write in a majesty."[61] Lightfoot means by this that the "wits and wisdom of all the men in the world should bow before it."[62] He is the God who spoke lightning and thunder at Sinai, and he does similar things in his writing of the Scripture. The Bible does not exist only for the benefit of mankind, it also exists to demonstrate how great God is, even confounding confidence in man's own wisdom. "Difficulties and things hard to be understood in Scripture, is one part of the majesticness of Scripture."[63]

Lightfoot's recognition of the obscurity of Scripture does not imply his belief in a lack of clarity. Lightfoot insists that he does not follow Rome in her understanding regarding the difficulties of Scripture. In fact, Lightfoot believes that obscure passages are only obscure in that intense study of them is required to arrive at conclusions. In a sermon largely about the difficulties of Scripture, he states two particulars regarding his view on obscurity:

> 1. Though we say, "There are difficulties in Scripture," yet we dare not say, "The Scriptures are difficult." Peter saith, "Some things in

---

58. Muller, *PRRD*, 2:327.
59. Ibid.
60. Lightfoot, *Sermons*, "Difficulties of Scripture," 7:207.
61. Ibid., 212.
62. Ibid.
63. Lightfoot, *Sermons*, "Difficulties of Scripture," 7:213.

Paul's Epistles are hard to be understood:" He will not say, "Paul's epistles are hard." The Holy Bible is like the holy land: some part, indeed, mountainous and rocky, and hard to be traveled over; but the greatest part, pleasant, plain, champaign, and valley. Like any clean beast or fowl that might be eaten,—some bones, but the far greatest part flesh. Now, it were but a mad kind of inference,— Never go about to eat the flesh, because thou canst not eat the bones.

Men, indeed, have made an obscure Bible, but God never did. As Solomon speaks, "God made man righteous, but they found out sundry inventions:" so God made the Bible plain, as to the main of it; but men have found out inventions of allegorizing, scepticizing, caviling, that would turn light into darkness, but that "the light shineth in darkness, and the darkness comprehends it not."—"That which God hath sanctified, do not thou call common;" and that, which God hath made plain, do not thou darken; nay, do not thou say, It is dark. How plain, as to the general, is the history in Scripture! How plain the commands, exhortations, threatenings, promises, comforts, that are written there! Take a sunbeam and write: and is it possible to write clearer? And what! must not the laity and unlearned meddle with Scripture, because it is too obscure? I doubt their meaning indeed is, Because it is too clear, and will discover too much.

2. These difficulties, that are in Scripture, which indeed are not a few,—are not a "noli me tangere," to drive us from the study of the Scriptures, as the inference would be made,—but they are of another kind of aim and tendency. They are not unriddleable riddles and tiring-irons, never to be untied, but they are divine and majestical sublimities; not to check our study of Scripture or of them, but to check our self-confidence of our own wit or wisdom. They are not to drive us from the holy ground, where God shines in majesty in the flaming bush,—but to teach us, to put off our shoes at the holy ground: not to stand upon our own skill or wisdom, but to strike sail to the divine wisdom and mysteriousness that shineth there: not to dishearten us from study of the mysteries of God, but to teach us, in all humility, to study the more.[64]

From this, we find that much in Scripture is plain and easily understood; its history, commands, exhortations, threatenings, promises, and comforts are generally plain and understandable. It is, in fact, largely the fault

---

64. Ibid., 214–15.

of man that Scripture is obscure. Lightfoot would insist that "the Bible is not like Persius in not wanting to be understood."[65]

He would, however, never assume that everything is equally plain to all people. After all, God "never intended to satisfy every man's curiosity, and crossness, and caviling; but he hath given the scriptures in authority and majesty."[66] Of course, he does not mean what Rome means by this—that the laity is not to meddle with the Bible. Rather, he means that some are more skilled than others, but that all are capable of some understanding. So even when it is mysterious by the very nature of its divinity, it is not so obscure that an answer cannot be found. When struggling with the proper understanding of "the feast of dedication" and "Solomon's porch," Lightfoot says, "Certainly the Holy Ghost would never have mentioned these things, if he would not have had us to have sought to know what they meant. But how should we know them? The Scripture gives not one spark of light to find them out; but human learning holds out a clear light of discovery."[67] It is difficult, but our struggles lead to great reward, and so the Scriptures must be understandable. He articulates this later in his sermon on difficulties when he says, "If the Lord were pleased that the Scriptures should not be understood,—he would never have written them, he would never have charged all to study them . . . that so being understood and practiced, they might become the means of salvation unto all."[68]

In some cases, it is not whether the Scripture is clear or not, but rather whether it is believable or not. In this case, we wrestle less with its obscurity and more with its profundity. Anthony Cotter says, "a mystery may be proposed clearly, though we may not be able to fathom its contents."[69] Lightfoot also insists that one understand obscurity and skepticism differently. Incredulity is natural in the case of divine mysteries; they appear to contradict our logical faculties, but this is not actually the case.

> What! Must we then believe things, that are clear contrary to reason? I answer, There are not points, in all the mysteries of divinity,

---

65. Ibid., 213–14.
66. Ibid.
67. Lightfoot, *Sermons*, "Communion of Christ with the Jews," 6:210.
68. Lightfoot, *Sermons*, "Difficulties of Scripture," 7:216.
69. Cotter, "The Obscurity of Scripture," 459.

> contrary to reason, if we resolve them into the right principle; that is, if we resolve them into the power, will, and working of God. That this vast universe should be created of nothing, in a moment; that God should become man; that dead bodies should be raised again. That this mortal should put on immortality;—are high mysteries, many regions above natural reason,—but not a whit contrary to reason, if you resolve them, as I said before, into the power, will, and working of God.[70]

These are indeed mysteries, but we can be assured that they are not contrary to reason, but easily resolved by understanding the power, will, and working of God.

Lightfoot, like his Reformation forebears and Protestant Orthodox contemporaries, holds that the Bible is generally plain and easily understood, but that some passages remain difficult. Often these difficulties exist because of men's lack of understanding and unwillingness to study. This ignorance can be resolved through serious study and proper methodology. Sometimes, however, the Bible contains mysteries that give rise to logical concerns and these are not so easily reconciled except to admit the greatness and majesty of God.

Unity and Coherency of the Testaments

The unity and diversity of the Testaments is not a discussion within Judaism, of course, but it has always been of utmost concern to Christian thinkers. All Christian thinkers, regardless of their varied positions, believe that Jesus Christ is somehow the key that binds them together. In his *An Outline of Biblical Theology*, Millar Burrows says that "the Bible's true unity and final significance are to be found in the general direction and the outcome of the process, culminating in the supreme and central revelation of God in Christ."[71] Floyd Filson says, "It has always been the position of the church that the Old Testament is a witness to Christ and that only as such can it claim a place in Christian Scripture."[72] Because of the universality of this sentiment and the considerable connection it has to the perspicuity and divinity of Scripture, an extended discussion of

---

70. Lightfoot, *Sermons*, "The Great Assize," 6:353.
71. Burrows, *An Outline of Biblical Theology*, 53.
72. Filson, "The Unity of the Old and the New Testaments," 141.

its history would have little value. I have limited myself to only a few examples in order to provide some context for examining Lightfoot himself.

Scriptural Unity and Coherency in Historical Thought

The early, medieval, and Reformation church all sought unity in different ways but most everyone at least included the ideas of prophecy and future hope. Origen began his *On First Principles: Book Four* with a discussion of the divinity of both the Old and New Testaments and sought to prove this largely by way of fulfillment of prophecy.[73] He said, "In demonstrating the divinity of Jesus in this somewhat summary fashion by using prophetic pronouncements about him, we also offer proof that the Scriptures which prophesy about him are inspired and that those writings that announce his coming and his teaching speak with full power and authority."[74] Augustine unified the Scriptures under the "love of God" and joined to that faith and hope.[75]

For the Reformers, the diversity was obvious. It appeared in regard to

> the ceremonial law and its abrogation, the gradual revelation of the manner of salvation in Christ despite the grounding of the entire covenant of grace in him from the beginning, the more complete revelation of the love of God for all people in the New Testament, the partial revelation of the trinity in the Old Testament and its full revelation in the New, and the clearer revelation of the last things in the Apocalypse as compared with the revelation of the end times in the Old Testament prophets.[76]

But none of this took away from its overall unity. One should identify the scope of the text as Christ or covenant. This substance or promise is what unified the Testaments because the New Testament interpreted and

---

73. "And what about the prophecy [from Gen 49:10]." Furthermore, a prophetic statement in the Song of Deuteronomy reveals the future election of foolish nations . . ." "But what about the prophecies concerning Christ which we find in the Psalms?" Origen, *Princ.* IV.I.6, cited in Froehlich, ed./trans., *Biblical Interpretation in the Early Church*, 50–51.

74. Origen, *Princ.* IV.I.6, in Froehlich, ed./trans., *Biblical Interpretation in the Early Church*, 52.

75. Zanchi, *In Mosen et universa Biblia, Prolegomena*, in *Operum*, VIII, col. 16, quoted in Muller, *PRRD*, 2:492.

76. Muller, *PRRD*, 2:492.

fulfilled the Old Testament. God recorded his love for his people in the Old Testament and revealed it even more in the New Testament.

SCRIPTURAL UNITY AND COHERENCY IN THE WORK OF LIGHTFOOT

Lightfoot recognizes the many difficulties that may lead one to doubt the unity of the Bible. Still, he believes that with diligent study, one could see that the two Testaments cohered. In his sermon on difficulties in Scripture, he readily admits, and gives five examples of, "passages in the New Testament which are directly contrary to the old, as if the two Testaments were fallen out, and were not at unity among themselves."[77] He does not reconcile any of these passages or discuss the unity in this passage, as the point of his sermon is only to encourage his readers to study more. Nevertheless, he loves to show the coherence of Scripture in other places. In one place, he says there are beautiful numerical harmonies between the Old and New, showing that "the Scripture is in concert."[78] He speaks of Old Testament passages having two different referents, showing that one of them resembled or prefigured the other in the New Testament.[79] He continues to speak of Matt 2:18, discussing the "fullness of this Scripture, as it is uttered by the prophet, and as it is applied by the evangelist."[80] "It was fulfilled in one kind, in the time of Jeremiah himself, and then was the lamentation and weeping in Ramah itself: . . . But now the prophecy is fulfilled in another kind, when Herod destroyeth so many children in Beth-lehem, and in the suburbs and borders belonging to it: and now the cry is in Bethlehem and it is heard to Ramah."[81] The Scripture is "full" only when the New Testament shows how the Old Testament has been fulfilled.

His most in-depth discussion on the unity of the Testaments appears in his *Miscellanies*, which includes various thoughts on numerous issues. He begins this section with the following:

---

77. Lightfoot, *Sermons*, "Sermon on 2 Samuel 19:29," 7:210.

78. For example, David reigned exactly as long as Jesus lived, and Elijah's drought, Antiochus' desolation and Christ's ministry are all 3.5 years long. Lightfoot, *Sermons*, "Wait the Time of God," 7:226.

79. See his example of the connection between Matt 2:15 and Hosea regarding the phrase "out of Egypt I have called my son." Lightfoot, *Harmony of the Four Evangelists*, 4:231.

80. Ibid., 232.

81. Ibid.

> The two Testaments, are like the apostles at Jerusalem . . . speaking in different languages, but speaking both to one purpose. They differ from each other only in language and time: but for matter, the New is veiled in the Old, and the Old re-veiled in the New. Isaiah, in his vision, heard the seraphins cry, "Zeh el zeh," one to another; "Holy, holy, holy, Lord God of Sabaoth." So the two testaments, like these two seraphins, cry . . . The old cries to the new and the new echoes to the old. The Old cries, "Holy is the Lord that hath promised"; the new answers, "Holy is the Lord, that hath performed." The old says, "Holy is the father that gave the law"; the New saith, "holy is the Son that preached the gospel": and both say, "Holy is the Holy Ghost, that penned both law and gospel, to make men holy."[82]

He continues in the same vein saying that the two cherubim in Solomon's temple had their wings touching the sides of the house and each other, so the Testaments reach from the beginning of the world to the end. He approvingly quotes Tertullian, who calls the prophet Malachi "'the bound' or skirt 'of Judaism and Christianity'; a stake that tells, that there promising ends, and performing begins,—that prophesying concludes, and fulfilling takes place: there is not a span between these two plots of holy ground, the Old and New Testament,—for they touch each other."[83]

He rebukes the "Papists" severely, because their Apocrypha puts a wall between the seraphims, removes "the landmark of the Scriptures." They remove the landmark of the scriptures when they "divorce the marriage of the Testaments, and so are guilty of the breach of 'that which God hath joined together, let no man put asunder?' These two Testaments are the two paps of the church, from which we suck 'the sincere milk of the word.' One pap is not more like to another, than are these two."[84] The Testaments are united and any attempt to ignore or reject this is abhorred and rebuked.

From Dual Authorship to Sensus Literalis

Lightfoot's dedication to the divinity of Scripture is what makes his desire to discover the literal sense so important. After all, if God spoke the words, then they were automatically significant. But the divine nature of

---

82. Lightfoot, *Miscellanies*, 4:51.
83. Ibid.
84. Ibid., 52–3.

the Bible also means that many things are difficult and obscure, and some things are truly beyond our understanding. The divinity also assumes that the two Testaments will cohere throughout; if God is their author, they can never contradict each other and will always be in harmony. The humanity of Scripture is what convinces him that simply by understanding the human author's meanings one can turn much of what is obscure into something more plain. Many things are obscure only in that we are not sufficiently learned enough to understand.

It is through Lightfoot's understanding of the divinity and humanity of the text that one better understands his interpretive techniques and therefore more easily arrives at his understanding of *sensus literalis*. Before looking at the exegetical methods that lead to Lightfoot's literal sense, it is important to discuss the problems inherent in its terminology.

WHAT IS SENSUS LITERALIS?

What exactly is the "literal sense" of Scripture? Brevard Childs is certainly correct that "there are few more perplexing and yet important problems in the history of biblical interpretation than the issue of defining what is meant by the *sensus literalis* of a text."[85] Some insist that "taking the Bible literally" is the only legitimate method, while others refuse to do so. Few, however, discuss what they mean by the term "literal." It could be "the sense the author intended," "the verbal or grammatical sense," "the sense for the writer's public," "the sense that God intends," "the sense a text has when included in the canon," "the sense Church authorities designate, or a host of other meanings."[86] This diversity of reference makes any consensus on the definition difficult and perhaps impossible. Furthermore, even among those who have basic agreement on the definition, there is a problem of consistency. They may insist on a wooden, by the letter, non-allegorical approach to interpretation, but it is doubtful whether they can be consistent in their practice.[87] James Barr says that Evangelicals are especially susceptible to the criticism of handling some passages in a literal

---

85. Childs, "The Sensus Litteralis of Scripture: an Ancient and Modern Problem" in *Beiträge zur Alttestamentlichen Theologie*, 80.

86. Tanner, "Theology and the Plain Sense," in *Scriptural Authority and Narrative Interpretation*, 63.

87. Barr, "Literality," 413. "Even among those who insist that they do 'take the Bible literally,' and that this is the only way to take it, it must be considered doubtful whether they do succeed in carrying out the same literalism on which they insist."

way, but ignoring the literality of others as their own religious position requires.[88] "Popular usage, then, seems to contain a goodly measure of confusion."[89]

It is, of course, not popular usage but rather Lightfoot's understanding of the literal sense that is the subject at hand in this chapter. Still, his writings come to us from within a historical context and for this reason, a brief survey of its use in both Jewish and Christian thought is necessary. While it is certainly the case that Lightfoot is first and foremost a Christian exegete, we must not ignore his desire to understand the inspired text through the writings of the rabbis. It is for this reason that we first turn to the literal sense in Judaism.

Sensus Literalis in Judaism

While Midrashic exegesis does not appear at first to include a literal understanding of the text, it is nonetheless the case that Jewish exegetes have always been concerned with the literal sense. One can see this in the popular dictum of the Babylonian Talmud, "*ein mikra yotze middei peshuto*" (No text may be deprived of its *peshat*).[90] And it has generally been assumed, at least since R. Samuel en Chofni, that *peshat* corresponds to a simple, plain, and literal sense.[91] Even English translations of texts like *Sabb.* 63a translate it as such: "R. Kahana objected to Mar son R. Huna: But this refers to the words of the Torah?—A verse cannot depart from its plain meaning [peshat], he replied. R. Kahana said: By the time I was eighteen years old I had studied the whole Shas, yet I did not know that a verse cannot depart from its plain meaning [peshat] until today."[92]

J. Z. Lauterbach, in his articles in the *Jewish Encyclopedia* summarizes *peshat* as "simple scriptural exegesis."[93] If this is the case, then the rabbis of the Talmud not only insisted on retaining this simple and plain sense, but also making it superior to the *derash* (applied meaning). Unfortunately, neither "simple" nor "plain" are self-defined. Some might

---

88. Barr, *Fundamentalism*, 40–55.

89. Barr, "Literality," 413.

90. b. *Šabb.*, b. 63a, *Yebam.* 11b, 24a.

91. Loewe, "The 'Plain' Meaning of Scripture in Early Jewish Exegesis," 140–85; Halivni, *Peshat and Derash*, 10.

92. *Šabb.* 63a; Isidore Epstein, n.p., *Soncino Classics Collection* on CD-ROM. Version 3.0.8, 1996.

93. Lauterbach, "Peshat," 653.

suggest a wooden-literalism as opposed to a more figurative *derash*. Raphael Loewe and M. Meilziner prefer to define simple and plain in a way that is nearly equivalent to authorial intention. Loewe says, "that only is properly to be regarded as plain, straightforward, or simple exegesis which corresponds to the totality of the meaning(s) intended by the writer."[94] Meilziner defines the literal sense as that straightforward, simple exegesis which corresponds to the meaning intended by its author.[95] But Jewish exegesis included the extreme "physicality" of the literal sense, to use Barr's terminology, and the tremendously figurative as well as everything in between.[96] The variety of understanding is natural considering the long period of time and different communities of interpretation within Judaism.[97] Weiss suggests that what one regards as literal, straightforward exposition is a question to which people of different periods, intellectual climates, and even individual temperaments will give varying answers.[98]

As early as Homer, allegorizing was accepted, and it survived Platonic criticism, because readers insisted that the "ancient poets were divinely wise and accomplished teachers of mankind," and therefore their work was primed for a more-than-straightforward exposition.[99] Both Stoic and Philonic "exegesis" relegated Plato's logic to the lowest division of philosophy and was heavily allegorical as a result. Philo insisted that one should understand anything tending towards derogation of Scripture in an allegorical sense. Even before rabbinic exegesis, interpreters began to apply extraneous devices of speculation to the traditional *halakhah* in order to extract from it hitherto unexposed knowledge of God and unsuspected possibilities of legal and ethical development.[100]

In Post-Tannaitic times, *peshat* and *derash* became nearly interchangeable and it was not possible to equate *peshat* with any single type

---

94. Loewe, "The 'Plain' Meaning of Scripture in Early Jewish Exegesis," 141–42. Although Loewe proffers this definition, he also suggests its irrelevancy to his larger point.

95. Mielziner, *Introduction to the Talmud*, 117, quoted in Childs, "The Sensus Litteralis of Scripture," 80.

96. Barr, "Literality," 414.

97. Halivni calls this idea "time-bound exegesis" in *Peshat and Derash*, 3–22.

98. Weiss, *Dor dor ve-dorshav: hu sefer divre ha-yamim le-Torah she-ba'al peh 'im korot sofreha ve-sifreha.*, i, chap. 18, 158, quoted in Loewe, "The 'Plain' Meaning of Scripture in Early Jewish Exegesis," 176.

99. Tate, *Plato and Allegorical Interpretation*, 10.

100. Loewe, "The 'Plain' Meaning of Scripture in Early Jewish Exegesis," 152.

of biblical exegesis.[101] Maimonides is well known, due to Spinoza's critiques, for his "rash and excessive" deviations from the *sensus literalis*.[102] A. Geiger rebuked the Talmudic authors for their "deficient sense of exegesis" because they neglected the "natural meaning" of the text.[103] Rashi certainly argued for a literal sense (the primary meaning of the biblical author), which included a close look at syntax, proof texts, and logical reasoning, but he continued to hand down the haggadic interpretations of his fathers. It seems apparent, either, that scholars ignored the ancient tradition of *Sabb* 63a or that they understood by it something different than a wooden literalism. Perhaps, as Barr suggests, "the obviously opposed pair of literal and allegorical, actually display a remarkable degree of common ground and interdependence."[104]

Were the rabbis really violating the simple, literal meaning of the text by using allegory or other figurative interpretations and if so, was it intentional or unintentional? In other words, did they prioritize this simple literal meaning or were they completely unconcerned? It does appear that the rabbis began their interpretations with the simple, literal meaning of the text, but felt no need to cling too closely to it. It was not, however, that they were abandoning the *sensus literalis*, but that their understanding of *sensus literalis* included a wider scope of interpretations; it was simply more inclusive.[105]

While we consider this further in chapter 6 on Lightfoot's ecclesiastical approach, it is necessary here at least to introduce what has become the more accepted understanding of *peshat*. S. Kamin says that *peshat* corresponds either to the text itself or to the semantic meaning of the text.[106] David Weiss Halivni argues convincingly that *peshat* carries the traditional meaning of the verb "extension," with the additional connotation of *context*.[107] And based on a "natural semantic development of the meaning *extend*," Raphael Loewe suggests that "the essential notion con-

---

101. Ibid., 156, 160.
102. de Spinoza, *A Theologico-Politcal Treatise*, 114–19.
103. Geiger, "Das Verhältnis des naturlichen Schrftsinnes zur talmudischen Schriftdeutung," 234–59. See also Halivni, *Peshat and Derash*, 3.
104. Barr, "Literality," 414.
105. Halivni, *Peshat and Derash*, 12.
106. Kamin, "Rashi's Exegetical Categorization," 31–32.
107. Halivni, *Peshat and Derash*, 52–88.

veyed by the root [of *peshat*] . . . is *authority*."[108] None of these leads to a wooden, plain sense. Loewe even states that notions of 'plain literalism' as a formal branch of rabbinic exegesis ought, up to the end of the period of the Talmuds and midrashim, be abandoned.[109] Even Lauterbach "is careful to point out that a distinction between 'peshaṭ' as the literal sense of Scripture and 'derash' as the interpretation and derivation could not have been made in antiquity for the simple reason that the Tannaim believed that their Midrash was the true interpretation and that their 'derash' was the actual sense of Scripture, and therefore 'peshaṭ'"[110] The suggestion is that the "literal sense" is equivalent to a community accepted meaning—an authoritative voice. Whether this is accurate or not, one must agree that the literal sense in Judaism has a considerable range of meaning.

It is this ever-fluid understanding of "literal" that Lightfoot is so familiar with in his reading of the Jews and which must have influenced his thinking. But Lightfoot was far less exegetically indebted to Jewish understandings than he was to his Christian faith and especially to the dominant Protestant and dogmatic thinking.

Sensus Literalis in Christianity

While discussions of the "perspicuity of Scripture" may be somewhat anachronistic, Christian interpreters, like their Jewish counterparts, have claimed that the Bible could be plainly understood as a witness to God. But this universal agreement has not resolved the question of a Christian *sensus literalis,* especially in regard to the Old Testament. In fact, the following brief review will demonstrate that interpretive methods in Christianity spanned the same extremes as Judaism.

The first few centuries after Christ included the Gnostic interpretations of Marcion, who was suspicious of allegorical harmonizations,

108. Loewe, "The 'Plain' Meaning of Scripture in Early Jewish Exegesis," 158.

109. Ibid., 180. Loewe later says on page 183: "The conventional distinction between peshat and derash must be jettisoned . . . derash is exegesis naturally, or even experimentally propounded without secondary considerations; if it is popularly received, and transmitted into the body of conventional or 'orthodox' opinion, it crystallizes into peshat."

110. Lauterbach, "Peshat," 653. Lauterbach continues, "Only later, in the period of the Amoraim, when on account of the development of hermeneutic principles the interpretation of the Midrash often seemed forced and artificial, did scholars come to the conclusion that the natural and simple sense of Scripture was different from that given in the Midrash; and a distinction was, accordingly, made between the simple literal sense, called 'peshaṭ,' and the interpretation, called 'derash.'"

and the Valentinians, who moved from simple literal exposition to a more esoteric instruction on ethical and spiritual truth.[111] Against these heretical sects were Justin Martyr, who believed that Jesus fulfilled messianic prophecies both literally and typically and Origen who believed that all texts had a spiritual sense, but not necessarily a literal one. The spiritual meaning included a deeper sense and a higher truth and the entire Old Testament, received for Origen, "a kind of independent allegorical interpretation."[112] Alexandrian and Antiochene schools developed around hermeneutical theories that tended towards the more allegorical and the more literal respectively.

The Middle Ages continued the dichotomy of interpretational methodology. Augustine interpreted both literally and figuratively and insisted they worked well together.[113] He distinguished between figurative and proper conventional signs and reigned in overly-figurative interpretations by the use of the Rules of Faith and Charity.[114] During the sixth and seventh centuries, the *quadriga* became well established and most interpreters accepted the idea that one could find more than one sense in a text.[115] Obscurities were quickly resolved using allegorical exegesis. Although Childs bemoans the implicit denigration of the literal sense of Scripture during this time, it seems important to remember that the *quadriga* was not inimical to a powerful interest in the literal sense of

---

111. Froehlich, ed./trans., *Biblical Interpretation in the Early Church*, 10–12.

112. Frei, "The 'Literal Reading' of Biblical Narrative in the Christian Tradition," 40.

113. Discussing diverse translations he comes to Isa 58:7 and concludes: "For the one is explained by the other; because 'flesh' may be taken in its literal sense, so that a man may understand that he is admonished not to despise his own body; and 'the domestics of thy seed' may be understood figuratively of Christians, because they are spiritually born of the same seed as ourselves, namely, the Word" (Augustine, *On Christian Doctrine*, 2:12).

114. *City of God*, 15.7, 26; *On Christian Doctrine*, Book 2 more specifically on the signs and Book 3 on the Rule of Charity.

115. The division into three spiritual senses is found in the work of John Cassian (d. 435), later worked into Augustine's rules, and eventually accepted by all. Cassian, *Conlationes* XIV, c. 8: De spiritali scientiae" (*Corpus Scriptorum Ecclesiasticorum Latinorum*. Vienna, 1866 ff.) "Spiritalis autem scientiae genera sunt tria, tropologia, allegoria, anagoge, de quibus in Proverbiis ita dicitur: 'tu autem discribe tibi ea tripliciter super latitudinem cordis tui.'"

the text.¹¹⁶ In fact, the other three senses were based on the solidity and authority of the literal sense.¹¹⁷

St. Gregory and Venerable Bede's spiritual interpretations dominated medieval scholarship in the seventh and eighth centuries. By the eleventh century, dialectic pedagogy was used to help determine the original sense, but even then theology often overshadowed exegesis.¹¹⁸ The Victorines, and later Aquinas, were not far from the understanding of Jewish interpreter Rashi regarding the literal sense. The Victorines also stressed authorial intention but allowed a literal sense intention to include a figurative meaning. Hugh of St. Victor, whom Spicq calls the greatest theorist of medieval exegesis, heavily emphasized the literal sense.¹¹⁹ Andrew stressed Hebraic truth and the historical sense, largely dismissing spiritual exegesis and theological questions.¹²⁰ Aquinas was much more specific about exegesis, distinguishing between the single meaning of the words and the various spiritual senses. He did this not by dismissing authorial intentionality but by extending its meaning to include the intention of the Holy Spirit.¹²¹ Nicholas of Lyra accepted Aquinas' connection between the things signified and a second thing, but is perhaps best known for his wide use of Jewish contemporary interpretation. He insisted on the literal sense as his starting point, but he also argued that the New Testament authors were interpreting the Old Testament literally. "He attempted to hold together an historical exegesis of the Old Testament according to the best Jewish scholarship along with a Christian understanding of the New Testament's authority without departing from the literal sense in either instance."¹²² By the time of Andrew of St. Victor, scholars had equated the

---

116. Childs, "The Sensus Litteralis of Scripture," 82. Muller, "Biblical Interpretation in the sixteenth and Seventeenth Centuries," *Dictionary of Major Biblical Interpreters*, 22–44.

117. Greene-McCreight, "Literal Sense," *Dictionary for Theological Interpretation of the Bible*, 455. See also Hans Frei who says that "allegory tended to be in the service of literal interpretation." Frei, "The 'Literal Reading' of Biblical Narrative in the Christian Tradition," 40.

118. Of course, theology always affects exegesis, but it does not always dominate it as it did at this time.

119. Spicq, *Esquisse d'une histoire de l'Exégèse Latine au Moyen Age*, 94.

120. Brown, "The *Sensus Plenior* of Sacred Scripture," 59.

121. Childs, "Sensus Litteralis," 85.

122. Ibid.

literal sense with Jewish interpretation, although as we have already seen, Jewish interpretation had no definitive *sensus literalis* either.

The Reformation is known for its decisive acceptance of a literal sense because Luther had, over time, grown considerably more hostile to allegory and spiritualizing, and called for interpretation to be by the letter. At the same time, he rejected Erasmus' *sensus grammaticus* as "flat, sterile and fully inadequate for interpretation."[123] Luther accepted Lyra's work, but was concerned with his acceptance of Jewish interpretation since Jewish interpreters were blind to the Old Testament's witness to the gospel.[124] Luther used what he called the *sensus propheticus*, which was the letter of the text properly understood as promise. This enabled the Old and New Testament to have one central message.[125]

John Calvin argued for a single sense, which included both literal and spiritual and had no historical and theological tension. His emphasis on the text as the faithful vehicle for communicating God's word kept him from spiritualizing since the literal sense was its own witness to God's divine plan.[126] But even Calvin's literal sense often included figurative and anagogical readings.[127] Hans Frei aptly sums up the tension:

> Whenever the Old Testament is seen as "letter" or "carnal shadow," spiritual and literal reading coincide, and figural and allegorical reading are one. "Spiritual reading" in this context is that of those who are in the first place privy to the truth directly rather than "under a veil," and who know, secondly, that the reality depicted is "heavenly," spiritual or religious, rather than earthly, empirical, material, or political. But since it is the story of Jesus taken literally that unveils this higher truth, the "literal" sense is the key to spiritual interpretation of the *New Testament*.[128]

Once again, we see that the *sensus literalis* of a text goes far beyond a "by the letter" approach. Having traced the two interpretive trajectories of Judaism and Christianity, we see even more clearly the difficulty of

123. Ibid., 86.

124. Ibid.

125. Preus, *From Shadow to Promise*, 267. Childs, "Sensus Litteralis," 86.

126. Childs, "Sensus Litteralis," 87.

127. Greene-McCreight, *Ad Litteram: How Augustine, Calvin, and Barth Read the "Plain Sense" of Genesis 1–3*, 95–149.

128. Frei, "The 'Literal Reading' of Biblical Narrative in the Christian Tradition," 40–41.

arriving at an agreed upon understanding of what is literal. It seems that Halivni's time-bound exegesis is correct in assuming that every era, community, and individual is involved in and continues this *sensus literalis* conversation, and each may define it differently. We have seen that interpretive communities tend to develop around similar assumptions, and it is these assumptions that lead to one's chosen methodology.

CONCLUSION

For centuries, scriptural exegetes have debated the meaning of Scripture and how one should approach it. The meaning, it was thought, came from the *sensus literalis* of the text. But even the meaning of *sensus literalis* and what is to be included within it has been hotly contested. Definitions have run the gambit from a wooden, "by the letter" approach to a considerably more allegorical one. This was bound to be the case since determination of meaning depended not only on the context of the text but on the context of the interpreter. The assumptions one brought to the interpretation greatly influenced what one thought was the literal sense.

Lightfoot like most other interpreters insists that meaning is found in the literal sense of the text, and his definition of "literal sense," again like most other interpreters, is dictated at least in part by his presupposition regarding the dual authorship of Scripture. Lightfoot insists that the authorship of the Bible is both human and divine. Since God is the author of the Bible, it is bound to have a higher meaning than what one finds on the surface. This higher meaning is not always obvious and requires diligent study to determine the answers to the mysteries of the text. Still, because it is divine, Lightfoot expects that the Holy Spirit would indeed make it clear enough for sufficient understanding. The divinity of the entire text also leads him to believe that both the Old and New Testament tell one cohesive story and cannot be properly understood without both pieces.

On the other hand, the fact that Scripture has human authors means that there may be normative means for arriving at meaning. Skill in ancient languages, knowing historical chronology and adhering to laws of reason, for instance, often clarify Scriptural content that at first looked obscure. Its divinity and mystery do not prevent Lightfoot from using typical hermeneutical "rules" to determine meaning. It is with this larger presupposition in mind, that we can now look into the exegetical methodology of John Lightfoot.

3

Lightfoot's Use of Logic, Reason, and the Scholastic Method

INTRODUCTION

THE USE OF HUMAN reason to determine the meaning of Scripture was a matter of great concern in the seventeenth century. John Wilson argued that human reason was depraved and that Scripture should be its own interpreter over against the normative claims of reason and philosophy.[1] On the other hand, Spinoza thought that philosophy (and thus rational truth) was better able to determine the nature and character of God then was Scripture, which offered only moral guidance and lacked a clear perception of God.[2] Ludwig Wolzogen "attempted to draw the line between legitimate and illegitimate use of reason in exegesis and theology," and ended up justifying his own Cartesian views.[3] Leonhardus Rijssen and Samuel Maresius criticized Wolzogen's Cartesian views as far too rationalistic.[4] The incongruity among the Scholastics of this time period makes Lightfoot's delineation of a divine and human text all the more significant. Since the text is human, perhaps it must necessarily follow basic rules of logic and reason. On the other hand, since the text is divine, perhaps its meaning ignores or supersedes human logic and goes far beyond our reasoning capacity. Lightfoot believes that human reason

---

1. Muller, *PRRD*, 2:137.

2. He insisted that theology and philosophy be strictly separated. Muller, *PRRD*, 2:138.

3. Muller, *PRRD*, 2:137.

4. Ibid.

did indeed play a part in interpretation but that it was not sufficient in itself.

Lightfoot's context within Reformed Scholasticism had obvious influence on his ideas and methodology. At the same time, his ardent reading of the Jewish writings was bound to sway his thinking. Besides these two, Rome and the infiltrating liberal perspective must have influenced Lightfoot as well.[5] Was there some middle ground that one could legitimately adopt? Could one use the hermeneutical methods of heretics and not succumb to their theological errors? These questions seemed to travel in the background of all that Lightfoot did as he sought to use the methods of Judaism, Rome, and "liberal" Protestants while holding firmly to his Reformed presuppositions. This chapter will trace Lightfoot's collaboration of reason and divine enlightenment by showing his rejection of much of Scholastic philosophy—or Rationalism, and his embracing of much of Scholastic methodology—or rationality.

RATIONALISM AND RATIONALITY

The seventeenth century was a time of growing interest in rationality and critical methods and most scholars were trained in an argumentative methodology.[6] In-depth questions were asked of the text and answers discovered and documented in logical formation. It was the age of syllogisms, brilliant logic, and minute distinctions. It was the period of Scholasticism and Lightfoot reveled in it. But Scholasticism was not new and it meant different things to different people. Both medieval Rome and Judaism had embraced scholastic thinking for centuries. And a new world was appearing that used a scholastic approach coupled with humanism that went so far as to insist that reason was the ultimate criterion of truth and the sole ground of certainty.

In order to understand Lightfoot's world, it is first important that definitions are in place. After all, Scholasticism can be understood either to be a philosophy or a methodology. It could apply to belief or to

---

5. I recognize that "liberal" is somewhat anachronistic. I mean by liberal, simply those who go significantly further than Lightfoot would prefer in regard to questioning the Scriptural text. It includes all those who do not stay within his "orthodox" understanding of what is allowable.

6. The word "critical" suggests different meanings depending on context. As will be shown, seventeenth-century critics are nothing like those of the next century. What they have in common is a willingness to question the text as it then stood.

function. With regard to it being a belief system, Jack Rogers claims that Scholasticism is a form of Aristotelian philosophy and therefore equates scholastics with rationalists.[7] Certainly there were rationalistic tendencies and Descartes was a seventeenth century thinker, but equating scholasticism and rationalism is somewhat anachronistic. The Reformed Orthodoxy or Scholastic Protestantism that Lightfoot embraces predated fully developed Rationalism by nearly a century.

Even more significant than a question of chronology is the question of the relationship between the beliefs of Scholasticism in general and those of Rationalism. Even the Pre-Rationalists held distinctive doctrines that could not be accepted by Reformed Scholastics. Descartes had pressed that reason was the ultimate criterion of truth and the sole ground of certainty. And this system of thinking developed further in the next century and gained even more solidarity. *The Dictionary of Catholic Theology* states that Rationalism was "the exclusive or at least predominant use of reason, which is to say, of rational speculation and criticism . . . in the study of religious moral, or metaphysics."[8] Rationalism was an understanding that claimed "to resolve religious and moral questions solely on the basis of the natural light [of reason], excluding all recourse . . . to divine authority as manifest in revelation."[9] Stated more succinctly, Rationalism is the view that reason, however defined, is the ultimate foundation of knowledge.[10] If Rationalism assumes that reason is the foundation and that divine enlightenment is to be rejected or at least that reason is to be held above divine authority, then most Scholastics, whether Reformed, Roman, or even Jewish, would dismiss Rationalism entirely.

Lightfoot, an immediate heir to the Reformation, could never be considered a Scholastic if Rationalism was encapsulated in the definition. His sermon on Acts 17:31 denounces those who give priority to reason.

> Then cometh the "disputer of this world," such as these scholars of Athens, that Paul was now discoursing with,—that will have nothing believed, but what may be grasped by human reason; and he will tell, that it is very unlikely, there should be a universal judgment; because it is very unlikely, there should be a resurrection. That bodies in the grave, that have been dust these thousand

---

7. Rogers, "The Church Doctrine of Biblical Authority," 15–46.
8. Constantin, "Rationalisme," *Dictionnaire de théologie catholique*, 13:2.
9. Ibid.
10. "Rationalism," *ODJR*, 573–74.

thousand years, should live and rise again the same—O! how many arguments he frames to show you, that it is against all logic, philosophy, nature, reason.

I shall first reply to him, as Paul to Agrippa, "King Agrippa, believest thou the scriptures? I know that thou believes." Oh! thou disputer, believest thou there is a God? I hope thou believest. If not, I shall give thee the answer, much like that I gave the atheist before,—"God will be God, whether thou wilt or no": as Scripture will be Scripture, whether thou believest it or not. But if thou believest that God is, and that he is what he is,—then, why does thou go about to measure the great things of God, by the pitiful, scant measure of poor human reason?[11]

Lightfoot believes that not only is reason not the ground of truth, but that using reason in this way actually carries atheistic assumptions.

Most scholars now agree that, rather than a philosophy or system of belief, Scholasticism is a method of inquiry. This means that it was more concerned with function than content, including logical argumentation and dialectical methods. Richard Muller, perhaps the most respected scholar on this time period, says that the label "Scholastic" was applied to an entire group of thinkers because they shared a dialectical method characteristic of the schools in which they taught.[12] The Scholastic enterprise assumed the necessity of drawing out, debating, and as far as possible, resolving apparent disagreements between theology and philosophy.[13] Elsewhere, he argues that a Scholastic is one who follows a five-part method:

> A discourse is scholastic only when it . . . concentrates on 1) identifying the order and pattern of argument suitable to technical academic discourse, 2) presenting an issue in the form of a thesis or question, 3) ordering the thesis or question suitably for discussion or debate, often identifying the "state of the question," 4) noting a series of objections to the assumed correct answer, and then 5) offering a formulation of an answer or an elaboration of the thesis with due respect to all known sources of information and to the rules of rational discourse, followed by a full response to all objections.[14]

11. Lightfoot, Sermons, "The Great Assize," 6:352.
12. Muller, "Calvin and the 'Calvinists,'" 126.
13. Ibid.
14. Muller, "Scholasticism and Orthodoxy in the Reformed Tradition," 4. Turretin's name is virtually synonymous with the term Protestant Scholasticism. His system, the

De Rijk supports this methodological understanding of Scholasticism, defining it as an "approach which is characterized by the use, in both study and teaching, of a constantly recurring system of concepts, distinctions, definitions, proposition analyses, argumentative techniques and disputational methods."[15] It may have originally been derived from the "Aristotelist-Boethian logic," but it was in no way "bound, in terms of both method and content, to any one philosophy, such as the Aristotelian."[16] Carl Trueman says, "Scholastic method does not demand a particular doctrinal or philosophical position; it is simply a basic way of arranging, investigating, and describing objects of study, which was developed in the schools (hence it is *scholastic*), and which demands no single philosophical or theological conviction."[17] Trueman, Muller, and de Rijk, along with other scholars such as John Platt, Olivier Fatio, and Donald Sinnema, agree that Scholasticism is first and foremost a methodology with a wide-ranging set of beliefs.[18]

SCHOLASTICISM AMONG THE FAITHS

Christianity as Scholastic

As mentioned previously, one can find scholastic methodology in Romanism, Judaism, and the more Reformed variety of John Lightfoot. In fact, there was more in common with the methodology of medieval Rome, Judaism, and Protestant Orthodoxy then there was between Protestant Orthodoxy and the Reformers themselves. Protestant Orthodoxy was not the methodological heir, but the theological heir of the Reformation. Lightfoot and his Protestant contemporaries took the doctrines of the Reformation and put them into a scholastic format. Bert Loonstra even defines Reformed Scholasticism as the "academic elaboration of the

---

Instittio theologiae elencticae (1679–85) stands at the apex of the development of scholastic theology in the post-Reformation era, prior to the decline of Protestant system under the impact of rationalist, pietism, and the Enlightenment of the eighteenth century." Muller, *After Calvin*, 138.

15. From de Rijk, *Middeleeuwse wijsbegeerte. Traditie en vernieuwing*, 25; cited in Asselt and Dekker, eds., in *Reformation and Scholasticism*, 25.

16. De Rijk, *Middeleeuwse wijsbegeerte*, 111, cited in Vos, "Scholasticism and Reformation" in Asselt and Dekker, eds., *Reformation and Scholasticism*, 107; Asselt and Dekker, *Reformation and Scholasticism*, 26.

17. Trueman, "Rage, Rage against the Dying of the Light," 10.

18. Asselt and Dekker, eds., *Reformation and Scholasticism*, 26–28.

Reformation principles."[19] This is not to suggest that the Reformers were not rational in their thinking. To be sure, Calvin did state that the witness of the Spirit is stronger than all proof and that the highest proof of Scripture derives from the fact that God in person speaks it. His *Institutes* even downplay reason to the extent of saying that Scripture bears its own authentication.[20] Still, the Reformers and even Calvin himself had many positive things to say about reason. Calvin even followed up his chapter on the self-authentication of Scripture with an extended discussion of the rational evidences of the divinity and credibility of Scripture.[21] The church throughout the ages had not dismissed reason even in their emphasis on a divinely inspired Scripture.

But the Reformers were not as scholastic in their approach as were their medieval predecessors or their Protestant Orthodox heirs. It was up to Lightfoot and his contemporaries to take Reformation theology and develop it in a logically consistent way. Muller summarizes: "Orthodoxy did provide Protestantism with an increasingly lengthy and detailed doctrine of Scripture that maintained the fundamental principles of the Reformers in an increasingly technical and scholastic form."[22]

Judaism as Scholastic

While the Reformation church was certainly less scholastic in its approach, the church at large had had a long history of scholastic methods and Lightfoot was certainly influenced by his medieval counterparts. One might argue, however, that the bulk of the influence came from Judaism, which also had significant scholastic tendencies. Judaism was in general agreement that the Bible was perfect, including even its grammar. People expected that God himself would adhere to the canons of correct style. For this reason, when something appeared to be grammatically or logically flawed, Jewish exegetes assumed there was a special message that they were to uncover. Precise and exacting language in the Scripture was there for a reason; never was the language mere embellishment or rhetorical flourish.[23] Nothing in Scripture was "adventitious, casual, or

---

19. Loonstra, "Scholasticism and Hermeneutics," in Asselt and Dekker, eds., *Reformation and Scholasticism*, 301.

20. Calvin, *Institutes of the Christian Religion* I.vii. 4–5.

21. Ibid., viii.

22. Muller, *PRRD*, 2:119.

23. Bland, "Issues in Sixteenth-Century Jewish Exegesis," 63.

superfluous."[24] In fact, twentieth-century German philosopher Hermann Cohen said that Judaism was the prototype of the "Religion of Reason."[25] Jewish medieval writing was famous for its close reading of the texts, its minute questioning, and its logical reasoning.[26] Judaism was scholastic in both its pedagogy and intellectual inquiry. It employed the stereotypically scholastic question and answer format and the logical arguments that often went with it. For example, the *Mishna Tractate Sanhedrin*, over a millennium earlier than Lightfoot, utilized this format with a *qal wahomer* argument:

> Caesar said to Rabban Gamaliel, "You maintain that the dead will live, But they are dust, and can the dust live?"
> His daughter said to him, "Allow me to answer him. There are two potters in our town, one who works with water, the other who works with clay. Which is the more impressive?"
> He said to her, "The one who works with water."
> She said to him, "If he works with water, will he not create even more out of clay?" (*M. Sanh.* 11:1.11)[27]

Gamaliel taught Caesar using a logical scholastic method. He asked questions and then responded with the logical argument that if one can do an impossible thing (working with water), then so much more a naturally easy thing (working with clay).

Kalman Bland, the Duke Professor of Religion who specializes in medieval and modern Jewish intellectual history, has written a telling article on Jewish exegetical principles. He implies that long before Lightfoot, but continuing to his day, most Jewish exegetes believed strongly that "Scripture is meant to be cross-examined and that the study calls for a process of active intellectual inquiry."[28] In the century leading up to Lightfoot, Jewish exegetes continued to share a desire for finding God in the microscopic scrutiny of biblical language. Furthermore, their

---

24. Ibid.

25. This is the entire premise of his work. Hermann Cohen, *Religion of Reason*.

26. Of course, the logic was what we call midrashic and therefore often differed from syllogistic reasoning.

27. I am using Neusner's own system for organizing the text, but disregarding his line designations. Jacob Neusner, *The Talmudic Anthology in Three Volumes*, 2:240. He explains his unique numbering system on pages 53–54.

28. Bland, "Issues in Sixteenth-Century Jewish Exegesis," 56. The entire article makes the point that this is not limited to medieval Judaism, but the quote is limited in scope.

reading habits were conditioned by a common set of hermeneutical principles that informed the rabbinic mode of analyzing sacred texts. By the sixteenth century, this rabbinic mode had been firmly established and, in fact, had reached new heights.[29] The Jewish exegetes sought out gaps in the narrative and responded to them with ever-increasing complexity. They structured their homilies with an initial, relentless questioning and followed it with a series of answers that heightened the syntactic, thematic, and linguistic unity of the passage as a whole.[30] They assumed that biblical authors were dialecticians who governed themselves in the "cold light of deliberate thinking and logical procedures" and that it was therefore the job of the exegete to discover the truths that only a like-minded methodology would uncover.[31] Even immediately prior to Lightfoot, we find examples of numerous Jewish texts that contain all five of Muller's tenets of Scholasticism.[32] No doubt, Jewish methods influenced Lightfoot.

Lightfoot Rejects Some Use of Method

Lightfoot cannot help but use the methodology of those around him and those whom he read, regardless of whether they were theological friend or foe. This does not mean that he is satisfied with the answers either of Rome or of Judaism. In fact, he uses reason and logic as apt weapons in his attack on these two groups especially. He ridicules Rome regarding their doctrine of transubstantiation, saying that it is against all sense and reason:

> I hope every one laughs at the doctrine of transubstantiation, which will fetch Christ from heaven at every sacrament: the master piece of the delusion. Satan shows here, how much delusion he can practice in the greatest ignorance, for a man, against sense and reason, philosophy and divinity, to believe a priest can call Christ out of heaven, and turn a piece of bread into his very body;—the strangest madness in the world! I see it, feel it, bread; and yet must believe it flesh. I know, it was made yesterday by the baker; yet now, I must believe it turned into my Creator. I know Christ is in

29. Ibid., 58.
30. Ibid., 61.
31. Ibid., 62.
32. For a great example of this see Rabbi Yizhak Caro, *Sefer Toledoth Yizhak* (Warsaw, 1877; facsimile reprint, Jerusalem: Makor Publishing, 1978), 48ff. In this example you see the scholastic structure, the disputational method, and the logical argument are revealed.

heaven; and yet must believe that he is here on earth. The heathen were never more blind.³³

Not only Rome, but he also ridicules the Jews for their fables and figments which they created without any evidence. Lightfoot wrote that they create myths and then follow up with an argument to give the myth credence. For example, writing about the Red Sea, he mentions that Jonah's whale was able to swim through the Red Sea showing Jonah the place where Israel crossed over during the Exodus.

> A whetstone; yet they will needs have some reason for this loud lie; and this is it, because Jonah, in chap. ii. 5, saith, "suph hhabhush leroshi," which is, "the weeds were wrapped about my head:" which they construe, "the Red sea was wrapped about my head." And to help the whale thither, Rabbi Japhet saith, that 'the Red Sea meets with the Sea of Japho, or the Mediterranean:' unless the Rabbin means, that they meet under ground, guess what geographer he was: and if he finds a way under ground, guess what a deep scholar. A long journey it was, for the whale to go up to Hercules' Pillars into the ocean, and from thence to the Red Sea, in three days and three nights.³⁴

He concludes this section saying that "the fabling Jews must find some sleight to maintain their own inventions."³⁵ Lightfoot saw that they used their arguments to support the myth they had already created. The evidence did not lead to the answer; the answer needed some evidence to make sense. While justifiably critical of poor exegesis, we will see later that Lightfoot deserves similar criticism himself.

Scholasticism can be seen in Romanism, Protestantism, and Judaism and each one influences Lightfoot for good and for bad.

LIGHTFOOT'S USE OF THE SCHOLASTIC METHOD

The fact that Lightfoot rejects certain arguments of Rome and Judaism does not imply a wholesale rejection of either broad-spectrum reason or the specific details of the methodology. In fact, we have already suggested that Lightfoot is a proponent of reasonable arguments, disputational for-

---

33. Lightfoot, cited without reference by Strype, "Preliminary Matter to Lightfoot's Genuine Remains," in Lightfoot, 1:191.
34. Lightfoot, *Miscellanies*, 4:27.
35. Ibid.

mats, and logical rules. Having said that, we should note that it was not his intention to get involved in scholastic disputes.

In his *Horae Hebraicae et Talmudicae*, Lightfoot claims only to deal sparingly with scholastic disputes:

> Those things which, both here [John 17:24] and elsewhere, in the discourse of our Savior, might give occasion for scholastical discussion, I leave wholly to the schools, omitting many passages, about which a great deal might be said, because they have been already the labours of other pens. It was my design and undertaking, only to note some things which were not obvious, and which others had not yet taken notice of; and, not forgetting the title of this little work (being "Horae Hebraicae et Talmudicae"), I have the more sparingly run out into scholastic or theological disputes.[36]

Not only in his *Horae*, but much of his chorographical work is largely lacking in scholastic approach. While these contributions are perhaps the greatest of his work, it remains that the vast majority of Lightfoot's contributions follow a scholastic method. And although Edward Leigh, a contemporary of Lightfoot, would say that a method of confirmation by reason is not technically scholastic, most modern scholars would embrace this and all catechetical theology as largely scholastic.[37]

Since Lightfoot is intent on deriving the proper meaning of a text, he cannot afford to ignore credible methods for obtaining answers. Difficulties and obscurities in the text are best resolved by asking proper questions of the text—this is the *quaestio* or disputational approach; a classic scholastic method. This method may be for heuristic reasons only

---

36. Lightfoot, *Horae*, 12:396.
37. His three categories are:

   1. Succinct and brief, when Divine Truth is summarily explained and confirmed by Reasons, and this Divinity is called Catechetical, Systematical.
   2. Prolix and large, when Theological matters are handled particularly and fully by Definitions, Divisions, Arguments, and Answers; and this is called handling of Common-places, Scholastical and Controversial Divinity . . .
   3. Textual, *which consists in a diligent* Mediation of the Scriptures, the right understanding of which is the end of other instructions.

   Edward Leigh, *A Systeme or Body of Divinity Consisting of Ten Books, Wherein the Fundamentals and Main Grounds or Religion are Opened* (London, A.M. for William Lee, 1662), I. i. Cited in Richard Muller, "Scholasticism and Orthodoxy in the Reformed Tradition: An Attempt at Definition" (Inaugural Address at the Calvin Seminary Chapel, 7 Sept 1995), 6.

or it could be an attempt at intellectual inquiry. In fact, de Rijk divides scholasticism into "both study and teaching."[38] While intellectual inquiry obviously went far beyond pedagogical organization to involve syllogisms, speculative gapping, critical investigation, logical implications, and reasonable conjecture, it is the case that both study and teaching in the scholastic period included questions and answers. Muller insists that the core of the scholastic method, in every period, consists in the "*quaestio* technique."[39] One can see this technique in Lightfoot's Old and New Testament writings as well as in his sermons.

A wonderful example of Lightfoot's use of the disputational method to challenge one's thinking in the New Testament is found in *The Harmony of the Evangelists*. In trying to understand the 390 years which take place in between the falling away of the ten tribes and the captivity of Judah, he suggests establishing a chronology by setting the years into parcels and making a chronicle table of the collateral kingdoms parallel to each other. Of course, by systematizing it so, there will arise "considerable scruples" before the student, and he will "find of more obscurity, and challenging more serious study and consideration."[40] It is this intellectual inquiry that both opens up new questions and is the first step in arriving at answers. It is then that he proceeds to his question-and-answer structure:

> Now how can there, possibly, be twelve years' reign between Asa's thirty-first and thirty-eighth?
>
> *Answer*: Omri began to reign, as soon as ever he had slain Zimri,— which was in the twenty-seventh of Asa: but he was not sole and entire king till his thirty-first: for Tibni, his competitor and corrival for the crown, held him in agitation and wars till Asa's thirty-first. And then was he overcome, and Omri acknowledged absolute king, by Tibni's soldiers; and so, from thenceforward, he reigned sole king in Tirzah.
>
> But yet doubt remaineth, how Omri, beginning his monarchy in the thirty-first of Asa, and ending it in his thirty-eighth, can be said to have reigned but six years;—whereas it was eight current.
>
> *Answer*: The six complete years are only reckoned:[41]

---

38. De Rijk, *Middeleeuwse wijsbegeerte*, 111, cited in Vos, "Scholasticism and Reformation," 106.

39. See Muller, "Scholasticism and Orthody in the Reformed Tradition," 4; Muller, *PRRD*, 2:32.

40. Lightfoot, *Harmony of the Four Evangelists*, 4:103–4.

41. Ibid., 4:105.

Lightfoot continues for several pages asking questions and providing resolutions:

> Now the resolution of this ambiguity is thus . . .
>
> *Answer*: The book of Chronicles, in this place meaneth not that Ahaziah was so old when he began to reign; . . .
>
> There is yet one scruple more arising, concerning the beginning of the reign of this Ahaziah. . . ."
>
> *Answer*: The resolution of this doubt will be easy to him that hath such a chronical table, . . .
>
> There is a scruple of no small difficulty about the reckoning of this twentieth year of Jotham, . . .
>
> *Answer*: In this very difficulty, hath the text fixed the time of Uzziah's becoming Leprous, . . .
>
> but yet there ariseth another doubt in the computation of the times of Hezekiah, parallel with the times of Hoshea: . . .
>
> *Answer*: The beginning of Hezekiah's reign, is of a double date: . . .[42]

This disputational approach includes both pedagogy and intellectual inquiry as Lightfoot is teaching his readers to ask the questions that he asked and teaching them how to arrive at the proper answers.

Lightfoot not only uses the disputational method in his exegesis of the New Testament, but also in his exegesis on the Old Testament. In *A Handful of Gleanings out of the Book of Exodus,* he discusses why Zipporah was so "lately delivered of child." Before he lists his reasons, he first mentions that it "is plain by observing these things."[43] First, regardless of where Moses was, Jethro would have circumcised the baby. Second, children are named at their circumcision; did the child not have a name all of this time? Third, Eliezer's name, "God is my helper" was given that Moses might escape the danger of Pharaoh.[44] Once again, Lightfoot uses logical arguments and numbers them for pedagogical reasons making his scholastic tendencies more evident. He uses this same pedagogy in his comments on Psalm 88 when he mentions a significant chronological problem.

42. Ibid., 4:105–10.
43. Lightfoot, *A Handful of Gleanings out of the Book of Exodus*, 2:364.
44. Ibid., 2:364–65.

> "*Objection.* But David is named frequently in the Psalm, who was not born, of many hundreds of years, after Ethan was dead.
>
> *Answer.* 1. This might be done prophetically."[45]

Once again, Lightfoot asks the right questions, setting himself up to teach the correct interpretation of the passage.

He also uses the disputational method in his sermons. In a sermon on Revelation, for example, where he is arguing for John the Apostle's authorship, he lists three reasons in normal scholastic style. When Lightfoot comes to the name of John in the text, he questions the identity of the man, whether he is the apostle or some other. It is this kind of intellectual inquiry that lends to his question-and-answer construction. He is involved in both intellectual inquiry and pedagogical method.

Few, if any, would doubt Lightfoot's scholastic style. These few examples only seek to buttress what most would naturally assume considering his social context and ancient texts he avidly read. However, more significant than the structure is the questions that he asks and the way in which he chooses to answer them. There are, for Lightfoot, three primary ways to answer the questions that he presents—basic reason, more sophisticated logical reasoning, and prayer that God might illumine the mysteries of his word.

LIGHTFOOT ANSWERING HIS OWN QUESTIONS

Basic Reason

Lightfoot insists that reason is a necessary skill in interpreting Scripture. It is through reason that one is able to arrive at the plain sense of the text. Moreover, Lightfoot believes that God has given reason to all men. In a discussion on Exod 20:5, he says that the first commandment should be easy to keep. Israel would be foolish to worship a golden calf after having just been to Sinai and having witnessed the defeat of Egypt. He states, "Reason, the light of nature, and common sense (one would think) should cry this down to men, that have their wits about them, that there might not any such command from God be needful."[46] What God has provided innately is sufficient for many things.

---

45. Ibid., 2:356.
46. Lightfoot, *Sermons*, "A Sermon Preached upon Exodus xx. 5," 7:351–52.

Not only has he given it to all men, there is scriptural support for using reason to understand the divine text. It is justified because Stephen himself speaks not from Scripture but from good and necessary consequence. Regarding Moses' education, Stephen says that he was "learned in all the wisdom of the Egyptians," but Lightfoot finds no text that states this expressly. Still, "it could not otherwise be conceived of the adopted son of a king, and of a king of Egypt, which nation was exceedingly given to learning and study."[47] Our ability to reason is from God and Scripture supports this.

Of course, some things require almost no reasoning ability at all. In a discussion on Babel's confusion of languages, Lightfoot says that there is no reason to give proof, because it is obvious to our senses that languages are distinct and confusing. "That the world, from Babel, was scattered into divers tongues, we need no other proof, than as Diogenes proved, that there is motion, by walking,—so we may see the confusion of languages, by our confused speaking."[48] Most things, however, are not so palpably clear.

While clarity is not always immediate, basic reason makes things abundantly clearer. The aforementioned example regarding the identity of the author of the book of Revelation is not so clear as to be able to dispense with inquiry. But, proper reasoning will produce the answer:

> I. That it is disagreeable to all reason to think, that our Savior,—when he intended to do some man so much honour and favour, as to impart such noble and glorious visions and revelations to him, as are recorded in this book,—should pass by and skip over his own apostles and disciples, and should pick out a man, that, we all know, was not apostle,—that no one knows, whether he were a disciple or no. But,
>
> II. It is agreeable to all reason to conceive, that, as the man, to whom God vouchsafed the revelation and discovery of the times and occurrences, that were to intervene betwixt his own times and the fall of Jerusalem, was "Daniel, a man greatly beloved;"—so that the John, to whom Christ would vouchsafe the revelation and discovery of the times and occurrences, that were to intervene betwixt the fall of Jerusalem and the end of the world, was John the disciple "greatly beloved."[49]

47. Lightfoot, *Harmony of the Old Testament*, 2:112.
48. Lightfoot, *Miscellanies*, 4:40.
49. Lightfoot, *Sermons*, "The New Jerusalem," 7:112.

Lightfoot's argument is one of basic reasonability. Why would God give this privilege to anyone other than the apostle John that we all know? This would be unreasonable and so John is evidently the author. One needs neither Scriptural argument nor illumination.

Scripture is often a part of the general argument, but one needs reason to make sense of it all. In his discussion on letters, he says that "letters were so long in use before the giving of the law, I am induced to believe, upon these reasons:—"

> First; Josephus is of this mind, that letters were before the flood. And the Scripture cites Enoch's prophecy,—which whether it were written by him or not, is uncertain: yet, if there were any such thing, those many places, which we find of it in Tertullian, Clemens, and others,—do argue, that so much could not punctually be kept by word of mouth.
>
> A second reason to move me to think of letters before the giving of the law, is, to think of Joseph's accounts in Egypt, which seem almost impossible without writing.
>
> Thirdly; But, omitting that, I cannot see how all arts and sciences in the world should then flourish, as (considering their infancy) they did, without the ground-work of all learning,—letters.
>
> Fourthly; Again, for the Jews, upon the writing of the law, to be put to spelling (as they that had never seen letters before), and not to be able to read it, had been a law upon the law, adding to the hardness of it.
>
> Fifthly; Nor can I think, that, when Moses saith, "Blot me out of thy book," that he taketh the metaphor from his own books (which, it is probable, he had not yet written); but from other books which were then abounding in the world.
>
> Sixthly; The Egyptian chronicles, of so many thousand years, in Diodorus and Laertius, I know, are ridiculous; yet their carefulness of keeping records, I have ever believed. "The Greeks were boys to them," as it is in Plato: and Moses was "scholar" to them, or their learning.
>
> Now, I cannot think, that this their exceeding human learning, was kept only in their brains, and none in writing: nor do I think, that, if it were written, it was deciphered only in their obscure hieroglyphics; but that some of it came to ordinary writing of familiar letters.[50]

---

50. Lightfoot, *Miscellanies*, 4:45–46.

Phrases such as "I cannot see how . . ." and "I cannot think . . ." make clear Lightfoot's approach to these difficulties. The proofs need no argument from Scripture; rather, they are only indirectly connected.

Lightfoot often intimates that the Bible interprets or hints at an issue, but that the answer appears when reason is brought into the equation. For example, the answer to how the angels sinned "is not spoken out in plain terms in other places of scripture. And yet, out of other places, and reason and argumentation from Scripture, it may be reasonably collected and conjectured what it was. . . ."[51] Reason is to confirm all interpretations of the Bible.[52] Satan's dismissal from heaven (Rev 12:9) was speedy even though there was "not mention of its speed . . . the word intimates and all reason confirms, the quickness of the thing."[53] Regarding Jesus' comment in Luke 24:44 about the "missing" category known as the writings, he explains: "That he did not exclude them, reason will tell us; for in several books of that division is he himself spoken of, as well as in the Psalms: and that he did not include them in the title of the 'the prophets' reason also will dictate: because we would not suppose him speaking differently from the common and received opinion of that nation."[54]

In Lightfoot's comments on Matt 17:2, reason again dictates the answer: "Here that is worthy observing, which some Jews note, and reason dictates,—namely, That the cloud of glory, the conductor of Israel, departed at the death of Moses . . ."[55] In discussing the letters of the Hebrew Bible, he again argues based on reason (and dignity) that the law could not have been given by Moses in Assyrian letters: "For to think that the divine law was writ in characters, proper to the cursed seed of Cham, is agreeable neither to the dignity of the law, nor indeed to reason itself."[56]

In his attempt to determine the *sensus literalis* of the text, Lightfoot insists on the use of basic reason. God gives it to all men and they are to employ it even in their understanding of a divinely inspired book. Without reason, Scripture remains obscure in many areas.

---

51. Lightfoot, *Explanation of Divers Difficult Places of Holy Scripture*, 5:352.
52. Lightfoot, *Sermons*, "The Sabbath Hallowed," 7:375.
53. Lightfoot, *Explanation of Divers Difficult Places of Holy Scripture*, 5:357.
54. Lightfoot, *Horae*, 12:217.
55. Ibid., 11:231.
56. Ibid., 102.

Logical Rules and Reason

Some biblical inquiries require additional reason to arrive at answers; they require the rationality of logical rules. This is not to suggest a large difference between basic reason and logical formulations, it is just to say that one is simple and the other is structurally more complex. Logic is a characteristic feature of both early and contemporary Scholasticism. Antonie Vos says as much in his discussion on Scholasticism: "This old tradition of logical analysis is the methodological *Sitz im Leben* of reformed scholasticism."[57] For Lightfoot, the purpose for following the rule of logic (like all of them) is to make the Bible plainer.

Logic is usually delineated via syllogism: if premise 1 and premise 2, then conclusion. This was characteristic of contemporaries like John Cotton as well as many seventeenth-century commentators up through the end of the century.[58] It was not, however, typical of Lightfoot's writings.

Not only did Lightfoot lack syllogistic form, he was, despite his attempts to be logical, not always successful. While justifiably critical of others misuse of logical principles, he himself was not immune to mishandling the text. In a discussion on Matt 27:38 and the parting of Jesus' garments, Lightfoot considers what Jesus wore on the cross. One tradition states regarding stoning: "When he is now four cubits from the place of stoning, they strip him of his clothes; and if it be a man, they hang a cloth before him; if a woman, both before and behind. These are the words of R. Juda: but the Wise say, A man is stoned naked, a woman not naked."[59] Lightfoot continues, "so that it is plain enough, he was crucified naked." This seems to be a large leap in logic. Stoning and crucifying are two very different punishments and even the tradition itself suggests two different answers. Lightfoot has a tendency, which we will note throughout, to come to a conclusion without argument and then make an argument to fit his presupposition.

His logical lapses were often evident when he dealt with minute textual difficulties. In these cases, his great respect for the divinity of Scripture and his avid reading of the Jewish writings compelled him almost into Cabbalism and mystical messages that defied reason and logic.

---

57. Vos, "Scholasticism and Reformation," 108.

58. His method was "basically syllogistic." Edward H. Davidson, "John Cotton's Biblical Exegesis," 133.

59. Lightfoot, *Horae*, 11:349.

The Jews were concerned with the mystical significance embedded in the shape of the letters of the Hebrew alphabet, the mystical significance of the Hebrew vowels, and the Masoretic system of Tropes and punctuation as well as techniques of permutation, substitution gematria, and notariqon.[60] Lightfoot himself falls prey to these tendencies in his writings. For instance, commenting on Deut 29:28, Lightfoot insists that the dots over each of the words of "to us and to our children" are there to warn against curiosity in prying into God's secrets, and that we should content ourselves with his revealed will.[61] Despite Lightfoot's consistent logical lapses, he remains adamant that reason and logic are important hermeneutical tools.

His neglect of syllogisms and his periodic lapses in logic did not keep Lightfoot from employing other rules of logic on a regular basis. For instance, he uses the "rule of contrary" in his comments on Luke 16:22. He says it is obvious that the angels carried the rich man to hell. "In the text, indeed, is not expressed so much; but that left it to be gathered by the rule of contrary: if angels carry good souls to heaven, devils carry bad ones to hell."[62] He also uses the rule of contrary regarding why there is a need for government. He says, "unhappy the sheep that are without a shepherd; like a man without conscience to govern and restrain him."[63]

Not only does Lightfoot use the rule of contrary but he also adapts Jewish hermeneutical methods such as *qal waḥomer* and *Binyan 'ab mishene kethubim*. By taking two passages together, he creates a principle that can be applied to a third. For example, based on the blessing to increase and multiply, Adam and Eve were to beget children agreeable to their own perfection and thus free from pain. This blessing did not utterly fail in Eve's sin. Furthermore, the Hebrew women in Egypt had a quick and easy delivery, no doubt assuming a lessening of the curse in their regard. If these two texts are true, Lightfoot assumes a *qal wahomer* addition: "much more may we think the travail and delivery of the Virgin to have been quick, lively, miraculous and painless."[64]

---

60. Bland, "Issues in Sixteenth-Century Jewish Exegesis," 64.

61. Bright, "Preliminary Matter to vol. 1 of the English Folio-Edition," *Lightfoot* 1:39–40.

62. Lightfoot, *Explanation of Divers Difficult Places of Holy Scripture*, 5:337.

63. Ibid., 319.

64. Lightfoot, *Harmony of the Four Evangelists*, 4:197.

Logic is so important to the production of understanding that it may even trump grammar. Despite Lightfoot's careful examination of grammar and his love for rabbis such as Kimchi and Levita who so ably expressed the intricacies of syntax, logic often took precedence.[65] In a conversation about lots, he says: "Sense and reason doth more bind us to understand casting of lots for this purpose, than the grammatical construction, or literal strictness, of the word; for though it signify, 'obtaining a thing by lot,' yet, not always by lot only . . . But undeniable reason telleth, that it must, of necessity, be understood of 'obtaining by lot', in its place."[66] Logic is of utmost importance to Lightfoot and even determines how literally one should take a word or passage. Lightfoot is obviously fond of logical arguments and uses them often in his quest for the *sensus literalis*.

Mysteries

Despite Lightfoot's prevalent use of basic reasoning and even the slightly more in depth logical rules, he does not believe that all things can be known through human knowledge. There are simply no rational resolutions to some biblical obscurities. For example, regarding the unfairness of the Gentiles' "2,000-year lack of true religion" and Paul's response in Rom 9, Lightfoot responds, "Some things are not resolved by reason, but into the will and sovereignty of God. As other points are above reason,—the incarnation, the resurrection: let reason scan them: and as the Athenian philosophers styled Paul 'a babbler,' when he treated of the resurrection, so the same reason will but laugh at them. But we must resolve them into the power, wisdom, and will, of God; and he knows not what God is, that believes them not."[67] We are incapable of rationally understanding why the Gentiles were unexposed to Yahwism and we will never truly understand the incarnation and resurrection.

In a sermon entitled "The Great Assize," he speaks at length about the Trinity and other mysteries of God.

---

65. Lightfoot, *Miscellanies*, 4:15. He says there regarding the rabbis that "in human arts, some of them have practised: Kimchi and Levita for grammar; Rabbi Simeon for logic; and others in other things,—as Buxtorfius in his collection of Jewish authors, will fully satisfy."

66. Lightfoot, *Harmony of the Four Evangelists*, 4:150.

67. Lightfoot, *Explanation of Divers Difficult Places of Holy Scripture*, 5:326.

> I remember the check in the story of him, that went about such a thing. He was deeply studying upon the mystery of the Trinity, and went about to fathom it by reason, and to suit it to reason. As he was thus studying at the sea-side, he saw a child that was about to empty the ocean into a ditch, with a spoon; and when he told him, how simple and vain a thing he went about; "Even so dost thou," saith the child,—or an angel, in likeness of a child,—"when thou goest about to draw out the profound and bottomless mystery of the sacred Trinity, by thy silly reason."[68]

Lightfoot compares the ludicrousness of emptying the ocean with a spoon, to trying to understand the Trinity by only using reason. Nevertheless, it is not that the Trinity is contrary to reason, as he makes clear in the following paragraphs:

> What! Must we then believe things, that are clear contrary to reason? I answer, There are no points, in all the mysteries of divinity, contrary to reason, if we resolve them in to the right principle; that is, if we resolve them into the power, will, and working of God. That this vast universe should be created of nothing, in a moment; that God should become man; that dead bodies should be raised again; that this mortal should put on immortality,—are high mysteries, many regions above natural reason,—but not a whit contrary to reason if you resolve them, as I said before, into the power, will, and working of God.
>
> Let philosophy and human reason, therefore, cavil, as much as they can, against the resurrection, as a thing unlikely, incredible, impossible; I shall only answer in the tune of them, that, when they saw a thing as unlikely and incredible, yet brought to pass by divine power,—viz. Elias's pouring water on and about the altar, and bringing fire,—they fell on their faces, and cried, "The Lord he is God, the Lord he is God."
>
> And if the Lord he be God, the Lord he be God,—he can raise all the dead in a moment and bring them to judgment, as he created the world in a moment, by the word of his power, if it be but his will so to do.[69]

The greatest mystery in the world is not *contrary* to reason; it is *higher* than natural reason, but it can be resolved within the power, will, and working of God. Lightfoot's rules of reason, logic and mystery all must

---

68. Lightfoot, *Sermons*, "The Great Assize," 6:352.
69. Ibid., 6:353.

necessarily be understood if there is to be any hope of properly understanding a divinely inspired human text.

CONCLUSION

Lightfoot belongs properly within Protestant Orthodoxy or Reformed Scholasticism. He is a theological heir of the Reformation and yet the *quaestio* technique used both as intellectual inquiry and pedagogical tool has come more indirectly through Rome and especially Judaism. This method of thought and writing is naturally organized and is a clear way to promote his rational approach to Scripture. He is not a Rationalist, but insists that one should never ignore reason. He nowhere devotes time to a lengthy discussion on reason, but his writings resound with his desire that his readers appropriate reason in their every exegetical task.

The fact that the Bible is a book written by human authors means that rational argumentation and basic reason can resolve many of its obscurities. Even its divine status does not negate the use of reason in interpretation, but its concepts are not always equally clear because it speaks of an infinite God clothed in mystery. Lightfoot has found a *via media* approach between Rationalism and spiritualism and would have others follow him on that path.

4

Lightfoot's Critical and Linguistic Approach

INTRODUCTION

Ever since 1440, when the *Donation of Constantine* was carefully compared to the Vulgate and the Greek Old Testament, and its early date was proven spurious, scholarship has been increasingly aware of the need for slow, systematic, linguistic, analysis. Lightfoot, two hundred years later, was a noteworthy proponent of paying close attention to a text's transmission, development, and origins. While he predates modern criticism by nearly a century, he is an astute reader of the original languages and demands a slow, careful, and critical reading of the text. He fully expects that his students and readers should understand the importance of original languages and that they would engage the text in the same critical way. He begins his *Rules for a Student of the Holy Scriptures* in this way: "The first to be looked after, is the 'language': the Spirit of God, upon the same occasions, using the same words in the original, This observed, which in translations cannot be so well expressed, giveth light to things, which, otherwise, were obscure."[1] The language of the text combined with this careful approach was essential to understanding Scripture's *sensus literalis*. His involvement in higher critical authorship debates and the lower textual discussions about scripts, Kethibs, vowel points, and other various markings as well as his consistent use of Aramaic, Greek, and dozens of other languages gives evidence of his critical approach. While his dogmatic beliefs somewhat hinder his critical approach, Lightfoot's work remains an important part of the evolving critical tradition.

---

1. Lightfoot, *Rules for a Student of the Holy Scriptures*, 2:2.

PROTESTANT ORTHODOX MILIEU: WERE THEY CRITICAL?

For some time, scholarship has ignored the exegetical advances of Protestant Orthodoxy. Claiming eighteenth-century rationalism as the beginning of the historical critical movement has unfairly corroborated the view that there was no real critical thinking before Reimarus and Astruc. In fact, however, there is not as large a gap between modern historical criticism and the so-called pre-critical scholars as once thought. Certainly Richard Bentley, writing in the early eighteenth century, is considered a father of modern textual criticism because of his argument that the Trinitarian comment in 1 John 5:7 was not original to John. He further insisted that a good exegete should always be on the lookout for contradictions and stylistic inconsistencies paving the way for future critical approaches.[2] However, these discussions were not original with Bentley. Renaissance humanism had already gone "back to the sources" and Erasmus worked on a Greek Old Testament and had already had the same Trinitarian questions in 1 John. In the period of Protestant Orthodoxy, Hyperius, Flacius, and Whitaker were arguing that circumstances and the context of the text were of utmost importance.[3] Scholars were doing critical work even before the advent of modern historical criticism.[4]

Despite the previous consensus on Protestant Orthodox criticism, John Lightfoot and many of his contemporaries insisted on a critical and linguistic approach to the Bible. Muller says that "the Protestant theologian of the seventeenth century was assumed to be fluent in Latin and highly competent in classical Greek and Hebrew. Many of the major theologians of the era added to this linguistic paraphernalia a fair ability in the ancient cognate languages, Aramaic and Syriac."[5]

This emphasis on languages, however, did not, in itself, make one critical. Chaim Schertz, the only scholar to treat Lightfoot's works comprehensively, would strongly disagree that Lightfoot himself was critical.

---

2. Muller, *PRRD*, 2:142.

3. Ibid.

4. It is perhaps helpful to share my conclusion up front, as the word "critical" might cause distraction for the reader. Lightfoot is not critical in the sense of modern criticism. Still, he is already suggesting some of the methodological moves of the next century. I will use the word "critical" in the sense of "careful and willing to question the text." Lightfoot does study and investigate biblical writings and seeks to make discerning and discriminating judgments about those writings.

5. Muller, "The Problem of Protestant Scholasticism," 63.

His dissertation on Lightfoot suggests that "Lightfoot does not belong in the tradition either of modern Biblical criticism or within the best tradition of Humanist scholarship. His approach especially to the Hebrew Bible and rabbinic writings was totally uncritical."[6] Schertz perhaps goes too far in saying that Lightfoot does not belong even "within the best *tradition* of biblical criticism" considering that Schertz himself devotes a full chapter to Lightfoot's intricate use of the Hebrew. The contradiction within Schertz's work is even more obvious when he says, "Lightfoot approached the Scriptures in a highly critical, rational and scholarly manner. His use of history and philology in some ways places him in the highest humanist tradition."[7] Besides that, Lightfoot is involved in controversial authorship questions and treats the Johannine Comma in considerable detail. Still, Schertz is correct that Lightfoot's devotion to divine inspiration, and therefore the perfection of the Hebrew text, prevented him from being as critical as many who would come after him. Lightfoot is both dogmatic and critical, but neither as dogmatic as Schertz propounds, nor as critical as those who would follow him.

In many ways, the Protestant Orthodox and the Reformers were similar, especially in their dedication to their dogmatics and literal exegesis. It is a mistake, however, to see this dedication in automatic opposition to a critical approach. In fact, they understood their critical approach more as a defense of both their dogmatics and their literal exegesis.

The Reformers and the Protestant Orthodox would not compromise their theology and it was often others' compromises that led them to a more detailed critical approach. William Fulke, writing in the late sixteenth century on the importance of accurate translations, bemoaned the fact that heretics erroneously expounded new doctrines in a way that was not in accord with the church and even altered "the very original text of the holy Scripture by adding, taking away, or changing it . . . for their purpose."[8] They were making "false translations . . . for the maintenance of error and heresy."[9] The works of the heretics actually "led to a doctrinal interest in the Hebrew and Greek texts of Scripture."[10] They became heav-

---

6. Schertz, "Christian Hebraism," 13–14.

7. Ibid., chapter 4, especially p. 75.

8. Fulke, *A Defense of the Sincere and True Translations of the Holy Scriptures in the English Tongue, against the Cavils of Gregory Martin*, 7–8, cited in Muller, *PRRD*, 2:110.

9. Ibid.

10. Muller, *PRRD*, 2:110.

ily involved in textual analysis, linguistic study, and historical contextual reading.[11] "They tried to produce a definitive critically acceptable text of scripture based on the best of the extant codices and a definitive interpretation of the whole of Scripture by carefully comparing text with text and by interpreting the obscure passages in the light of related but clearly stated texts."[12] The Protestant Orthodox scholar Johannes Maccovius, said that the internal means of interpretation included languages and hermeneutical nuances but that this was never to be divorced from theological non-negotiables. He states: "Concerning the words themselves, we must consider which are to be taken properly, which figuratively, which of them are more obscure and which clearer: the analogy of faith and context of the passage in turn govern these issues of interpretation."[13] The goal of a critical approach, in the latter half of the seventeenth century was, quite simply, to help clarify the text and, in so doing, defend orthodoxy. It was not intended to be "a negative approach or as a threat to orthodox system."[14]

Not only were dogmatics and a critical approach not opposed to each other, neither was the quest for a literal sense opposed to criticism. Childs says, "a fundamental characteristic of the critical movement was its total commitment to the literal sense of the text."[15] James Barr, on the other hand, says that this is "to miss the point that biblical criticism, as people understood it, was to show that—in many places at least—the literal sense of the Bible could not be true."[16] It was the quest for the literal sense that led to a critical approach. While this critical approach would later lead to a questioning of the literal sense, the Protestant Orthodox, at least, insisted that criticism was necessary. Whitaker continued to say with the Reformers that it was "the grammatical sense of scripture" which is "best

---

11. Ibid., 129. Muller also says "Not only was the era of orthodoxy a time of the flowering of textual criticism, it was also an era in which the critical establishment of the text of the Bible on the basis of collation and comparison of manuscripts and codices was understood as fundamental to the task of the orthodox exegete and theologian." Muller, *PRRD*, 2:398.

12. Muller, *PRRD*, 2:117.

13. Maccovius, *Loci communes theologici*, vii (48).

14. Muller, *PRRD*, 2:144.

15. Childs, "The Sensus Litteralis of Scripture," 88.

16. Barr, "Literality," 427 n5.

able to explain and interpret the scripture."[17] The literal meaning of the text remained that meaning given by the grammatical understanding of the narrative and one could comprehend it by using a critical approach to Scripture.

Despite their commitment to *sensus literalis* and Reformed dogmatics, the Protestant Orthodox remained critical in their approach. While Schertz is certainly correct that Lightfoot, and with him most of Protestant Orthodoxy, is not involved in historical criticism in a modern sense, it is unfair to diminish his advances in biblical criticism. His emphasis on philology did not lead directly into modern historical criticism and his devotion to the divinity of the text kept him from heretical questions. Still, Protestant Orthodoxy was scholastic and critical and "the distinction between 'late orthodox theologians' and 'textual critics' cannot be drawn with absolute clarity."[18] Most scholars emphasized original Biblical languages, cognate languages, dating of vowel points, oriental and Talmudic studies, and all areas of Judaica; Lightfoot himself was heavily involved in each of these.[19]

HIGHER CRITICISM

Although a modern distinction, both higher and lower criticism were significant in the supposedly pre-critical era. Certainly, Lightfoot is far more concerned with textual-linguistic issues, but he does not ignore questions of authorship and textual transmission either. In truth, the distinction between higher and lower criticism is somewhat arbitrary. Both types of criticism deal with similar issues, and in both, one must look carefully and critically at the text. Still, John Lightfoot and his contemporaries do have something to say about specifically higher critical issues.

The eighteenth century boasted the new modern critical age and serious controversy regarding science, text, and authorship questions.[20] Jean-Alphonse Turretin argued that one should not understand the Primeval History as a precise history or a scientific account. The Bible led people to

---

17. Whitaker, *A Disputation on Holy Scripture, against the Papists, especially Bellarmine and Stapleton*, IV.i, 362.

18. Muller, *PRRD*, 2:131.

19. Ibid., 452–53.

20. I do not mean that there were no precursors to non-Mosaic authorship. Andreas Masius' commentary on Joshua in 1574 hinted at similar things. See Muller, *PRRD*, 2:135.

faith and was not for rational and scientific knowledge. Richard Simon argued that the order of the biblical books and even the chronology within the books was inconsistent and therefore, one could not read Scripture chronologically. Furthermore, he was convinced that anonymous scribes gradually rewrote the Pentateuch, and he limited Mosaic authorship to only some laws specifically ascribed to Moses therein.[21] Both Rome and the Protestants refuted such beliefs, but the way had been paved for Jean Astruc's two-source theory and a more fully higher critical approach.[22]

Questions of authorship and chronology, however, did not begin in the eighteenth century. As early as Louis Cappel, there were questions regarding the historical development of the Hebrew language and of the text itself, and Cappel pointed out the many editorial comments of the Pentateuch and historical books. Certainly, the more "dangerous" critical steps were still to come, as Cappel stayed submissive to common dogmatic beliefs and was not willing to deny Mosaic authorship of the Pentateuch.[23] While staying true to Mosaic authorship, scholars of Protestant Orthodoxy were asking significant questions making clear that the gap between pre-critical and critical was not that large. Matthew Poole, for instance, was convinced that Moses could not have written some Pentateuchal statements. In his commentary on Deut 34, he said, "But it seems most probable, and is commonly believed, that this chapter was not written by Moses, but by Eleazar, or Joshua, or Ezra, or some other man of God, directed herein by the Holy Ghost; this being no impeachment of the Divine authority of this chapter, that the penman is unknown, which also is the lot of some other books of Scripture . . ."[24]

Furthermore, he was uncertain as to who wrote 1 and 2 Samuel, he denied the apostolic authorship of Mark, and even questioned whether the accepted attribution of John Mark is accurate.[25] Matthew Henry, another good example of a pre-critical critic, was a proponent of later

---

21. Muller, *PRRD*, 2:135.

22. It is in his work *Conjectures Concerning the Original Memoranda*, that he says that Genesis was composed of two sources based on the names of God: Yahweh (J) and Elohim (E). See Briggs, *The Higher Criticism of the Hexateuch*, 2–3.

23. Laplanche, *L'Écriture, le sacré et l'historie: érudits et politiques protestants devant la Bible en France au XVIIe siècle*, 370–71.

24. Poole, *A Commentary on the Holy Bible*, I: 407. This idea is actually considerably pre-reformation, dating at least as early as Jerome.

25. Ibid., II: 213 and III: 147.

post-monarchical redactors for the historical books. He said, "they were put into the form in which we now have them by some other hand, long afterwards."[26] Henry suggested that Jeremiah may be the compiler and redactor of the historical books and Ezra of the books that follow.[27] Modern higher critics still accept his six reasons for such conclusions. It is perhaps significant to note that while asking difficult authorship questions, neither Poole nor Henry questioned the authority of the text. Henry eloquently stated, "Though we are in dark concerning their authors, we are in no doubt concerning their authority."[28]

John Lightfoot was also not averse to entering into authorship discussions. These answers were not, for him, matters of dogma and one should consider these questions carefully in light of textual details. He willingly confirms the authorship of the book of Ezra by the priest Ezra but is not dogmatic regarding the authorship of Chronicles.[29] Furthermore, he disagrees with Bishop Patrick and many other contemporaries who argued that the man Joshua was the author of the book of Joshua; Lightfoot, rather, believes that Phinehas wrote this book.[30] His faith and theology does not appear to be contingent on the answers to these authorship questions.

Unfortunately, many still see Lightfoot as an extremist who refuses to entertain theories outside of his fundamentalism.[31] Chaim Schertz writes that Lightfoot believed God dictated the entire Pentateuch verbatim to Moses.[32] Schertz attempts to prove that Lightfoot held to a dictation theory through a single paragraph in the *Horae*.

> Aben Ezra will smile here, who, in that his obscure and disguised denial of the books of the Pentateuch, as if they were not writ by the pen of Moses, instances, in that chapter in the first place, as far as I can guess, as a testimony against it. You have his words in his commentary upon the Book of Deuteronomy, a little from

---

26. Henry, *Matthew Henry's Commentary on the Whole Bible wherein each Chapter is summed up in its contents: the sacred text inserted at large in distinct paragraphs; each paragraph reduced to its proper heads: the sense given, and largely illustrated with practical remarks and observations*, 2:1.

27. Henry, *Commentary*, 2:1.

28. Ibid.

29. Lightfoot, *Ezrae Synagoga Magna*, 10:524–31, esp. 530–31.

30. Henry, *Commentary*, 2:1.

31. Schertz, "Christian Hebraism," 80.

32. Ibid.

the beginning וְאִם תָּבִין סוֹד הַשְּׁנֵים עָשָׂר וְגו׳ if you understand the mystery of the twelve," &c, i.e. of the twelve verses of the last chapter of the book (for so his own countrymen expounded) "thou wilt know the truth;" i.e. that Moses did not write the whole Pentateuch;—an argument neither worth answering, nor becoming so great a philosopher.[33]

Schertz's point is that Lightfoot rejected Ibn Ezra's comments about non-Mosaic authorship. If God dictated all of the Pentateuch to Moses, then Moses must be the author of the entire corpus. This may appear, at first, to be a fundamentalist dictation theory, but a close reading of Lightfoot does not substantiate this and rather shows that he did not hold to a dictation theory as traditionally understood.[34] The problem with Schertz's citation is that the quote both begins and ends in the wrong place. Lightfoot has been discussing the division of the Old Testament and specifically the separation of the Pentateuch into a Heptateuch or even an Octateuch. The sentence before Schertz's quote is this: "But if any consent that he [Eulogius] owned the Heptateuch we have already mentioned, we should be ready to reckon the last chapter of Deuteronomy for the eighth part." So, the context of Lightfoot's comments is the possible separation of the Pentateuch into seven books. Still, it is this last line that most clarifies Lightfoot's point: "For as it is a ridiculous thing to suppose, that the chapter, that treats of the death and burial of Moses, should be written by himself,—so would it not be much less ridiculous to affix that chapter to any other volume than the Pentateuch. But these things are not the proper subject from our present handling."[35] Here Lightfoot is agreeing that Moses did not write this chapter, but is somewhat sarcastically at a loss for where this chapter would go if not at the end of the Pentateuch. While Lightfoot is indeed firmly entrenched in Reformed Orthodoxy, he is not as extreme as Schertz suggests. Lightfoot neither holds to fundamentalist dictation theory nor is he opposed to questioning the authorship of texts

---

33. Lightfoot, *Horae*, 12:215.

34. The word "dictation" must be used carefully as we have already shown that direct revelation from heaven might not have been the view of those who were once understood to believe in dictation. See Augustine and chapter 2 above (Divine and Human Authorship). See also Polman, *The Word of God according to St. Augustine*, 47–51. Augustine uses *dictare* and *suggerere* which certainly causes the reader confusion, but they seem to be used interchangeably.

35. Lightfoot, *Horae*, 12:215.

and this, again, places him in the midst of a vital transition into higher criticism.

Lightfoot never doubts the existence of redactors. Like the next generation's Richard Simon, Lightfoot sees the dischronology of biblical passages as evidence of these later editors. For instance, there is an obvious problem when we find David's name in Pss 88–89. After all, these are "the oldest pieces of writing that the world hath to show" because the authors of the psalm were Heman and Ethan, the sons of Zerah and were in bondage in Egypt.[36] How could they mention David if he did not become king, according to Lightfoot's chronology, until 436 years after the crossing of the Red Sea?[37] Lightfoot suggests possible solutions to this problem but the most probable for him is that later redactors add the name.

> It will be found in Scripture, that when some holy men, endued with the Spirit of God, have left pieces of writings behind them, indited by the Spirit,—others, that have lived in after-times, endued with the same gift of prophecy, have taken those ancient pieces in hand, and have flourished upon them, as present, past, or future occasions did require. To this purpose, compare Psalm xviii, and 1 Sam. xxii; Obadiah, and Jer. xlix. 14; and 1 Chron. xvi, and Psalm xcvi, and cv; and 2 Pet. ii, and the Epistle of St. Jude, ver. 18. So this piece of Ethan being of incomparable antiquity and singing of the delivery from Egypt,—in after-times, that it might be made fit to be sung in the temple, it is taken in hand by some divine penman, and that groundwork of his is wrought upon, and his song set to a higher key; namely, that whereas he treated only of the bodily deliverance from Egypt, it is wound up so high as to reach the spiritual delivery by Christ; and therefore, David is so often named, from whence he should come.[38]

Lightfoot clearly leaves room in his thinking for later redactors. The Holy Spirit, of course, endued these redactors with the same prophetic authorial abilities as the earlier writers, but they were editors nonetheless.

That acknowledging the existence of editors is significant to understanding the Scriptures is evident throughout his writings and most often in his *Harmony and Chronicle of the New Testament*, his *Harmony of the*

---

36. Lightfoot, *A Handful of Gleanings out of the Book of Exodus*, 2:356.

37. Lightfoot, *Harmony of the Old Testament*, 2:117 and 175. The Egyptians are drowned in the Red Sea on the 20th of Nisan, year of the world 2514. David is anointed King of Judah in the year of the world 2950.

38. Lightfoot, *A Handful of Gleanings out of the Book of Exodus*, 2:356–57.

Four Evangelists, and his *Rules for a Student of the Holy Scriptures*. Still, his *Horae* speaks of the book of Numbers being split into three books with chapter 10, verse 35 as an entire book in itself, "partly because it does not seem put there in its proper place."[39] Exodus 18 is also misplaced because it speaks of a burnt offering in which there is "no tabernacle nor altar for sacrifice yet built." He also mentions that Moses was to sit to judge the people and make them know the statutes and laws of God, but these statutes and laws had not yet come from Sinai. For these and other reasons, he moves this story to a place between Num 10:10 and 10:11.[40] These examples are evidence, for Lightfoot, that editors reworked the texts for later purposes although all within the purview of the Holy Spirit.

Lightfoot is not overly concerned with historical criticism as defined as reaching behind the text or seeking to correct the text, but he does ask and answer questions that place him within this historical-critical vein. He does not automatically accept commonly held views of authorship, nor does he discount the evidence of redactors in Scripture. Still, while he is certainly critical, he is indeed a man of his time. He is only willing to go so far: demanding that the Holy Spirit equally inspired all authors and editors and that no one should question the authority of the Scripture. This dogmatic, yet critical view flowed over into text criticism as well.

THE IMPORTANCE OF HEBREW

The Hebrew Bible is Sacred and Perfect

The background for higher and especially lower criticism in the period of orthodoxy is the great importance placed on the Hebrew text. For Lightfoot and many of his contemporaries, the Hebrew text is sacred and perfect and this fact demands not only honor and respect, but careful examination of it as well. The original words from God's mouth were in Hebrew and were obviously perfect, but so were the words on the page and even the script itself. Furthermore, the textual traditions were there for a divinely ordained purpose and God, at Sinai, gave Moses the vowel points themselves with the rest of the text. Lightfoot's extreme dedication to the text was almost that of a Jewish rabbi and he defended it with vigor.

---

39. Lightfoot, *Horae*, 12:214.
40. Lightfoot, *A Handful of Gleanings out of the Book of Exodus*, 2:379.

There is little question that in regard to the perfection of the Hebrew language and text, Lightfoot was heavily influenced by the rabbis he so avidly read. The Jews had not corrupted the text out of hatred for the Christians as Melchior Cano, in his *De locis theologicis*, had argued.[41] Their commitment was commendable and even praiseworthy. Lightfoot quotes with admiration the story of Solomon and the *yod* from Song of Songs Rabbah. Apparently, Solomon wanted to remove a *yod* from Deut 17:16 but either the *yod* or the book of Deuteronomy (different traditions) opposed him. For Lightfoot, the conclusion was simple: God himself had left assurance that even a *yod* will never pass away from the Torah.[42] Lightfoot again praises the rabbis who say, "whosoever changeth Cheth into He, destroys the world."[43] The Jews had, commendably, preserved the very words of God for every generation.

Even the fact that there were varying traditions did not concern Lightfoot. He used the generally accepted Masoretic Text, which had been derived from three distinct traditions.[44] The Talmud speaks of three texts of the Bible being found in the court of the second temple with various discrepancies among them.[45] The method for arriving at the commonly accepted text was simply to lay the three traditions next to each other for comparison. If two agreed against the third then the majority position was accepted. Even though there was speculation within the Babylonian and Jerusalem Talmuds over whether the language of the Bible was changed by Ezra after the Babylonian captivity, Lightfoot insisted that the Masoretic text that they used was preserved perfectly. He, rather uncriti-

41. Cano, *De locis theoligicis libri*, I.ii.

42. Lightfoot, *Horae*, 11:99. He attributes this to the Jerusalem Gemarah here, but I was only able to find this story in *SOS Rabbah*. In 5.13 it says, "So if all came together and tried to remove a yod, the smallest letter of the Torah, they would not succeed. From what can you learn this? From the case of Solomon; for because he sought to remove a yod from the Torah, an accuser rose against him. Who accused him? R. Joshua b. Levi said: The yod in Yarbeh accused him. R. Simeon b. Yohai said: The book of Deuteronomy went up and prostrated itself before the Almighty, and said before Him: 'Sovereign of the Universe, Thou hast written in the law that a testament of which part is cancelled is wholly cancelled. King Solomon seeks to remove a yod from the Torah.' The Holy One, blessed be He, replied: 'Solomon and a hundred like him will pass away, but a yod in thee will never pass away.'"

43. Lightfoot, *Horae*, 11:99.

44. Lightoot thought that the three texts originated in Judea, Babylon and Egypt. Lightfoot, *Horae*, 11:103.

45. *b. Ta'an* 18a.

cally, accepted the traditions in the Talmud that were in agreement with him and resulted in a perfect Hebrew text for his community.

The Jews believed, and Lightfoot agreed, that the Hebrew text was sacred and should be preserved because not only did the Patriarchs and Adam speak Hebrew, but also God himself did. "Other commendations this tongue needeth none, than what it hath of itself; namely, for sanctity, it was the tongue of God,—and for antiquity, it was the tongue of Adam; God the first founder, and Adam the first speaker, of it."[46] Not only is this the language of antiquity and of God himself, it continued to be the language of Old Testament mysteries and has continued for millennia. Even when Aramaic largely ousted Hebrew as the lingua franca, the Jews had insisted that, in the synagogues, one read Hebrew prior to the translation into Aramaic.[47] Not only that, but the Aramaic translation was originally to be done extempore so that the translation was not to be seen as a second kind of Scripture.[48] Even to Lightfoot's day, Hebrew remained prevalent among scholars and all Jewish children learned it. Certainly, it was not the Jews primary language, but children, as they grow up, "are taught the letters, and learn to read the Holy Scripture in the Hebrew tongue."[49] Lightfoot recognized that the Jews considered the holy books to pollute the hands and that every letter was important: Changing their language or characters diminished the nobility of these books.[50] The perfection and sacredness of the Hebrew was so important that one could rescue a Hebrew Bible from the fire on the Sabbath day, while saving other translations was against the law.[51] The Jews had kept a pure and holy translation.

Even if one doubted the Talmudic supports, Jesus himself justly defended Lightfoot's views. In Matt 5:18, Jesus argued for the preservation of every jot and tittle of the law. Lightfoot explained that this included the bare letters, the little marks that distinguished them, and every particle of the sacred sense.[52] Not only did Jesus support the Hebrew text, but so did the Holy Spirit. The unknown tongue in 1 Cor 14:2 is actually Hebrew.

---

46. Lightfoot, *Miscellanies*, 4:46.
47. *m. Meg.* 3a, based on Neh 8:8.
48. *m. Meg.* 74d.
49. Lightfoot, *Miscellanies*, 4:47.
50. Lightfoot, *Horae*, 12:577 citing *m. Yad.* 4:5.
51. Ibid., 578 citing *Sabb.* 115a.
52. Lightfoot, *Horae*, 11:99–100.

Special knowledge of the sacred Hebrew text was necessary because a large part of the ministerial task was to prove "the doctrine of the gospel, and the person, and the actions, and the sufferings of Christ, out of the Old Testament" during this transitional period.

> Now the original text was unknown to the common people; the version of the Seventy interpreters was faulty in infinite places; the Targum upon the prophets was inconstant, and Judaized; the Targum upon the law was, as yet, none at all: so that it was impossible to discover the mind of God in the holy text without the imedaiate gift of the Spirit, imparting perfect and full skill both of the language and of the sense; that so the foundations of faith might be laid from the Scriptures, and the true sense of the Scriptures might be propagated without either error, or the comments of men.[53]

When one spoke in a tongue (Hebrew) it benefited "because things were rendered truly, which that mystical and sacred language contained in it."[54] It was mysterious, it was sacred, and God had it faithfully preserved for the benefit of the church.

The Script

While Lightfoot is happy to use the Talmud when it supports his presuppositions regarding a sacred text, he is not so happy with the Talmud's lack of uniformity in its view regarding the script itself. Lightfoot assumes both the perfection of the text and with it the consistency of the biblical Hebrew text written in the Assyrian script. When the Talmud suggests that the Law changed letters during its history, Lightfoot feels compelled to disagree. In this he says that the argument of the Gemarists "rests upon so brittle and tottering a foundation."[55] Even though many of Lightfoot's colleagues argue against a sacred script, Lightfoot insists that it is more probable that the author originally wrote the Law in Assyrian letters and that later editors made no changes in them. The Talmud may not be consistent, but Lightfoot never compromises on either the sacredness of the text or even the script.

---

53. Ibid., 12:539.
54. Ibid.
55. Ibid., 11:102.

Every Word of the Hebrew has Meaning

If the text and script are perfect, then it naturally follows that everything on the page is there for a reason: every word, every letter, every marking. Even a single particle in Gen 4:1 is of utmost significance. Lightfoot's whole translation revolves around the אֶת in קָנִיתִי אִישׁ אֶת־יהוה. Through this particle, we have a prophecy of the coming Christ in human form. The אֶת translated "according to its most proper signification and use" results in the translation "that the Lord himself shall become a man."[56] Even a minor letter change alters the entire sense of passages. For example in Matt 12:24 it says Beelzebul, but some insist it should be Beelzebub. "Let them, therefore, who dare, form this word, in Matthew, into 'Beelzebub.' I am so far from doubting, that the Pharisees pronounced the word ['] Beelzebul,' and that Matthew so wrote it,—that I doubt not but the sense fails, if it be writ otherwise."[57] The change from בעל זבול to בעל זבוב is senseless. Since the text is perfect, one must pay careful attention to it and be alert to changes that some might suggest.

Even the Qere/Kethib traditions show the perfection of the text and compel us to believe that nothing has been lost. Despite 848 places that have marginal readings that appear to show at least a questionable text, Lightfoot insists that these readings actually support the sacredness and accuracy of the text. Sometimes Lightfoot ignores the tradition altogether and simply assumes the accuracy of one over the other. For instance, while he spends ample time tracking אֵשׁ דָּת, the Kethib of Deut 33:2, through both the Jerusalem and Babylonian Targums, he completely ignores the Qere tradition.[58] Still, both traditions are there to convince the reader further that God permitted nothing to be lost. Ezra himself was probably unaware of the differing traditions since he had only the original manuscript of the author.[59] Ezra's postexilic review of the Bible

---

56. Ibid., 12:555.
57. Ibid., 11:195.
58. Lightfoot, *Miscellanies*, 4:79.
59. Lightfoot, *Ezrae Synagoga Magna*, 10:531. His words here are in the Latin: "Librum suum conscripsisse Ezram non est cur negemus : Librosque Paralipomenon conscripsissi; cum, nec affirmabimus, nee inficiabimur. Ad quam rem statuminandam observentur quinque vel sex istae generations memoratae post captivitatem, 1 Par. iii. 19 . . . Prima et primaria Textus correctio est quoad Keri et chetib. Jam vero, 1. Ista correctio orta videtur excomparatione duorum pluriumve Exemplarium, Babylonici, ut videtur, et Hierosolymitani. 2. Cum ergo occurrat saepiuscule apud Libros Paralipomenon, apud Zachariam, Haggaeum, Maliichiam alternation istar tou Keri et Chetib, quinam, quaeso,

included many copies, and instead of ignoring the variances, they kept both.⁶⁰ Not one jot or tittle has vanished from God's revelation to us and we should continue to preserve both traditions accurately.⁶¹ We see this desire in Brian Walton's response on April 14, 1656, to a non-extant letter by Lightfoot. In the letter, he defended his own decisions regarding the Kethib tradition.⁶² Apparently, Lightfoot had questioned him regarding the missing Kethibs as compared to Buxtorff's text and had expected them to be included. Lightfoot believed that since every word was significant and God had preserved every word, we, too, should continue to preserve it.

Vowel Pointing

For many of the Protestant Orthodox, the importance and even sacredness of the Hebrew text went beyond the sentences, words, and letters to the vowel points themselves. While the Reformers never even questioned the antiquity of the points, the Protestant Orthodox encountered a critical polemic that focused specifically on the origin of the points.⁶³ The Roman Catholics, in order to support their view of the superiority of the Vulgate over the MT, were arguing that the points were a later Masoretic invention.⁶⁴ The purity of the Hebrew Text was being questioned and most Protestants could not tolerate its subjugation to the Vulgate. A defense was necessary.

Making the defense even more necessary was the fact that some, even among the Protestant Orthodox, were accepting the non-Mosaic authorship of the points. After all, if only the Catholics argued against Mosaic authorship, the Protestants might be justified in simply dis-

---

hujus rei observatio et correctio Ezrae adscribi potest? Aut si scripti, et ab eo visi, cum quonam tandem Exemplari comparatio hanc produxit variationem? Cum, praeter autographon manu ipsorum Prophetarum conscriptum, vix fuerit aliud Exemplar. Pitman comments on this in his "Preface to the Octavo Edition of Dr. Lightfoot's Works," 1: xcv.

60. Lightfoot, *Miscellanies*, 4:20–21. He does suggest that there is more to it than this, seeming to lean towards the more mystical saying that more than likely, "these marginals are not only human corrections."

61. Lightfoot, *Horae*, 11:104.

62. Walton, letter to Dr. Lightfoot on April 14, 1656. Lightfoot, *Letters to and from Dr. Lightfoot*, 13:358–59.

63. Muller, *PRRD*, 2:254. The Reformers almost universally assumed the pointing to be a late invention. See also Muller, *PRRD*, 2:143.

64. Muller, *PRRD*, 2:242.

counting the argument as unwarranted propaganda (as some did). But, famous Protestant scholars, like Louis Cappel, were also arguing for the late Masoretic addition of the points. And they seldom stopped there. Questioning the points led to questioning the text. If the vowel points were not original, then there was nothing to stop Cappel from using ancient versions to experiment with grammatical reconstruction and actually emend the text. Cappel, with support from men such as Thomas Erpenius, Andreas Rivetus, and John Weemse, did just that and the battle lines were drawn.[65]

Protestant Orthodoxy was becoming more rationalistic and individualistic in its exegesis, but, for most, a mutable text threatened the Protestant view of biblical authority.[66] Non-Mosaic vowel points meant mutability and so the antiquity of the vowels needed defense. After Buxtorff's death, his son refuted Cappel and many Hebraists, both Jewish and Protestant, defended him. John Owen, too, bitterly assaulted Cappel arguing, on totally doctrinal grounds, for the Mosaic origin of the points.[67] Over the next several decades, the views of Owen and his supporters were in the large minority, but the debate never completely abated.[68] In the eighteenth century, John Gill and Peter Whitfield put up scholarly defenses. Whitfield's *A Dissertation on the Hebrew Vowel-points: Showing that they are an Original and Essential Part of the Language* included ten well-argued points that went well beyond doctrine.[69] John Moncrieff did an exceptional job in the nineteenth century and his defense continues to find support today.[70] Mosaic authorship of the points has never been without defenders.

While there were some who denied the usefulness of textual criticism and others who were willing to emend the text haphazardly or without significant proofs, the vast majority of Protestant Orthodoxy

---

65. Ibid., 409. Laplanche, *L'Écriture*, 220–21; Muller, *After Calvin*, 151–52.

66. Muller, *PRRD*, 2:131.

67. Owen, *Of the Divine Original, Authority, Self-evidencing Light, and Power of the Scriptures*, in *Works*, vol 16. It is important to note that he was not attacking text criticism. He even owned a copy of the Polyglot. Muller, *PRRD*, 2:401.

68. Muller, *PRRD*, 2:133.

69. Whitfield, *A Dissertation on the Hebrew Vowel-Points. Shewing that they are an Original and Essential Part of the Language*

70. See Strouse's (Emmanuel Baptist Theological Seminary) arguments. Strouse, "A Review of and Observations about Peter Whitfield's A Dissertation on the Hebrew Vowel-Points."

found a middle ground.⁷¹ Some had suggested that it was not the points themselves that were original, but the sounds. Brian Walton believed that the Masoretes invented the textual vocalic markings, but that they, as Muller summarizes, "stood as an authentic representation of the oral tradition of pronunciation."⁷² In other words, the sounds were original, the written marks that symbolized the sounds were Masoretic, and the Masoretes were faithful to the original sounds. The *Formula Consensus Helvetica* (1675), the last orthodox Reformed Confession, seems to support this possibility. It argued for the purity of the "Hebrew original of the Old Testament . . . not only in its consonants, but in its vowels" but it did not stop there. It did not defend the Mosaic origin of the points, but rather said, "either the vowel points themselves or at least the power of the points, not only in its matter, but in its words inspired of God."⁷³ The purpose of this was to sustain the belief that the MT had supremacy over all translations and yet not to go so far as to claim the inspiration of the actual points. So, while there were varying views, most among the Protestant Orthodox supported the antiquity of the markings or at least the antiquity of the sounds that they represented.

Lightfoot writes sparingly on the vowel points, but he is not uninvolved. True to the fundamentalism that some accuse him of, Lightfoot strongly supports the antiquity of the points.⁷⁴ The Hebrew text was perfect and to question the vowels meant the potential unraveling of the inspiration and authority of Scripture.

The vast majority of Lightfoot's references to the Hebrew vowels simply show that he assumed their utmost significance. He consistently presupposes at least the antiquity of the sounds by making theological arguments hinge on specific pointings and the tenses that follow. For instance, he solves an Old Testament chronological problem by demanding that the conjunction of וְאָעִידָה in Isa 8:2 be pointed with a *sheva* and

---

71. Muller, *PRRD*, 2:399–401. Muller says that the Protestant Orthodox drew the line "at the point of emendation of an original language of the text on the basis of pure conjecture, or of the witness of a single variant codex, or of the sole witness of ancient versions, unconfirmed by the original languages."

72. Muller, *PRRD*, 2:409.

73. *Formula Consensus*, 2, cited in Muller, *PRRD*, 2:93–94.

74. Chaim Shertz agrees, although perhaps stating too strongly, "that what mattered most to him was Christian polemics and not 'objective truth.'" Schertz, "Christian Hebraism in the Works of John Lightfoot," 14.

therefore "rendered in the future tense, not in the preter."[75] He simply assumes the originality of the pointing.

While Lightfoot's assumption regarding the antiquity of the points probably stems, at least partly, from a desire to defend the sacred Scriptures from those who would seek to emend or subjugate them, he is probably equally influenced by the rabbis he reads. While some more modern Jewish authors had invented stories regarding the origination of the points by the Masoretes, and had received Lightfoot's condemnation, most rabbinic texts seemed unswerving in their dedication to the idea that the vowels were divine in origin—even the symbols themselves. [76] Being a master of the rabbinic literature meant that Lightfoot certainly knew the Mishnah. Question 3a in *m. Meg.* asked and sought to answer whether Onkelos, the proselyte, composed the Targum to the Pentateuch. The answer was that:

> R. Ika said in the name of R. Hananel who had it from Rab: What is meant by the text, And they read in the book, in the law of God, with an interpretation. And they gave the sense, and caused them to understand the reading? "And they read in the book, in the law of God": this indicates the [Hebrew] text; "with an interpretation": this indicates the targum, "and they gave the sense": this indicates the verse stops; "and caused them to understand the reading": this indicates the accentuation, or, according to another version, the massoretic notes?—These had been forgotten, and were now established again.[77]

This passage suggests that whenever one read the Law in antiquity, the rabbis were to help them understand the reading. They interpreted this help to refer to what people later called masoretic notes. This text presupposed the genuineness of the accents and notes and most scholars agreed that this included the vowel points.[78] Lightfoot too, agreed. In this, he

---

75. Lightfoot, *Horae*, 11:293. Another lengthy and worthwhile paragraph on Gen 4:7 is found in *Miscellanies*, 4:49.

76. John Owen understands Lightfoot's condemnation to be aimed specifically at Elias Levitas. Levitas argued a century prior to Cappel that the points were invented. Regarding the Jewish understanding of the vowel symbols: the rabbis believed that the symbols had originally been part of the divine gift of Torah, but that they had been lost and were restored by the Masoretes.

77. *m. Meg.* 3.a, Isidore Epstein, *Soncino Classics Collection*.

78. Lightfoot discusses vowels and accents together in *Miscellanies*, 4:20.

approved the view of the vast majority of Jews who followed the Talmud and were not in favor of a more recently invented vowel pointing system.

Lightfoot's belief in the antiquity of the vowels was, as we stated earlier, the commonly accepted view. Lightfoot however, steeped in dogmatic assumptions about the perfection and immutability of the text, believed not only that the sounds were original, but also that the very markings themselves were.[79] This extreme conservative view distanced him from those he otherwise respected like Brian Walton. Even though he worked closely on Walton's *London Polyglot Bible*, he simply could not agree with him regarding the points. Muller contrasts the brilliance of Lightfoot with his attack on those who held to a lately invented vowel system.

> Lightfoot continues—and rightly so—to be noted as one of the leading critical scholars and linguists of his time, particularly in view of his vast Talmudic learning and his ability to draw upon the Talmud and Midrash in order to reconstruct the historical, religious, and cultural context of the new testament. Nonetheless, in the same work in which he presented these insights to the scholarly community, the *Horae hebraicae et talmudicae*, Lightfoot also took up the philological cudgel against Walton and Cappel over the issue of the origin of the vowel points.[80]

While Lightfoot generally did nothing more than assume the antiquity of the points, on occasion he chose to make an actual argument on their behalf.

While none of his arguments compare to those of his contemporary John Owen, nor to later ones by Turretin and Whitefield, Lightfoot does, on three occasions make specific remarks regarding the points. We have already stated that Lightfoot believes in the antiquity of both the sounds and the markings, but a defense of this is necessary. His first argument discusses the competency of the Masoretes. He says that these doctors of the rabbis, these wise men of Tiberias, are the least capable of all men to accomplish so divine a task. The very nature of who they were was convincing enough that they could not have invented these points.

---

79. Lightfoot believed that the points had always existed although obviously not in all manuscripts. Even the manuscripts and versions available to him were not all pointed correctly. For instance in his sermon on Dan 12:12–13 he says, "Point the latter clause right, as you should do (for, I observe, in some Bibles it is mispointed), and the passage is much cleared: . . ." Lightfoot, *Sermons*, 7:223.

80. Muller, *PRRD*, 2:134.

> There are some, who believe the Holy Bible was pointed by the wise men of Tiberias. I do not wonder at the impudence of the Jews, who invented the story; but I wonder at the credulity of Christians, who applaud it. Recollect, I beseech you, the names of the Rabbins of Tiberias, from the first situation of the university there, to the time, that it expired: and what, at length, do you find, but a kind of men mad with Pharisaism, bewitching with traditions and bewitched; blind, guileful, doting; they must pardon me, if I say, magical and monstrous? Men, how unfit, how unable, how foolish, for the undertaking so divine a work! . . . And if you can believe the Bible was pointed in such a school, believe also all that the Talmudist write. The pointing of the Bible savours of the work of the Holy Spirit, not the work of lost, blinded, besotted, men.[81]

It seems abundantly clear that Lightfoot is strongly against the masoretic origin of the vowels. However, it is not quite so clear whether this included both the sounds and the markings. In fact, these comments by Lightfoot do not seem to bar the Masoretes from inventing symbols to work with the ancient and divine vocalization. After all, even Lightfoot heaps praise on the Masoretes in his second discussion of the points and considers them worthy observers and organizers, but not the authors of them.

> These men are held to be the authors of the vowels and accents: which opinion, received by some (and those no ordinary men neither), I must confess, I am not so fully satisfied for, as to believe it. I do, indeed, admire the Masorites' pains, in observation of them in the Bible; but I cannot guess by that, that they have done more than observed: when a word, either in letter or vowel, goes from ordinary rules of grammar, they have marked, that it does so; which a mean Hebrician may do; but why it does so, there is either a right Jewish reason, or none at all, given. To exemplify in one; the word rm[lrdk is so strangely pricked, that one cannot pass it: I myself observed it, before ever I saw the Masoreth: and when I came thither to them for a reason, they have done no more but observed it; viz. "Tebhah hhatha," &c. that Kametz is written with two Shevaes: and so, of others, they seldom say more. Admirable is their pains, to prove the text uncorrupt, against a gainsaying Papist. For they have summed up all the letters in the Bible to show, that one hair of that sacred head is not perished. Eight hundred eight-and-forty marginal notes are observed and preserved

---

81. Lightfoot, *A Chorographical Century: Searching out, chiefly by the light of the Talmud, Some More memorable Places of the Land of Israel; those especially, whereof mention is made in the Gospel of St. Matthew*, 10:150–51.

for the more facility of the text: the middle verse of every book noted; the number of the verses in every book reckoned: and (as I said before) not a vowel, that misseth ordinary grammar, which is not marked. So that, if we had no other surety for the truth of the Old Testament text, these men's pains, methinks, should be enough to stop the mouth of daring Papist.[82]

He does not greatly denigrate their abilities here. If the Masoretes are able so perfectly to observe the text and accurately document their findings, it seems difficult to believe that Lightfoot would not also assume they could create symbols that represent the sounds. Still, if this were the case, this would be the right place to expand on his view regarding vocalization. It would follow naturally that the Masoretes were observing the text and creating symbols that reveal the vocalic pronunciation. Here, however, his emphasis is on marking where vowels do not follow the normal rules of grammar. They are not simply observing a divine tradition of sounds, but a divine tradition of symbols as well. The Masoretes are observers of both the Assyrian letters and the already available vowel symbols. While Lightfoot is unclear whether the word "vowels" in the first sentence refers to the symbol or the sound, it seems logical to assume that in this case he is speaking of both.

Fortunately, we can greatly clarify his ambiguity on the points by interpreting these two previous paragraphs with further in-depth arguments found in his *Miscellanies*.[83] Here he admits that the LXX did not use a "pricked" Bible, whether by accident or purposely ignoring it, but will not suggest that it was unavailable. It must have been available since he is "fully resolved, that the letters and vowels of the Hebrew were,—as the soul and body of a child,—knit together at their conception and beginning; and that they both had one author."[84] He defends this with four arguments.

---

82. Lightfoot, *Miscellanies*, 4:20.

83. While *Miscellanies* was published 30 years prior to the *Horae* and there is always a chance that the previous text is a change in his thinking, it seems fair to interpret this text in the *Horae* in light of this earlier text. Lightfoot never openly admits to changing his opinion and Chaim Shertz says that "one can find the same comments and interpretations in all his works without discernable change between an early or late composition." Schertz, "Christian Hebraism," 15.

84. Lightfoot, *Miscellanies*, 4:50. The LXX writers purposely used an unpointed text so that they could more easily "conceal the truth and treasure of the scripture from the heathen, and, as much as they dare, to delude them." If they used a pointed copy then

1. For, first, a tongue cannot be learned without vowels, though at last, skill and practice may make it to be read without. Grammar, and not nature, makes men to do this, and this also helped out with the sense of the place we read.

2. That Masorites should amend that, which the Septuagint could not see,—and they should read righter than the other, who were of far greater authority,—I cannot believe.

3. Our Saviour, in his words of one "Iota" and one small keraia (*tittle*) not perishing from the law, seems to allude to the least of the letters, Jod, and the least vowel and accent.

4. Lastly, It is above the skill of a mere man to point the Bible: nay, scarcely a verse, as it is. The ten commandments may puzzle all the world for that skill.[85]

There is again no specificity regarding whether the vowels he speaks of here refer to the sound or the symbol. Argument two uses the LXX's antiquity to oppose it against an eighth-century vocalization and this could very well be speaking of the sounds and not the symbols themselves. Argument 4 is no clearer than the same argument we looked at in the *Horae*.

His first argument takes needed steps towards a resolution. It seems he must be referring to the actual symbols since he says that "skill and practice may make it to be read without" and it is "grammar, and not nature" that cause men to read with vowel sounds. We simply would not know the vowel sounds naturally.[86] His third "argument," however, is the most clear of all. Here he suggests that the tittle is not the stroke of a letter but rather the stroke of an accent or vowel that certainly suggests the symbols themselves are *ab originale*.[87] This third argument seems significant

---

they were vulnerable to those who would compare one to the other. By purposely using a non-pointed text they were better able to repoint it to make their transcription feasible. See Lightfoot, *Harmony of the Four Evangelists*, 4:327.

85. Lightfoot, *Miscellanies*, 4:50.

86. His argument is not convincing because it fails to consider that God may have given them the Bible orally before he gave it to them in written form. Still, it is not the cogency of his argument that we are looking at.

87. Of course, Lightfoot is wrong that the tittle is a stroke of an accent or a vowel; rather, it is the mark that distinguishes between a *dalet* and a *resh*. This may cause one to disagree with Lightfoot's conclusions, but it does not change Lightfoot's opinion on the matter.

enough to require that each of the other arguments actually refer to the vowels as symbols and not simply as sounds.

The sacredness of the Hebrew text was non-negotiable for Lightfoot. This meant, that not only did the authors faithfully record God's actual spoken words, but also that the words, the script, and the vowel points were original and flawless as well. Lightfoot's theological presuppositions meant that the Hebrew was superior to the Vulgate and all other translations and that one should reject any attempt at emendation. Both the rabbis and his place within conservative Protestant Orthodoxy influenced Lightfoot greatly and certainly proved to slow his text-critical advance. Still, Lightfoot's dogmatic beliefs did not completely keep him from significant insights and progress in the critical arena. In fact, one could still say that Lightfoot's work was a necessary part of the critical tradition.

LIGHTFOOT'S APPROPRIATION OF VARIOUS TRANSLATIONS

While the Hebrew text was unparalleled in regard to its trustworthiness, sacredness and perfection, other translations had their place as well. After all, the *sensus literalis* of the Hebrew text was not always plainly understood. It was Lightfoot's desire to "clear and open the sense all along," and this led him naturally to the "examination of translations in diverse languages."[88] These translations may have been right or wrong, but they were generally worthy of careful comparison with the MT.

While the use of multiple languages was already a part of standard scholarship at the time of Protestant Orthodoxy and even before, it was not generally acceptable to use it for establishing the original text itself.[89] Beza had often used the Vulgate in his work, as well as variants of the church fathers and Syriac. John Owen, who was more than a little disturbed by critical methods, still used Syriac and a host of other language helps throughout his work on the book of Hebrews. Ainsworth used the Targums, consistently comparing them with the Greek. Still, while everyone was using languages to help their interpretations, they were generally not to be used to emend the text. Cappel did argue that conjectural readings could be chosen above the Hebrew or Greek if it made better sense and enhanced the coherence of the meaning. Ussher and Walton were not too far behind him. But Muller again aptly summarizes Turretin and

---

88. Strype, *Appendix to Author's Life*, Lightfoot, 1:64.
89. The content of this paragraph comes largely from Muller, *PRRD*, 2:433–35.

with him the orthodox perspective: "The ancient version could never be placed on an equal level of authority with the Hebrew or Greek original."[90]

Not only was Lightfoot not averse to using the languages in interpretation, he was perhaps the most gifted master of languages of his time. This is obvious throughout all of his writings, but it is most evident in that nearly all of his extant correspondence is written regarding textual questions relating to various languages. Castell asked Lightfoot, "whether when the ordinary interpretation of any Hebrew words renders the sense hard and rough, recourse may not be had to the interpretation of those words according as they signify in Syriac, Chaldee, or Arabic."[91] The answer for Lightfoot would have been an enthusiastic yes. He references the Complutensian Bible, which was the first polyglot printing of the entire Bible (1517), and included Hebrew, the Vulgate, LXX, New Testament Greek, and Targum Onkelos.[92] He quotes with authority the Erpenian edition, an Arabic version printed in Leyden in 1616, to support his argument that John would not have mentioned the flowing of blood and water unless it had some preternatural meaning.[93] His comments on Ezek 8:17 were made taking into consideration the LXX of the Roman edition, the Alexandrian edition, and the Targums.[94] Lightfoot considered the languages most beneficial for use in interpretation and thereby giving a fair sense to the text.

Not only was knowledge of the various languages beneficial in scholarly writing, but sermons were also a great place for extended word studies. In the first four pages of his eleven page sermon comparing Paul to Bar Jesus, who is also called Elymas, Lightfoot quotes from the Arabic translation found in the Polyglot Bible, the translation of Erpenius, the interlineary Latin, the Greek, the Hebrew, the Syriac, and the Targums Jerusalem and Jonathan.[95] Discussing the result of Jephthah's vow in an-

90. Muller, *PRRD*, 2:435.

91. Strype, *Appendix to Authors Life*, Lightfoot, 1:93.

92. Lightfoot, *Horae*, 12:378. Referenced in regard to John 13:23. Other references to LXX and Targums can be found in his discussion on the didrachma in Exodus 30 in *Horae*, 11:238.

93. The Erpenian edition adds the word "right" in regard to the side where Jesus was pierced showing that it is obviously something strange since the left would have naturally flowed water and blood. The piercing of the pericardium would result in this mixture. See Lightfoot, *Horae*, 12:421.

94. Lightfoot, *Horae*, 12:387.

95. Lightfoot, *Sermons*, "Elymas the Sorceror," 7:102–5.

other sermon, he uses the Eastern languages to support his leaning that Jephthah sacrificed his own daughter.[96] Everyone, even congregations, should know not only the resultant meaning of Scripture, but also the language work that went into arriving at that conclusion.

While the ancient languages are generally helpful, Lightfoot does not always take these translations and translators at face value. He often disagrees with the translators. He is not always fond of the Vulgate or the interlinear and even disagrees with Beza's translations from time to time.[97] He disagrees with modern versions from the French and Italian and even the English saying they have been too loose or too narrow in their translation at particular times.[98] He notices details like the aorist tense, but often disagrees with the sense that others give to it.[99] Perhaps his greatest disagreements are with the Samaritan Pentateuch. The language and the sense is often the same, and yet he is often hostile to it and quotes from rabbis who despise it as well. Lightfoot references the Jerusalem Talmud which states, "R. Eliezer Ben R. Simeon said, I said to the scribes of the Samaritans, Ye have falsified your law, without any manner of profit accruing to you thereby. For you have writ in your law אצל אלוני מרה שכם near the oaken groves of Moreh, which is Sychem."[100] Lightfoot believes that they only "pretend to study the religion of Moses" when they are actually idolaters and accepters of the "deceit and witchcraft" of Simon Magus.[101] He further calls them impudent and heretical and says their version is not of that antiquity they claim for it.[102] In fact, it is fair to say that the Samaritan Pentateuch is never compared positively to the MT, and it is only used to show how remarkable the MT actually is. All languages and all translations are not created equal, and none compare to the sacred Hebrew.

---

96. Ibid., "Prudence in Making Vows," 7:155–56.

97. He disagrees with all three regarding John 13:1 and the addition of the word "day" when the common language consistently applies to the entire festivity. See Lightfoot, *Horae*, 12:373.

98. Lightfoot, *Horae*, 11:88.

99. Ibid., 2:373.

100. *Sotah* 21.3. The problem is with the addition of the word שכם which is not in the MT.

101. Lightfoot, *Horae*, 11:174–75.

102. Lightfoot, *The Chorographical Works*, 10:337–39.

LIGHTFOOT'S USE OF THE HEBREW COGNATE LANGUAGES

While Hebrew is the holy language, being the language of the patriarchs and of God himself, other languages remain significant to Lightfoot. Their significance, however, is not found in their own sacredness, but in their ability to help interpret the sacred Hebrew. Those languages best capable of being beneficial are Hebrew's cognate languages including Arabic, Syriac, and, most importantly, Aramaic.

We have already mentioned his fondness for quoting from the Erpenian edition as well as the Arabic version found in the Polyglot, but Syriac is even more hermeneutically helpful. The Peshitta actually confirmed Lightfoot's chronology of the world and especially of the events of day six. Lightfoot believed that the fall of Adam took place on the very first day of his existence.[103] John 8:44 says that Satan was a murderer from the beginning, but the Syriac clarifies by adding the important word "in": he was a murderer "from *in* the beginning." The Syriac is an interpretation of what Jesus meant when he said "from the beginning." The writers of the Peshitta were saying that what Jesus meant and what his hearers would have understood was a reference to the very first day of creation. The Jews heard Christ say that Satan was a "murderer from the beginning" and understood this to be that he was a murderer from the days of creation—that he murdered Adam on the very first day God created him.[104] The Peshitta is helpful in interpretation.

The Aramaic targums are perhaps the most significant of the cognate language texts, but one must never follow them blindly; asking questions of the texts is always necessary. After all, God did not give the targums on Mt. Sinai, as some of the Jews believe. The Mishna's insistence that Onkelos did not simply add his own sense based on an assumed liberty that he had, but rather restored what had been given with the Law is for Lightfoot a mistake of great proportion.[105] It is a great mistake because "the Targum

---

103. Lightfoot, *Sermons*, "The Sabbath Hallowed," 7:373, 378.

104. Ibid. 374. This was one of two biblical arguments (and several reasonable ones) to prove Adam's death in the sixth day. We will discuss his chronology and historical obsessions in chapter 5.

105. "The Targum was given in Mount Sinai; and when they forgot it, he came and restored it." Lightfoot, *Horae*, 12:540–41 citing *b. Kid.* 49:1. The background context is as follows: "R. Judah said: He must be able to read and translate it. Even if he translates it according to his own understanding! But it was taught: R. Judah said: If one translates a verse literally, he is a liar; if he adds thereto, he is a blasphemer and a libeller. Then what is meant by translation? Our [authorised] translation. 'Our translation' is generally

upon the prophets," for instance, "was inconstant, and Judaized."[106] One example of the error of the Targumists is in his Miscellanies in a discussion on the Tower of Babel. Lightfoot rebukes the Targumist here for taking away the "sweet mystery of the trinity" found there.[107] The Aramaic, upon these words of God, "come let us go down" says instead, "The Lord said unto the seventy angels that are before him, Come, now let us go down, and confound there their tongue." This addition of the seventy angels is destructive to orthodox theology and comments such as these are "strange fancies" that Lightfoot cannot understand. The Targumists are simply not completely trustworthy.

While not trustworthy in an absolute sense, the Targumists often do prove helpful especially in regard to making connections that were not readily apparent by looking at the Hebrew text alone. This is most helpful in our attempt to understand Lightfoot's hermeneutical methodology because Lightfoot often copies their gap-filling tendencies. One connection Lightfoot finds most helpful concerns the identity of Jannes and Jambres mentioned only in 2 Tim 3:8. Certainly, they were antagonists of Moses as this passage explains, but the Old Testament never mentions them. The Targumist not only imagines that they are the same sorcerers who compete against Moses in Exod 7:11, but they are also the ones found between the lines of Exod 1:14 and 15 who proclaim the birth of one who will destroy Egypt. Pseudo-Jonathan further connects them to Balaam's intention to curse Israel in Num 22:22; there they are two dutiful scholars or perhaps even Balaam's sons.[108] *Tg. Ps.-J* Num 22:24 shows a less intricate connection between Balaam and Jacob. Apparently, the place where Balaam is surprised by the angel is the same place where Jacob and Laban erected a mound, a pillar, and a watch post.[109] Lightfoot does not suggest that the reader do anything other than notice these connections. Lightfoot himself makes similar geographical and chronological connections. For example, Lightfoot suggests that Abraham was circumcised in Hebron in

---

agreed to be Onkelos." See Bacher, *Die Terminologie der Tannaiten*, 205 et seq., also art. "Targum" in J.E.

106. Lightfoot, *Horae*, 12:539.

107. Lightfoot, *Miscellanies*, 4:42.

108. Ibid., 33. It is interesting that Lightfoot fails to notice the further connection with Balaam in the Exod 7:11 passage. Here Balaam is seen by the Targumist as one of the three magicians present at the competition.

109. McNamara, *Targum Neofiti 1 and Pseudo-Jonathan: Exodus*, 253.

the month of Abib or Nisan, which is the same time and place that John the Baptist was born who brought us baptism instead of circumcision.[110] God is apparently working carefully in history making connections for our overall blessing. The Targum paraphrases are not automatically and necessarily significant, but they may help in understanding the overall sense of the Scriptural passage and one must consider them.

Perhaps even more significant than the help the Targums offer in making geographical, chronological, and historical connections, is the benefit they are in proving the superiority of the Scriptural languages. One thing that is particularly helpful is comparing words or phrases found in both languages. It is helpful to know, for instance, that the title "the word" which appears in the first verse of the gospel of John is not unique to John and may have theological significance of which John is aware. It occurs frequently among the Targumists and Lightfoot gives a useful list of where מימרא occurs.[111] Neither is the often-used self-designation of Jesus, "the Son of Man," a unique phrase. One can find it in the Chaldee and Syrian and it is Ezekiel's captivity in a Chaldean land that is the reason for its use in the book of Ezekiel as well.[112] One can put the Targums to great use in defending the Scripture's use of certain words and phrases.

Even knowing the spelling patterns in the "Syrian" is beneficial because Syrian often leaves out letters and the authors are "writing not as they read."[113] For example in 2 Pet 2:15, Peter speaks of Bosor and not Beor as it is supposed to be. This slight change of letters from *Ayin* to *Sin* is normal in the Aramaic language and he says that Peter did not make a mistake, and that this was not a later redaction. Rather, this change is purposeful as Peter is in Babylon when writing and is doing so according

---

110. Lightfoot, *Chronicle and Harmony of the Old Testament*, 2:91.

111. Lightfoot, *Horae*, 12:230–31.

112. Lightfoot, *Miscellanies*, 4:13. Chaldee is the language beyond the Euphrates, which the people of Israel picked up during their exile in Babylon. It is quite similar to Scripture's Hebrew but it is spoken post-exile and is what we now call Aramaic. "Under the Name 'Hebrews,' there is none but would place the Palestines, the Babylonians, the Assyrians, the Syrians, if they knew what was the common mother-tongue of all these countries; were placed by the Talmudists themselves, in effect, under the same rank and alliance of customs and privileges, as well as under the same language." Lightfoot, *Addenda to 1 Cor. XIV*, 12:566.

113. Lightfoot, *Miscellanies*, 4:13; See also *Horae*, 11:348 where he criticizes Beza for not taking this knowledge into account in his comments on Golgotha from Matt 27:33.

Lightfoot's Critical and Linguistic Approach   97

to the normal idiom and propriety.[114] Once again, Lightfoot's "critical" use of language leads him to stand by the absolute authority and inerrancy of Hebrew and Greek originals as they stand.

Both Onkelos and Jonathan translate the Gen 6 בְּנֵי־הָאֱלֹהִים as "sons of the potentates or judges" and this pleases Lightfoot considerably.[115] Still, most of the time Lightfoot does not make judgments on the Targumists' or the Peshitta's translations. He prefers, rather, to give the information and leave the reader to make necessary conclusions. After all, there is great disagreement between the varied versions. For instance, Rom 11:10 shows that Paul followed the Greek of Ps 69, which Lightfoot translated "Bow down their back always." This is a problem since the Hebrew, וּמָתְנֵיהֶם תָּמִיד הַמְעַד would be translated "make the loins to quake continually."[116] Exacerbating the problem is the fact that the Targum sides with the Hebrew while the Arabic and Syriac incline towards the Greek. Lightfoot's attempt at harmonization is minimal leaving the solution somewhat undetermined except for those with the background knowledge that Lightfoot always chooses the Hebrew.

Sometimes Lightfoot does not make conclusions about the accuracy of another translation, choosing rather to use it as an illustration, regardless of its accuracy. Regarding עַל־פִּי יְהוָה in Deut 34:5 he says that the Targumist renders these words "At the kiss of the Lord." Whether this is correct or not is of little importance to Lightfoot. He mentions it simply to be able to express the Jewish way of speaking that shows the favor of God on the dying person and how sweet the death of God's saints is to them. He needs to say this, so that he can compare it to the death of the ungodly man, which involves wrath and fire. In this, he refers to the Targum for illustrative purposes alone.

While the Targums and other cognate languages did not come to Moses on Sinai, Lightfoot generally considers them very helpful in trying to determine the sense of Scripture. Despite their paraphrastic nature and the fact that they often contradict the Hebrew, Lightfoot uses them as

---

114. Lightfoot, *Sermons*, "A Sermon preached at Ely, November 5, 1672," 7:80–81. He recognizes that some suggest this is referring to Rome, but disagrees because of this change that takes place in Aramaic.

115. This is the same translation as is found in Exod 22:28 and while Lightfoot is satisfied with that answer he goes a step further saying that the sons of God are the church—the progeny of holy Seth. Lightfoot, *Miscellanies*, 4:12–13.

116. Lightfoot, *Horae*, 12:446.

illustrations, as chronological and geographical gap-fillers, and as proof that the sacred words are without flaw. They are necessary pieces of the text-linguistic approach to Scripture.

LIGHTFOOT'S USE OF THE GREEK

Lightfoot was not only a master of Hebrew and its cognate languages, he was a master of Greek as well. In order to understand the Old Testament, he resorted often to the Greek. However, his use of the Greek was a constant source of tension for Lightfoot. He believed neither that the Septuagint was a Greek version, nor did he believe that the actual Greek version was at all a worthy one. Once again, we see that the rabbinic writings as well as his own careful reading of the text heavily influenced Lightfoot and this caused him to reject many commonly accepted views regarding the Greek Scripture.

The LXX Was Neither Inspired Nor Even a Greek Version at All

There were many problems when dealing with the Greek translation, but the most significant for Lightfoot was the mistaken notion by many that the LXX was inspired. After all, seventy translators had each arrived at the same Greek translation, and the apostles themselves chose to quote from the LXX. If both of these things were true, then there could be no doubt that the Greek version of the Old Testament was just as holy and perfect as the Hebrew MT. Lightfoot, however, strongly disagreed.

The common belief regarding the inspiration of the Septuagint was wrong primarily because of the mistaken understanding of what the Septuagint was. Lightfoot believed that the Letter of Aristeas and Josephus were simply wrong on this subject. Rather than the legend of the seventy having anything to do with a Greek version, Lightfoot believed it referred rather to a Greek transliteration. [117] He finds evidence of this as

---

117. There is some ambiguity in the work of Lightfoot as his *Harmony of the Four Evangelists*, in contradistinction to his *Horae*, assumes the general accuracy of the Letter of Aristeas. The *Harmony*, furthermore, never differentiates between the seventy and the Greek version, as does the *Horae*. Part of the reason for this is likely the different times these books are published. The *Harmony*, being published from 1644 to 1650, would not have contained the lucidity of his *Horae* published between 1658 and 1674. There is no reason to assume that Lightfoot did not evolve in his own thinking. It is also possible that Lightfoot was accommodating the generally held position regarding the seventy and the Greek version in order to make a more significant point in his writing. Either way, it seems that by the time of his masterpiece his thinking was clear that the Septuagint was

he compares Aristeas and Josephus with the contradictory information found in the Talmud. For instance, Josephus and Aristeas mention great sums of money paid to the interpreters, whereas the Talmud mentions none. This would be strange since the talmudic authors are always quick to mention the wealth of the Jews and so glorify their own Jewish people.[118] Lightfoot notes another discrepancy between Josephus and the Talmud. Josephus writes that the king sent a letter to the interpreters requesting them for the job while the Talmud says the interpreters convened with no knowledge of their task.[119] Quite simply, Josephus says the seventy turn the Law into Greek, but the Talmudists are not clear that there was anything translated at all.

Another significant problem with the so-called Septuagint is that both Talmuds say that the Seventy changed thirteen places in the law, but no one has been able to find these thirteen places in the Greek version. While many scholars conclude therefore, that the Talmudists are not being truthful, Lightfoot insists that the reason it does not appear in the Greek is that they made the change in the Hebrew transcription, not the Greek version. A Greek version simply would not make sense considering the changes that the Talmud mentions.[120] "There is no reason, therefore, why that tradition of the thirteen places changed should bear so ill a report, and be accounted for a fiction, because those thirteen alterations are not met with in the Greek Version: for the Talmudists plainly treats of the Seventy-two, not translating out of the Hebrew, but transcribing the Hebrew books themselves."[121] For Lightfoot, the evidence is incontrovertible. The Talmudists do not acknowledge a version of the seventy-two because there is no version, only a transcription.

> But if any should say, that they *transcribed*, indeed, in Greek, that is, the Hebrew text in Greek letters, and *translated* not,—you would scarcely refute him out of the Talmudists; especially, when

---

not a Greek version, but simply a transliteration of the Hebrew. For the most exhaustive discussion of this, see Lightfoot, *Addenda to 1 Cor XIV*, 12:580. Lightfoot uses the seventy interchangeably with the seventy-two.

118. Lightfoot, *Addenda to 1 Cor XIV* 12:580. "They are not silent of the gifts of Monobazus and Helena, Nicanor, Ben Cattin, &c; of the gifts of princes either given or lent to their Rabbins; but of these vast expenses of Ptolemy, there is not one syllable."

119. Lightfoot, *Addenda to 1 Cor XIV*, 12:580.

120. Ibid., 581–82.

121. Ibid., 582.

elsewhere they distinguish between writing out בכל לשון, in any language, that is, in the characters of any language; and writing out תרגום בכל לשון "by a version into any language": . . .[122]

As transcribers of the Hebrew only, and not creators of a new version, they were not inspired.

The True Greek Version Was Purposefully Deceptive

Of course, the fact that the seventy-two did not create a Greek version does not mean a Greek version did not exist. Despite widespread disagreement with Lightfoot's views, he insisted that the scholars did indeed create a Greek version, but that the story of the seventy-two with miraculous results was a fiction. Rather, it was created by five elders and the Sanhedrin and there were dreadful problems.[123] Lightfoot believed that Ptolemy was a prudent king who, hosting many Jews in Egypt, wanted to look into their manners and institution.[124] Unable to read Hebrew, he called the five elders to translate it for him. The Sanhedrin too were compelled to translate the rest of Scripture into Greek.

While they had to write a Greek version, it was neither inspired nor was it even a consistently accurate translation. The Sanhedrin were careful and wrote with a clear agenda.[125] They wanted to protect the Jews from friction with the present or future kings, but at the same time, they wanted to hide the mysteries of the holy text from the Gentiles. In order to do this, the text must be purposefully deceptive: it must satisfy the readers but not concede too much. Lightfoot says, "This they established, and strengthened by their own authority, not as a pure version, and such as was to be recommended to their countrymen, but as fit enough to stop the mouths, and satisfy the curiosity, of the heathen."[126] Strype sums up

---

122. Lightfoot, *Horae*, 12:580–81.

123. Strype, *The Preface Relating to the Author*, Lightfoot, 1:165. Strype, wrongly, I think, speaks of Lightfoot's view of the translation of the Seventy. What Strype is really referring to is what Lightfoot believed was the translation of the five elders. This confusion is certainly understandable since Lightfoot himself chooses to refer to it by what others commonly believed it was: the LXX.

124. Lightfoot, *Addenda to 1 Cor XIV*, 12:580.

125. Ibid., 590.

126. Ibid., 591. Lightfoot says that the LXX contains many willful errors and is arranged so as to favor the manners, traditions, and ordinances of the Jews and to conceal from the heathen the truth and reassurance of the Scripture. Lightfoot, *Miscellanies*, 4:34;

Lightfoot's Critical and Linguistic Approach 101

the political motivation admirably: "as that the Bible might be represented after that manner to the heathen, among whom the Jews dwelt, that they might have no occasion from any passages therein to revile, or cavil with them; and that the Jewish nation might live the more securely; concealing in the mean time as much as they could, the mysteries and truths contained therein."[127] The rabbis rejected this Greek version, commonly called the LXX. The Talmud never quotes it, even though they are willing to quote Sirach, a prohibited book, and the Greek version of Aquila. They fully understood the deceptive purpose of the text.

The Problems of the Greek Version

Even if one did not accept Lightfoot's account of the Greek version, there was still the matter of dealing with the numerous textual problems that came when one compared the Hebrew to the Greek.[128] These difficulties were widely recognized throughout the history of the church.[129] For Lightfoot, these details alone were enough to prove that the Greek is "a botching translation," is not to be authorized above the Hebrew, and is therefore far from an inspired text.[130] It is, he insists, faulty in infinite

---

Harmony of the Four Evangelists, 4:326; *Horae*, 10:419; *Addenda to 1 Cor. XIV*, 12:579. "I will only mind, that they did the work of this translation against their will, and, therefore, we must expect but slippery doing: and that appears by them." Lightfoot, *Miscellanies*, 4:30. Lightfoot even believes that it is not the Greek copy that is the closest to the Hebrew text that is most original, but the one that is closest to the minds of the translators who were overly crafty in hiding things from their readers. See Lightfoot, *Addenda to 1 Cor. XIV*, 12:591.

127. Strype, *The Preface Relating to the Author*, Lightfoot 1:165.

128. The contradictions had to prove something: either the Greek was deceptive or else the Jews, who knew the Greek version was for the heathen, stayed pure in their rendering of the heathen copy (the so called LXX), but corrupted their own Hebrew text. This second option was simply not reasonable to Lightfoot. Lightfoot, *Addenda to 1 Cor. XIV*, 12:583–87.

129. Seventeenth-century scholars were not the first to notice the discrepancies between the LXX and the MT. Although scholars such as Bellarmine had argued that the Seventy ought to be viewed as prophets and not as interpreters, Jerome had said exactly the opposite. Many of the Church Fathers on up through the Reformation noticed difficulties based on contradictory translations. See Muller, *PRRD*, 2:371–441. Certainly Luther and Zwingli questioned the Vulgate as contrasted with the MT and Calvin had much to say about the differences between the LXX and the Hebrew. See Muller, *PRRD*, 2:407.

130. Lightfoot, *Sermons*, "A Sermon Preached upon Dan. 12:12, 13," 7:223.

places, "paraphrastic," and allusive.[131] Even when he is not explicit, it is obvious that he deems the Hebrew to be superior. For example in a discussion on Deut 33:2, he notes that the LXX mentions angels whereas the Hebrew mentions fire. Lightfoot does not bother to prove one translation superior to the other; instead, he simply ignores the LXX and quotes the MT in its entirety. Lightfoot has blatantly assumed the quality of the Hebrew over the LXX.[132]

While he is sometimes reserved, Lightfoot is more often severe in his criticism of the Greek. For example, the LXX of Gen 5 has added hundreds of years to men's ages before and after the flood. How they do this, Lightfoot says, "few scholars but they know."[133] He spends a whole chapter on this in his *Miscellanies* quoting example after example of the Greek errors. The LXX even helps "Job's wife to scold, adding there a whole verse of female passion."[134] Regarding the Greeks placing Methuselah on top of the ark during the flood, Lightfoot says that the differences found in this chapter should "incite men to apply themselves to the Hebrew text, where is no falsifying nor error."[135] He is consistently negative saying that "the Greek interpreters, what Jews soever they were, do sometimes frame a sense of their own, and that not seldom, very foreign from the Hebrew truth."[136]

The Sanhedrin guard their deceptions by always using an unpointed Hebrew text.

> Thirdly, Therefore they strive, as much as they can, to conceal the truth and treasure of the Scripture from the heathen, and, as much as they dare, to delude them. Their chief means for this, is, to use an unpricked Bible, in which the words written without vowels, might be bended divers ways, and into divers senses, and different from the meaning of the original; and yet, if the translation were questioned, they might prick or vowel the word, so as to agree to

---

131. Lightfoot, *Horae*, 12:539, 446. He calls it allusive because of their tendency to make word connections with the Old Testament that may or may not have any relevance to the New Testament translation.

132. Lightfoot consistently refers to the Greek Old Testament as the LXX, choosing to accommodate his language to the commonly accepted terminology of his time.

133. Lightfoot, *Miscellanies*, 4:68.

134. Ibid., 30.

135. This is similar to the Jewish writings where we often find Og on top of the ark. Lightfoot calls these words ridiculous. Lightfoot, *Miscellanies*, 4:69.

136. Lightfoot, *Horae*, 12:445.

their translation. How they have dealt in this kind, there is none that ever laid the Hebrew Bible and the Septuagint together but hath observed.[137]

They are able to turn the text however they want and in so doing keep the Gentiles in the dark. One example Lightfoot mentions is found in Gen 47:31 where it relates that Israel bowed himself upon his מטה.[138] The Sanhedrin have chosen to point this as מַטֶּה (staff) while the original Hebrew has מִטָּה (bed). Lightfoot, of course, insists that the Hebrew is correct and openly criticizes the error of the Greek.

Explaining Why the Apostles Use What Is Commonly Called the LXX

While Schertz perhaps goes too far in saying that Lightfoot was embarrassed by the apostles use of the Greek Old Testament and even renounced reason in his formulations of faith, it is certainly the case that Lightfoot had some struggles with the apostolic use of the LXX. His general explanation was simple: the apostles simply used what was available and commonly readable.[139]

> Those holy writers had to do with two sorts of men, Jews and Gentiles: the volume of the New Testament was in the hands of both. A gentile desires to examine the quotations, which are brought out of the Old Testament: but not understanding the Hebrew, wither should he go, but to the Greek version, which he understands? So that it was not only ἐκ συγκαταβάσεως, "out of condescension," that those holy writers followed the Greek version, but out of pure necessity: for otherwise it was impossible, that their allegations out of the law and the prophets could be examined by the Gentiles, And if a Jew, having the New Testament in his hand, should complain and quarrel, that, in their quotations, they departed from the Hebrew text, they had an answer ready,— viz. this very version which is cited, is that very same, which ye have writ, published, and propounded to the world, as the symbol and token of your law and religion, and as your very own Bible.[140]

---

137. Lightfoot, *Harmony of the Four Evangelists*, 4:327.

138. Lightfoot, *Chronicle and Harmony of the Old Testament*, 2:107.

139. It is interesting that he also criticizes those who prefer the LXX saying that this is true for many not because they truly prefer it, but because they cannot read the Bible in Hebrew. Lightfoot, *Miscellanies*, 4:32.

140. Lightfoot, *Addenda to 1 Cor. XIV*, 12:592. "It is apparent, by most of the fathers, both Greek and Latin, how they followed the Greek, though, I think, not so much for

And elsewhere: "Whereas the New Testament was to be wrote in Greek, and come into the hands chiefly of the Gentiles,—it was most agreeable,—I may say, most necessary, for them, to follow the Greek copies, as being what the Gentiles were only capable of consulting; that so they, examining the quotations that were brought out of the Old Testament, might find them agreeing with, and not contradicting, them."[141] The Greek Old Testament was good for something. It provided the means for the holy apostles to give proof of the gospel. This is further confirmed when Lightfoot quotes Clemens Alexandrinus' reason why God turned the Bible into Greek. He says "For this were the Scriptures interpreted in the Grecian's tongue,—that they might have no excuse for their ignorance, being able to understand our (Scriptures) if they would."[142]

The larger concern was that the apostles quoted the LXX even though it differed from the sacred and holy MT. For instance, Luke quotes the LXX which adds the name of Canaan to the genealogy in Gen 5:24.[143] In other words, the MT, which is perfect, has one less name in the genealogy than does the LXX and Luke chooses to quote the errant LXX text. Schertz aptly summarizes the problem: "If the Greek text of the Old Testament was known to be incorrect, its errors no less, purposefully inscribed by vain and deceitful men, why should the Gospel with consent of the Holy Ghost refer to such a text for its validation? Would not the New Testament have risen in prestige if its source was the uncorrupted Hebrew original?"[144] This must have bothered Lightfoot and his answer is interesting:

> There could be nothing more false as to the thing itself, than that of the apostle, when he calleth the preaching of the gospel μωρίαν, foolishness, 1 Cor. i. 21; and yet, according to the common conceptions of foolish men, nothing more true. So neither was this true in itself, that is asserted here; but only so in the opinion of those, for whose sake the evangelist writes. Nor yet is it the design of the Holy Ghost to indulge them in any thing, that was not true;

---

affectation, as for mere necessity; few of them being able to read the Bible in Hebrew." Lightfoot, *Miscellanies*, 4:32.

141. Lightfoot, *Horae*, 12:59.

142. Lightfoot, *Miscellanies*, 4:32.

143. Luke 3:36, "the son of Cainan, the son of Arphaxad, the son of Shem, the son of Noah, the son of Lamech . . ." (NIV)

144. Schertz, "Christian Hebraism," 91.

but only would not lay a stumbling-block at present before them. "I am made all things to all men, that I might gain some."[145]

The New Testament is factually incorrect, but not by a mistake of the Holy Spirit. Lightfoot says, "In following the assertion of the Seventy, he [Luke] embraceth not their error, but divinely draweth us to look at their intent."[146] The Holy Spirit was completely purposeful and we readers who notice the problem are, instead of emphasizing the "error," to examine the intent. This is no different from Jude mentioning Michael's striving with Satan about the body of Moses. Jude knew this was nothing more than a parable but he uses it simply as an argument against them for their instruction. So, while the New Testament was factually incorrect, it served the higher purpose of helping the Gentiles to see the Savior.

Lightfoot's mastery of both Greek and Hebrew led him to numerous contradictory comparisons. True to his tendency to side with the Talmud and the Hebrew, Lightfoot readily assumes the inaccuracy of the Greek. Still, he is not content merely to assume. He references numerous examples of the Greek mistranslations and insists that most of these contradictions were purposeful and intended to deceive. The Greek version should not have been dubbed the Septuagint, but more importantly, it was essential that no one be enticed into elevating this Greek version above the Hebrew. He quotes approvingly St. Augustine's remarks against those who held to the legitimacy of the Greek version: "Let that tongue be rather believed, out of which a translation is made into another by interpreters."[147] For Lightfoot, the Hebrew text is not only superior to the Greek; it is really the only legitimate word of God.

CRITICAL AND CABALISTIC

Lightfoot's brilliance in the ancient languages was unsurpassed, and his attention to detail made him a necessary albeit early and not fully mature part of the historical critical tradition. Unfortunately, this same attention to detail coupled with his dogmatic belief in the divine status of the Hebrew text often pushed Lightfoot into areas that are more dangerous and often beyond legitimate scholarship. It was perfectly natural that by

---

145. Lightfoot, *Horae*, 12:60.

146. Lightfoot, *The Harmony of the Four Evangelists*, 4:330.

147. Lightfoot, *Miscellanies*, 4:32. Augustine further states, "the truth of things must be fetched out of that tongue, out of which that that we have, is interpreted." Lightfoot cites this as *De Civitate Dei*, 11.13–14.

the constant ingestion of the rabbinic works, Lightfoot would not only adopt their various viewpoints, but would also adopt, albeit accidentally, their extreme exegetical methods. He descended into the mystical interpretive methods known generally as Cabalism despite his great animosity towards it.

Lightfoot loves and praises the Jews, on the one hand, for their accurate preservation of the Hebrew text and their devotion to even the smallest of details. They are to be admired for their conviction that "there is no tittle in Scripture, but even mountains of matter hang upon it" and for their belief that the changing of even one letter destroys the world.[148] Still, their great contributions do not keep Lightfoot from rebuking them for being ignorant. For Lightfoot, even the great "textualists and grammarians" are not the wisest of men and not the best at the text.[149] It is this ignorance that leads them into Gematria and even Cabalism and Lightfoot condemns both tendencies strenuously. One chapter of his *Miscellanies* is devoted entirely to the problems of the Cabalists. "These should be men of great account, for their trading is chiefly in numbers but the effects of their studies prove but fetches 'nullius numeri,' of no reckoning. Their strange tricks and sleights of invention, how to pick out a matter of nothing, out of a thing of no matter, is so intricate, that I do not much care, if into these secrets my soul do not come."[150] He continues, "Their Rashe and Soph tebjoth, their Notericon, and Geometeria, whether to call them Cabalistical, Masoretical, or fantastical, I know not:—they have paid the margin of the Bible with such conceits."[151] Lightfoot is amazed at their exegetical imaginings but wants nothing to do with them. They create things out of nothing.

> The Alchymistical Cabalists, or Cabalistical Alchymists, have extracted the name קפו or number, whether you will,—out of the word Jehovah, after a strange manner. This is their way to do it.

> ופעמים י" הפעמים כה" הרי קכה"
> ופעמים ו' לו" הרי קסא הפעמים ה' כ"ה
> הרי קפו

---

148. Lightfoot, *Sermons*, "A Sermon preached at Ely, November 5, 1672," 7:80. One letter destroying the world is from *Tanhuma* on Gen 1.

149. Lightfoot, *Miscellanies*, 4:14–15.

150. Ibid., 4:18.

151. Ibid.

Which great mystery is, in English, thus: "Ten times ten is a hundred; five times five is twenty-five; behold 125: six times six is thirty-six; behold 161: and five times five is twenty-five; behold וּפַק, or 186." Thus runneth their senseless multiplication, multiplying numberless follies in their foolish numbers;—making conjectures, like sibyls' leaves, that, when they come to blast of trial, prove but wind.[152]

The arguments are senseless and prove nothing at all.

Not only the rabbis, but also the church fathers and the Targumists are often mysterious in their attempt to find meaning in the Hebrew text. Irenaeus has a "mystical stir" about the name Jesu (יֵשׁ), saying the shortened name signifies the Lord and contains in it heaven and earth.[153] The Targumists, he mentions, write the name of God with two *yods* above and a vowel under and some see this as a sign of the Trinity in that the vowel (Holy Spirit) proceeds from the letters and they are all equidistant from one another. This is their story, but Lightfoot insists that he has a more sure word of testimony quoting 1 John 5:7 as a Trinitarian proof.[154] Lightfoot does not like Cabalism.

Despite Lightfoot's abhorrence of Cabalistic tendencies, he himself is not immune to the same exegetical errors. The strange markings, like letters that are larger or smaller than others are and letters placed off the main line, out of order, or reversed, must be there by the intention of the Holy Spirit, and therefore one must reckon with them. "There is a letter א in the very first word of the book, וַיִּקְרָא written less than all his fellows: and it seemeth, by such a writing, to hint and intimate, that though this were a glorious oracle, yet was it small in comparison of what was to come, when God would speak to his people by his own Son, whom the ark, mercy-seat, and oracle, did represent."[155] Malachi 4:4 begins with זִכְרוּ and the first letter "is a great letter, and above ordinary size; either, as some say, to intimate to them the great cause they had to remember the

---

152. Ibid., 10.

153. Lightfoot, *Miscellanies*, 4:10–11. Lightfoot cannot make out what Irenaeus is doing. He only repeats that "the name Jesu, according to the proper speech of the Hebrews, consisteth of two letters and a half, as the skilful amongst them say: signifying, the Lord, which containeth heaven and earth: for 'Jesu,' according to the old Hebrew, signfieth 'heaven' and the earth is called 'Sura usser.'" Lightfoot says he can only critique Irenaeus's words in deep silence because he doesn't understand the mysticism.

154. Lightfoot, *Miscellanies*, 4:11.

155. Lightfoot, *Harmony of the Old Testament*, 2:120.

law; or, as others, to call upon them to remember the five books of Moses, and the book of the prophets, and the book of Hagiographa, according to the great Zain's numeral, which is seven."[156] He notes a transposition of the Hebrew letters in the alphabetical chapters of Lamentations. Apparently, Lightfoot's copies had the verses that begin with פ set before the verses that begin with ע. His reasoning is that it may have hinted at the seventy-year desolation of Jerusalem since ע's numerical value is seventy.[157] Even the letter nun has special significance when it is reversed in Num 10:25 and 11:1.[158] According to Lightfoot, the backwards nun in the phrase "and the ark went forward" in Num 10:25 signifies the loving turning back of God to his people. In Num 11:1, the letter nun is again backwards in "the people became as murmurers" and the reason, so the Jews say, is the perverse turning of the people from their God. While he qualifies both statements by saying these are the words of the Jews, he also says that if this is not a good answer, students should look for a better one. "Such strange passages as these, in writing some words in the Bible out of ordinary way (as, some letters above the word, some letters less, and some bigger than other), observed constantly by all copies and books, cannot sure be for nothing."[159]

Sometimes, Lightfoot thinks that there are hidden messages in the text that refer specifically to Christ. Isaiah 9:7 has the word *lemarbeh* which is a *Mem clausum*,—"to show the hiddenness and mysteriousness of Christ's kingdom, different from visible pomp,—and to hint the forty years before Jerusalem's destruction, when this dominion increased through the world."[160]

Lightfoot's rhetoric regarding the important work of the Jews and their great contribution to the *sensus literalis* is confusing since he also rebukes them for their fanciful imaginations. It is even more difficult to follow Lightfoot's admonishments when he himself falls prey to the same

---

156. Lightfoot, *Sermons*, "Funeral Sermon upon Sir R. Cotton," 6:203.

157. Lightfoot, *Harmony of the Old Testament*, 2:298. But as George Bright recognizes, it is just as possible that it refers to eighty years since that is the numerical value of פ. Bright, *Preface to the Reader*, Lightfoot 1:40.

158. Lightfoot, *Miscellanies*, 4:19.

159. Ibid. He adds that if for no other reason, these letters may be different simply to show us that the text is punctually kept and not decayed since these are observed in all Bibles.

160. Lightfoot, *Harmony of the Old Testament*, 2:251–52.

fanciful interpretations. His comments on Deut 29:29 summarize well his bifurcated thinking. Lightfoot believes that the points above each letter in this verse are warnings against the curiosity of prying into God's secrets, and that we should content ourselves with his revealed will.[161] Lightfoot expects that his readers will use the mystical nature of these points and at the same time only concern themselves with God's revealed will. It is the mysterious points that mystically inform us that we should only concern ourselves with his revealed will. But how does one come to such a conclusion without speculating on his unrevealed will found in the strange points? So, while Lightfoot ridicules the Jews for their speculations, Lightfoot expects his own readers to accept his equally strange speculations. It seems that despite Lightfoot's disgust towards the Jews for their own Cabalistic methods, he has, through constant reading of them, become somewhat of a Cabalist himself. His close, critical reading has actually somewhat frustrated his literal endeavors.

CONCLUSION

Lightfoot's second rule, as I have organized it, is that students should proceed slowly and critically through the Hebrew text and compare it with the many other versions available. In this, Lightfoot was both on the cutting edge of textual controversies and firmly entrenched in dogmatic resolutions. Both of these tendencies came from his *via media* approach between the Reformation and the rabbinic literature. He stressed the importance of the original Hebrew because of its divine origin and insisted that its perfection was mandatory. He was innovatively involved in both higher and lower criticism. Although full-fledged critical methods had not yet surfaced, Lightfoot is on the edge of and one who helped clear the path to modern critical methods. He insisted on the cognate languages and multiple copies involved in translation and interpretation. He did not blindly accept the authorship of certain books but questioned them in opposition to many of his contemporaries. At the same time, he was not a text critic in the tradition of Cappel or Buxtorff and trusted far more in his dogmatics then in his critical speculation. Moreover, since he often succumbed to the same methods that he criticized, one must admit that his social and academic context did not help in his search for a *sensus*

---

161. Ibid., 2:137. Bright says it is likely copyist errors. Bright, *Preface to the Reader*, Lightfoot, 1:40.

literalis. Still, we have found that the meaning of the text, Lightfoot's plain sense could properly be determined by placing different versions and translations against the ancient Hebrew and MT.

5

Lightfoot's Use of Chronology and a Historical Approach

INTRODUCTION

THAT THE BIBLE IS divine and therefore inerrant is never in question for Lightfoot. He would insist that rejecting the Bible due to seeming contradictions derived from literal reading is an egregious error. Still, reading the Bible literally does indeed lead to many obscurities concerning the historicity and chronology of biblical stories. In order to escape many of these difficulties, Lightfoot urges his students to lay the books and chapters in their true or chronological order. This chapter will discuss a third hermeneutical rule that Lightfoot utilizes much time, effort, and paper in getting across to his readers: that of chronological reading.

History

Dating of events, based on the biblical text, is certainly not something new to Lightfoot; the church throughout its entire history has created biblically based time lines.[1] The early church had a rather detailed chronological understanding based primarily on the LXX that the earth came into existence about six thousand years before the Christian era. They based this idea especially on the six days of creation prefiguring the six thousand years during which the earth in its first form was to endure.

---

1. It might be pertinent to add that this chronological interest seems to have begun even as early as the last stages of development of the Hebrew Bible. Some of the data in our Bible may come from late editing after comparison with Samaritan and Greek texts. The book of Jubilees is well known to be a chronologically rewritten Genesis. See James Barr, "Why the World Was Created in 4004 BC," 601.

The second Adam would come on the sixth day or sixth millennial period. Those who revered the Hebrew text as supreme like Eusebius and St. Jerome held to an even shorter existence for the earth and mankind, but all agreed that the earth was created somewhere between four thousand and six thousand years before Christ. Augustine insisted that belief in a longer duration was heresy. The Venerable Bede, in the eighth century, came close to calling into question the idea that a day represents a thousand years and confirmed the short time period of Jerome. Maimonides came to a similar conclusion in his research on the Hebrew text. Luther said that the world was not older than six thousand years and Melancthon fixed the creation of man at 3963 BC. Pope Urban XIII said that the creation of man was in 5199 BC. De Vignolles, in 1748, after forty years of computations, said that he had arrived at more than two hundred computations based on Scripture and none were alike.[2]

Despite this earlier proclivity towards biblical chronology, we remember the time of Protestant Orthodoxy as a time when the dating became standardized. John Cotton is a good example of one who was more than a little enamored by chronologies and numbers. He said that God designed the sequenced numbers not only to clarify the presentation in the Bible but also to conform to God's very own direction. Edward Davidson describes Cotton's interest in numbers in the following way: "Scripture was, accordingly, a system of divine counting which, as God had revealed it, was so precise that it could be reckoned in centuries, years, months, days, and even hours and minutes. Number encompassed the divine order, the structure of Scripture, the world of men and things, and the smallest particles. In number God had given man an instrument to search and discover the truth."[3]

Perhaps the most well-known biblical chronologist was Archbishop James Ussher. His chronology, which detailed the events from Adam to his own time, was a beautiful piece of scholarship in its time. So accepted was his chronology, that it was included in the marginal notes of many editions of the Authorized Version affirming all the more its acceptance among present and future lay readers. Ussher believed that one could in-

---

2. This paragraph is taken largely from White's *A History of the Warfare of Science with Theology in Christendom*, 254–56. I recognize that White has taken much criticism in the last century as one who did not always read history well and did more to add to the scientific myths of the past, but these statements here are generally accepted.

3. Davidson, "John Cotton's Biblical Exegesis: Method and Purpose," 126.

deed arrive at an exact date and, working within a community that held to an accepted methodology, he dated the creation of the earth to 4004 BC.[4]

THE USSHER-LIGHTFOOT CHRONOLOGY

People often connect Ussher's name with John Lightfoot's. In fact, people of later generations often referred to this famous chronology as the Ussher-Lightfoot Chronology. The numbers of Scripture are indeed of utmost importance to Lightfoot and chronology of events is one of the most significant tools needed for understanding the Bible. In fact, for those who are only able to read in translation, developing a chronology is Lightfoot's first rule.[5]

> The first thing, then, for them, that only read translations, to be looked after, in reading the Scriptures, is,—to lay the books and chapters in their true order. The Holy Spirit hath, in divers places, purposely and divinely, laid stories and passages out of their proper places, for special ends. The evangelists especially witness this. Here the skill of the reader is, first, to reduce each thing to his own place and secondly, to seek the Divine reason, why it is misplaced.
>
> The only way to come to this skill, is by casting the story of the Bible into a continued chronicle; which as the Spirit hath given undoubted helps to draw,—so being drawn, it is the most satisfactory, delightsome, and confirmative of the understanding, mind, and memory, that may be. This settles histories in your mind this brings the things, as if done, before your eyes: this makes you mark what else you would not; and this suffers you not to slip over the least tittle of a word: and sometimes, in things of doubt and scruple, this strikes all out of question.[6]

This was so important to Lightfoot that he spoke boldly and with great conviction when the issue surfaced in the Westminster Assembly regarding whether to examine candidates for the holy orders in regard to their

---

4. This is not only true for theologians but for scientists as well. For example Johannes Kepler suggested a creation date of 3992 BC and Sir Isaac Newton rigorously defended Ussher's chronology. He says, "For an educated man in the seventeenth or even eighteenth century, any suggestion that the human past extended back further than 6000 years was a vain and foolish speculation." Sir Isaac Newton, *The Chronology of Ancient Kingdoms Amended* (London: printed for J. Tonson, 1728) cited without page number in Renfrew, *Before Civilization*, 22–23.

5. Lightfoot, *Rules for a Student of the Holy Scriptures*, 2:3.

6. Ibid., 2:3–4.

chronology. Lightfoot urged the necessity of it, saying that he read not Scripture, who was not expert in chronology.[7] He did not believe, however, that the Bible was perfectly chronological and gave many examples of passages that were out of order. He believed that numbers in the Bible were mostly there to give literal and detailed understanding of significant things. He further believed that the numerical chronology of the Old Testament corresponded perfectly to New Testament events and significantly even to Post-Reformation events that he was currently involved in. However, he was not nearly as dogmatic about the literalism of the New Testament numbers. Because of the great impact that chronology has on Lightfoot's exegesis and because several entire treatises and more than a third of his works are designed to help us understand the biblical world in the proper event order, we will examine each of these issues: exact ordering, purposeful displacement, and lack of New Testament literalism.[8]

Numbering and Exact Ordering

While most connect the chronologies of Ussher and Lightfoot, and it is true that their methodologies were similar, there were significant differences between the two. Andrew Dickson White is perhaps the cause of their close association. In 1896, he wrote the following in his *A History of the Warfare of Science with Theology in Christendom*:

> [T]he general conclusion arrived at by an overwhelming majority of the most competent students of the biblical accounts was that the date of creation was, in round numbers, four thousand years before our era; and in the seventeenth century, in his great work, Dr. John Lightfoot, Vice-Chancellor of the University of Cambridge, and one of the most eminent Hebrew scholars of his time, declared, as the result of his most profound and exhaustive study of the Scriptures, that "heaven and earth, centre and circumference, were created all together, in the same instant, and clouds full of water," and that "this work took place and man was created by the Trinity on October 23, 4004 B.C., at nine of the clock in the morning."[9]

---

7. John Strype, *Appendix to Author's Life*, in Lightfoot, 1:72.

8. For his works that emphasize chronology, see Lightfoot, *Harmony of the Old Testament*; Lightfoot, *Rules for a Student of the Holy Scriptures*; Lightfoot, *Harmony and Chronicle of the New Testament*; Lightfoot, *Harmony of the Four Evangelists* vol. 1, 2, and 3; and *Horae Hebraicae et Talmudicae*.

9. Dickson, *A History of the Warfare of Science*, 9.

Lightfoot's Use of Chronology and a Historical Approach 115

In truth, however, this date is not from Lightfoot, but rather from Ussher.[10] Lightfoot said that the world began in 3928 BC.[11] He even narrowed it to a month and day of the year being "the twelfth of September . . . without all doubt."[12] Although White said it was at nine in the morning, this quote from Lightfoot was actually in reference to the creation of man.[13] Still, despite the differences between Lightfoot and Ussher, in terms of general computations, they both remained within the "orthodox" dating system.

While, certainly orthodox for the time, Lightfoot actually differed quite a lot from his contemporaries regarding the dating of biblical events. He differed as to the time of Christ's birth, the time from Christ's baptism to his death, the two terms of Daniel's seventy weeks, and the time from the flood to Abraham's birth.[14] In fact, it would be hard for him to agree with anyone considering the amazing detail and precision of his dating. Exactly three hours after the sin of Adam God came to censure them.[15] He says that the first day of creation was thirty-six hours long, the flood came 1,655 years after creation, and Noah died two years before Abram was born.[16] At the same time, he does agree with others in many intermediate intervals, but because of his different starting points the numbers are generally off by about sixty years.[17]

---

10. Even this is difficult to determine. Warfield says Ussher dated the beginning of the world to 4188 B.C. and Barr finds a chronological discrepancy, albeit only a year, in Ussher's *Annales*. Warfield, "On the Antiquity and Unity of the Human Race," 3 and James Barr, "Why the World Was Created in 4004 BC," 580, n9.

11. Lightfoot, *The Harmony of the Four Evangelists*, 4:97, 112. On page 97 he gives the exact date of 3928 while on page 112 he gives the conclusion of his computations, "And now, he that desireth to know the year of the world, which is now passing over us,—this year, 1644,—will find it to be 5572 years just finished since the creation; and the year 5573 of the world's age, now newly begun, this September, at equinox." This conclusion seems to imply a dating of 3929, but the contradiction is irrelevant to our purposes.

12. Lightfoot, *Sermons*, "The Sabbath Hallowed," 7:372.

13. Lightfoot, *A Few and New Observations on the Book of Genesis*, 2:335.

14. John Bright, "Preface to the Reader," in Lightfoot, 1:41.

15. Lightfoot, *Rules for a Student of the Holy Scriptures*, 2:12; Lightfoot, *Chronicle of the Times, and the Order of the Texts of the Old Testament*, 2:74; Lightfoot, *Meditations upon som Abstruser Points of Divinity, and Explanations of Divers Difficult places of Holy Scripture in Three Decads*, 5:362.

16. For Creation see Lightfoot, *Rules for a Student of the Holy Scriptures*, 2:10. For the flood see Lightfoot, *Rules for a Student of the Holy Scriptures*, 2:14. For Noah's death, see Lightfoot, *Chronicle of the Times, and the Order of the Texts of the Old Testament*, 2:86.

17. John Bright, "Preface to the Reader," in Lightfoot 1:41.

116 WHAT IS THE LITERAL SENSE?

His method of arriving at dates and a detailed chronology rests completely on the genealogies and other chronological inferences in the Scripture. He is not opposed to using extra-biblical texts like Josephus in his computations, but sees the computation of the heathen Persian Monarchy stories as a thing of "utter improbability;" the conclusions just prolong the Persian monarchy unjustifiably.[18] These historians have made the same mistakes regarding the king lists that a careless scholar of the Bible might make. Lightfoot mentions these mistakes and in so doing, warns his own readers about the difficulties of chronicling kings. He works out the details of the king lists, beautifully harmonizing the different accounts mentioning that kings sometimes begin ruling even before officially becoming king due to an overlap with their fathers. He notices that the Bible sometimes mentioned full years when the king only reigned for a very small percentage of the year. New kings often take the place of an old one and both have that year counted as included in their reign.[19] Lightfoot insists that a student with a "chronical table before his eyes" is able to make the scruples and difficulties quite plain.[20] One can find similar issues throughout his writings including a great example from the seventy years of captivity in Babel.[21] He lists several reasons and then states, "these reasons do plainly and sufficiently demonstrate, that the seventy years of Judah's captivity in Babel, did begin from the third year of Jehoakim . . ."[22] We also know that the return of the Jews to the death of Christ is exactly 490 years. He says regarding this that "he doth so clearly fix the time, the two 'termini' of its extent, and some particular links of it, as it passed, that nothing can be more clear, evident, and perspicuous."[23] Chronological tables help one hold to the clarity of Scripture and one should certainly take them in their plain sense.

The numbers are exact and although they may have symbolic significance, this does not take away from the literality of the numbers. For

---

18. Lightfoot, *A Prospect of the Temple*, 9:472.

19. Each of these resolutions can be found in the Prolegomena to *The Harmony of the Four Evangelists, among themselves, and with the Old Testament*, 4:97–112. Cf. *A Prospect of the Temple*, 9:472.

20. Lightfoot, *The Harmony of the Four Evangelists*, 4:107.

21. For sake of clarity, I have chosen to use Lightfoot's terminology despite the fact that Babel is no longer the proper verbiage for Babylon.

22. Lightfoot, *The Harmony of the Four Evangelists*, 4:111.

23. Ibid., 112.

instance, Job lived 210 years and while Lightfoot recognizes that this is exactly twice again what he had already lived, he makes no comment that shows even a hint of uncertainty regarding the literal numbers. He apparently thought that God had so orchestrated this beautiful happenstance. Likewise, Enoch's 365 years was literal. Lightfoot, recognizing this as the length of the sun's course, still does not imply that one should understand this any differently than the exact length of Enoch's life.[24] He also insists that history is broken down into similar chronological units. The time from Samuel to the exile is 490 years as is the time from the end of the exile to Christ's death. The seventy years in between are a seventh part called by Habakkuk the midst of years.[25] Furthermore, these 490 years conclude at the very hour that Christ begins to suffer.[26] The forty years of wilderness wandering was apparently exactly forty years and the fact that the Bible uses the word forty so often is no reason to doubt its literal interpretation. Christ himself appears as an armed angel "40 years to a day since they came out of Egypt."[27] Again, the numbers are part of the Holy Spirit's plan and one should understand them as actual, literal, historical years to be figured out down to the very hour. Modern hermeneutical distinctions like those of literal intention vs. literal truth would have been appalling to Lightfoot. Lightfoot would never have considered rejecting the length of Methuselah's thousand-year life span as literally intended but not literally historical or physically true.[28] The authors intended that their readers understand the numbers literally.

Lightfoot, like many of his contemporaries, was convinced of the importance of literally understood Old Testament numbers. They were literal, he insisted, even when they were also obviously symbolic. Although he differed in significant areas, the presuppositions and the methodology seemed largely the same.

---

24. Lightfoot, *Sermons,* "Wait the Time of God," 7:224.
25. Lightfoot, *A Handful of Gleanings out of the Book of Exodus,* 2:360.
26. Lightfoot, *Sermons,* "Wait the Time of God," 7:224.
27. Lightfoot, *Harmony of the Old Testament,* 2:139.
28. For a worthwhile introduction on this, see Barr, "Literality," 412–28. For his examples concerning chronology see especially page 414.

Order Displacement

He did not base his hermeneutical understanding regarding chronology merely on dogmatic presuppositions but rather on the generally compelling historical markers found in the Bible. This did not mean, however, that the Bible was orderly throughout. In fact, the Bible is not always in the correct chronological order and it is for this reason that he insists that charting the order is a great way to help understanding.

Displacement of the order of historical events is rampant throughout Scripture. For example, Lightfoot insists that a plain reading of Jethro's story in Exod 18 demands that it is misplaced. He does this first by looking closely at Exod 18:12–16, which says:

> Then Jethro, Moses' father-in-law, brought a burnt offering and other sacrifices to God . . . The next day Moses took his seat to serve as judge for the people, and they stood around him from morning till evening . . . Whenever they have a dispute, it is brought to me, and I decide between the parties and inform them of God's decrees and laws (NIV).

"But," Lightfoot responds, "as the story lieth here, there was not tabernacle nor altar for sacrifice yet built: neither, as yet, did Moses know the statutes and laws of God himself; for as yet, they are not come to Sinai."[29] As further support, Lightfoot adds that Moses says in Deut 1:6–19 that it was at the leaving of Horeb that he recruited elders to help. Despite the fact that the event recorded here properly took place between the events of Num 10:10 and Num 10:11, Lightfoot does not think that either Moses or the Holy Ghost was mistaken in placing the record of the event in Exod 18. If a text is out of place, there is certainly a reason and it is up to the diligent student to determine this divine intention. In this particular place, "the Holy Ghost might show that Jethro, who dwelt among the Amalekites, did not fall under this curse [of the Amalekites in Exod 17:14–16]."[30] Apparently, the Holy Ghost placed the story in Exodus "in the very next place after that curse is related; not thereby to conclude, strictly, that his coming was at that very time, as soon as the curse was denounced; but to show, that he once came, and so avoideth and escapeth that curse."[31]

---

29. Lightfoot, *A Handful of Gleanings out of the Book of Exodus*, 2:379.
30. Lightfoot, *Harmony of the Old Testament*, 2:127.
31. Ibid.; for more details see Lightfoot, *A Handful of Gleanings out of the Book of Exodus*, 2:379–80.

For Lightfoot, the storyline of the book of Judges is considerably jumbled. In the last few chapters of this book we find mentioned the idolatry of Micah and the Danites as well as the horrid wickedness of Gibeah. Lightfoot insists that while everyone agrees these took place before there was any king in Israel, these events also took place before there was any judge in Israel. The events of the end of Judges properly took place at the beginning of the book.

> Consider, that the beginning of this book is the proper place for these histories, though they be laid in the latter end. For,
>
> 1. The Israelites follow idols after the death of the elders, Judg. iii: Micah is the first that sets it up.
> 2. There is not king in Israel then; that is before any judge rose.
> 3. The Danites are not yet settled; that could not be long after Joshua's death.
> 4. Phinehas is yet alive, chap. xx. 28: so that we must needs cast things into the thirty-second year, ascribed to Othniel's judgeship, before Chushan did afflict them.[32]

He then adds an additional argument for "why the stories are so mislaid" and concludes that chapters 17–21 properly belong between 2:10 and 2:11.[33]

The entire book of Job is out of order in regards to the canon. While most scholars who still hold to the historicity of a person named Job tend to place his existence in the period of the Patriarchs, Lightfoot, never questioning his historicity, considers Job's suffering at least to be post-patriarchal. He is likely the grandnephew of Abraham and likely existed sometime between Joseph and Moses due to the comment that no one on earth was like Job.[34] It is for this reason that he must come after the likes of Abraham, Isaac, and Jacob and before Moses. After all, these ancestors were as equally reputable as Job. The author of the book would not raise Job to such a status if men like Abraham were still living. Moreover, since

---

32. Lightfoot, *Harmony of the Old Testament*, 2:37.

33. Ibid.

34. Lightfoot, *Harmony of the Old Testament*, 2:110. He says that Job likely lives sometime in the fourth generation from Esau, since Eliphaz is a Temanite and he thinks this means an actual son of Teman. He deduces other theological reasons why Job's suffering should come at the same time as Israel's suffering in Egypt. Cf. Lightfoot, *Miscellanies*, 4:75.

Lightfoot holds to such a strict chronology, he insists also that Job was still living during the exodus and likely outlived Moses himself.[35]

Chronological restructuring of texts not only makes the history clearer, but it also leads to doctrinal clarities. For instance, Exod 10 states that the ninth plague is darkness but Ps 105:28 suggests that darkness is the first. This can only be, Lightfoot surmises, because Psalms understands it to be the most terrible of all the plagues. He then moves to Ps 78:49, a passage which also includes the plagues but which does not include darkness among them. In place of the darkness, Ps 78 refers to evil angels and so Lightfoot concludes that what happened during the darkness of the Exodus plagues was actually far more than darkness; it included "fearful apparitions of fiends and devils, and horrible visions, which so hideously affrighted, and even distracted them, that they were, as it were, in hell already."[36] He has now come up with an entirely new meaning to the plague of darkness in Exod 10.

As is the case in the previous example, Lightfoot is so chronologically passionate that he sometimes finds patterns where perhaps none should be. A close look at Ps 78 makes this evident. Not only does the psalm fail to mention the plague of darkness, but it also ignores four other plagues. This makes the chronology somewhat perplexing if this is to be a literal one-for-one correspondence with Exod 10. Furthermore, the one that appears prior to the death on the firstborn may simply be a general personification of bad things happening in general. This is not the only time Lightfoot forces an order on something which may not be intended to be chronological or orderly in any way.

All of this shows his dedication to the "Scripture interprets Scripture" dictum. He is neither arguing for perfectly consistent chronologies throughout the Bible, nor is he insisting that genealogies are complete. He does insist that when we find an incomplete genealogy or a discrepancy in order, there is most likely a theological reason for it, which another passage often explains. Matthew 1:8, for instance, fails to record several names, but Ps 37:28 reconciles the problem. By placing these texts next to each other and by using some sophisticated Gematria (some would say Cabalism), Lightfoot says that it is because the wicked have been cut off (Ps 37) that the names have been blotted out of the genealogy in Matt 1.

---

35. Lightfoot, *Harmony of the Old Testament*, 2:112.
36. Lightfoot, *A Handful of Gleanings out of the Book of Exodus*, 2:371.

Exodus 20:5 speaks of God's jealousy to the third and fourth generations. Considering the idolatry of Joram, it is only fitting that God would erase Joram's name from the genealogy. This is sufficient to show that Lightfoot, although helped greatly by genealogies, is not bound to individual ones, but rather uses all of Scripture to understand individual chronologies.

It is because of the chronological difficulties that Lightfoot insists on the importance of working through the Bible with "chronical" tables laid out. The Holy Spirit purposely penned all the disorder in the Bible and therefore requires his people to work out the seeming discrepancies. It is in the working out that we find numerous helps to our historical as well as to our theological understanding.

New Testament Numbers Not Exact

While Lightfoot insists on the literality of Old Testament numbers, even allowing him to conclude the exact day of man's creation, New Testament numbers are not subject to the same rigorous literality. For instance, Daniel's numbers are always exact and refer to a definite time when the misery of the people will end. This, however, is not the case in Revelation—the 1,290 days does not refer to that time so definitely. God is using the memorial of the Old Testament sum to refer to a less definite future time. Still, the fact that he uses these expressions at all shows that God defined and determined the times. Lightfoot says that "though the time intended be not exactly and punctually the time named,—yet when so punctual a sum is named, it must needs argue, that the time intended is punctually determined with God."[37] The reason God no longer gives definite times regarding the end of our ministry is quite simply because it is not for us to know the times and the seasons.[38] What is interesting is that there seems to be no basis given for why one should not take this as literally as the Old Testament numbers. Lightfoot neither tells the reader, nor even insinuates that this is based on the genre of Revelation. His commentary on Acts is the only thing that comes close to a reason:

> Now, as for those stories that we are to follow in the "Acts of the Apostles," the Holy Ghost hath not been so punctual and exact, to give us the times of the things, as to give us things themselves. The chronicle-chain of the times, indeed, is drawn up by the Scripture

---

37. Lightfoot, *Sermons*, "Wait the Time of God," 7:226.
38. Ibid., 7:222–23.

from the creation, to the death of our Saviour (which was the fullness of time), with all care and accurateness: but, from thenceforward, not so strictly or observantly exhibited and held forth; nor, indeed, was it requisite, that it should so be . . . because the Holy Ghost hath been very sparing, if not utterly silent, in giving account of the times in the New Testament, from the death of Christ forward; that great business in his death being accomplished and fulfilled, for which alone the succession of times was reckoned and recorded.[39]

Both the detailed numbers in Revelation and the sparse chronology of the New Testament events after Christ are not helpful in arriving at chronological conclusions. Often Lightfoot simply states that this is the case, but he seems to base it on the consistent assumption that the times pointed to Christ; once that event was fulfilled, there was no reason for the continued detailed chronology.

Corresponding Texts

While one should not necessarily take literally all timeframes in the New Testament, one must understand the dates given in historical narratives in precisely this way. The reason for this is that the Old Testament events correspond so perfectly with other Old Testament events and most importantly with similar New Testament events. To see them as anything other than literal might imply that God is not in charge of the times and seasons. This, all the more, confirms the coherence of the Old and New Testaments.

One example, which should suffice regarding the confirmation of some Old Testament dates by other Old Testament dates, is found in his writing on Gen 1:1. Scholars have translated the word *bereshith* in many ways, but Lightfoot is content to recognize simply that God created the heavens and the earth in the beginning. Although content in this, he continues to add that some "Jews do invert the word 'Bereshith,' and make it 'Betisri,' that is, 'in the month of Tisri' was the world created."[40] Even though he has already accepted another interpretation, he admits this one rings true to him as well.

---

39. Lightfoot, *A Commentary on the Acts of the Apostles*, 8:103.
40. Lightfoot, *Miscellanies*, 4:64.

> This month is about our September; and that the world was created in this month (to let other reasons alone), this satisfies me,—that the feast of tabernacles, which was in this month, is called the end of the year: and this I take to be the reason, why the Jews began to read the Bible in their synagogues, at the feast of tabernacles; viz. that they might begin the lecture of the creation, in Gen. i at that time of the year that the world was created.[41]

Lightfoot is convinced of this interpretation because of the incredible correlation that is evident here.

Old Testament dates do not simply correspond to other Old Testament dates, but they correspond to actual events in the New Testament as well. For instance, it is not simply a coincidence that Abraham was circumcised in Hebron in Abib or Nisan and that this is the same time and place that John the Baptist was born who brought us baptism.[42] Lightfoot reasons that the purpose of changing the beginning of the year from September to March (in Exod 12:1) was to make it cohere with something that was to take place in the New Testament.

> The equity or life of this law,—that their years should begin from March, or Abib,—was, because the preaching of the gospel should begin, and the redemption be consummate, from that time. For it was just at that time of the year, when John began to baptize, which was the beginning of the gospel; and it was at that time of the year, when our Saviour suffered, and fulfilled that which this prefigured,—viz. our redemption.[43]

Neither is it coincidental that Christ began his forty-day fast about that very time of the year when Moses ended his last forty day fast.[44] The first day of creation is thirty-six hours long just as was Joshua's day of battle and "so long was our Savior clouded under death."[45]

There is tremendous correspondence between the fall and redemption.

> Redemption was wrought on the sixth day, as the fall had been on the sixth day. And when Christ had wrought that great work, he

---

41. Ibid.
42. Lightfoot, *Harmony of the Old Testament*, 2:91.
43. Lightfoot, *A Handful of Gleanings out of the Book of Exodus*, 2:374. Cf. *Sermons*, "The Sabbath Hallowed," 7:386.
44. Lightfoot, *Horae*, 12:64.
45. Lightfoot, *A Few and New Observations on the Book of Genesis*, 2:334.

rested the seventh day in his grave; as God rested on the seventh day, when he had wrought the great work of creation. To this purpose, I might also apply the particular times of the one, and the other. About the third hour, the hour afterward of sacrifice and prayer, it is very probable Adam was created. And Mark tells you, chap. xv. 25, "And it was the third hour, when they crucified him"; that is, when they delivered him up to Pilate to be crucified. About the sixth hour, or high noon, Adam most probably fell, as that being the time of eating. And John tells you, chap. xix. 14, that, about the sixth hour, he was condemned, and led away to be crucified. And about the ninth hour, or three o'clock afternoon, Christ was promised, which Moses calls the cool of the day: and, about the ninth hour, Christ "cried out with a loud voice, and gave up the ghost." Such harmony may be found betwixt the day and hours, of the one and the other . . .[46]

While Lightfoot is not always certain regarding Old Testament dates or times, he, by using the New Testament and the Talmud together, is able to come to strong conclusions about these dates and times. For instance, we are not certain how old Solomon was when he judged the case of the dead baby, but various analogous texts put him near the age of twelve. First, it is at twelve years old that children begin their training for their future occupations.[47] It is also the time when children are to begin training in regard to fasting so that they will be ready on the Day of Atonement.[48] Then, of course, R. Chama says that Moses was twelve when he was taken from his father's house.[49] Lightfoot would be happy to accept these traditions but it is only verified by Luke 2:42 which says that Christ was twelve when he entered the temple and began the work of his father.[50] The biblical numbers correspond so perfectly in Lightfoot's understanding and the

---

46. Lightfoot, *Sermons*, "The Sabbath Hallowed," 7:377.

47. *b. Ketub.* 50a. Epstein, *Soncino Classics Collection* on CD-ROM. "It was ordained at Usha that a man must bear with his son until [he is] twelve years [of age]. From that age onwards he may threaten his life."

48. *b. Yoma* 82a. Epstein, *Soncino Classics Collection*. The Mishna states that one should "not afflict Children at all on the Day of Atonement. But one trains them a year or two before . . ." The Gemara then explains that a healthy child should be fasting all day by the age of twelve. Soncino electronic edition.

49. *Exod. Rab.* 5:2. Epstein, *Soncino Classics Collection*. "R. Hama said: Moses was twelve years old when he left his paternal home." This is derived from the words "who made thee for a man?" (Exod 2:14) and obviously means that Moses was still a minor; i.e., under the age of thirteen.

50. Lightfoot, *Horae*, 12:41–42.

Holy Spirit has worked out the history so that the diligent student can make these determinations. The two Testaments exist in perfect harmony and noticing this brings great refreshment to the saints.

> His harmonizing of times in so sweet a union as he hath done, doth not that show that he is the "wonderful numberer" of times, and numberer of times of the affliction of his people? The Scripture is most copious, and the providence of God most sweet and heavenly, in this kind of concert; and it may much refresh and ravish the reader of Scripture to observe such harmony . . . David, to reign exactly so long a time in Jerusalem, as Christ, the son of David, lived here upon earth, "thirty two years and a half"; no rain in Elias's time, "three years and a half"; Antiochus's desolating of religion, "three years and a half," in the verse before the text, and Christ's ministry to be "three years and a half"; doth not this harmony tell, that God is the wonderful "numberer" of time, and "weigher" of all affairs?[51]

The harmony is apparent in the text if we simply look for it and in the finding, we are refreshed with the understanding that God is in control of all history.

IS THE CHRONOLOGY OUTDATED?

Scholars in the last century have largely abandoned the chronologies of the early, medieval, and Reformed Orthodox church. In 1890, William Henry Green made "the most important biblical discovery of our time" when he refuted the formerly entrenched chronology. Green's article, entitled "Primeval Chronology," criticized early genealogical assumptions and with it Lightfoot's precise chronology arguing that the Bible is not chronologically informative regarding life before Abraham.[52] He further concluded that the Mosaic records were "not intended to fix the precise date either of the Flood or of the creation of the world."[53] A senior colleague at Princeton Seminary, Charles Hodge, agreed that

> the chronology of the Bible is very uncertain. The data are for the most parts facts; that is, not stated for the purposes of chronology . . .

---

51. Lightfoot, *Sermons*, "Wait the Time of God," 7:224–25.

52. George Macloskie to G. F. Wright, 23 November 1904, G. G. Wright Papers, Oberlin College Archives. Cited in Numbers, "The Most Important Biblical Discovery of Our Time," 257.

53. William Henry Green, "Primeval Chronology," 303.

> Under these circumstances it is very clear that the friends of the Bible have no occasion for uneasiness. If the facts of science or of history should ultimately make it necessary to admit that eight or ten thousand years have elapsed since the creation of man, there is nothing in the Bible in the way of such concession. The Scriptures do not teach us how long men have existed on the earth.[54]

B. B. Warfield said that genealogies "cannot be intended to supply a basis for chronological calculation, and it is illegitimate and misleading to attempt to use them for that purpose."[55] He then expressed his willingness to go up to two hundred thousand years if necessary, arguing that the biblical genealogies were "so elastic that they may be commodiously stretched to fit any reasonable demand on time."[56]

Today, it is fair to say that most have discarded precise chronologies like those of Lightfoot. Nevertheless, it would be unfair to judge Lightfoot as anything other than a man of his time. Hugh Ross is incorrect in more than one way when he ridicules Lightfoot's chronology. He says the following: "Both Lightfoot and Ussher ignored Hebrew scholarship and assumed that no generations were omitted from mention in the biblical genealogies. They also assumed, based on the wording of the King James Version, that the numbered days of the Genesis creation account could only be six consecutive twenty-four-hour periods."[57] He is incorrect, as we have seen, that Lightfoot based his arguments on the King James and that he ignored Hebrew scholarship. In fact, Lightfoot was a master of Hebrew and many other languages. Furthermore, even if Lightfoot was mistaken in both his chronology and his interpretive methodology, it is unfair to judge him based on our more modern understandings.

It is perhaps important to remember that Stephen Gould defends Archbishop Ussher and with him most of those who practice pre-critical chronology arguing that it was "an honorable effort for its time" and "that

---

54. Charles Hodge, *Systematic Theology*, 2:40–41. Warfield agrees stating that "The Bible does not assign a brief span to human history: this is done only by a particular mode of interpreting the Biblical data, which is found on examination to rest on no solid basis." Warfield, "On the Antiquity and Unity of the Human Race," 2.

55. Warfield, "On the Antiquity and Unity of the Human Race," 5.

56. B. B. Warfield, Editorial Notes, *Bible Student*, 241–52, cited in Numbers, "The Most Important Biblical Discovery of Our Time," 272. Numbers mentions several other applicable citations. See also Warfield, "On the Antiquity and Unity of the Human Race," 11.

57. Hugh Ross, *Creation and Time*, 26–27.

our usual ridicule only records a lamentable small-mindedness based on mistaken use of present criteria to judge a distant and different past."[58] Regarding the accusation that these may have delayed the establishment of an empirical geology, he says that this "is much like blaming dinosaurs for holding back the later success of mammals. The proper criterion must be worthiness by honorable standards of one's own time."[59] Not only he, but also James Barr and J. D. North say that Lightfoot was a "highly careful and rational person" "of an erudition seldom matched by that of his critics."[60] One can say the same thing of Lightfoot in regard to his chronological proclivities. As Barr said in a letter to David Watson,

> probably, so far as I know, there is no professor of Hebrew or Old Testament at any world-class university who does not believe that the writer(s) of Genesis 1—11 intended to convey to their readers the ideas that . . . the figures contained in the Genesis genealogies provided by simple addition a chronology from the beginning of the world up to later stages in the biblical story . . . Or, to put it negatively, the apologetic arguments which suppose the "days" of creation to be long eras of time, the figures of years not to be chronological, and the flood to be a merely local Mesopotamian flood, are not taken seriously by any professor, as far as I know . . .[61]

It was simply not strange for Lightfoot to put such importance on the biblical chronology. After all, if the Bible was highly interested in the proper times of events, than the student of the Bible should be as well.

CONCLUSION

As is obvious from the discussion among the Westminster Divines, Lightfoot was one of many masters of chronology, although unique in some of his conclusions. While perhaps these ideas are outdated, Lightfoot's skills did set him apart from his colleagues and colored all of his scholarly conclusions. He is often strict in his numerical assertions almost demanding a wooden, literal understanding. At other times, like when he looks at the New Testament, the plain sense is more malleable.

58. Gould, "Fall in the House of Ussher," 10.

59. Ibid., 12.

60. Barr, "Why the World Was Created in 4004 BC," 575. North, "Chronology and the Age of the World," 307.

61. Barr, "Letter to David C.C. Watson, 1984," cited by Ham, "Do the Days Really Matter," http://www.icr.org/article/689/.

He even suggests that one cannot understand the New Testament chronologies as definitely as one can their Old Testament counterparts. While perhaps not as defined, one must still understand them literally. However, this literality lacks specificity and the ambiguity allows him to see figures and types that were not visible to all. He was more than content to use non-biblical history to arrive at conclusions and was confident that the Bible's record and the actual history would never contradict. He was not as interested in the form of the text as he was that it correlated properly with the rest of the Bible and with the historical events themselves. Perhaps we can adduce most of all from his views on chronology, language, and rationality that he believed in such a strong coherence between the Testaments that none would be justified in disputing its divine nature.

6

Lightfoot's Understanding of Community and Authority

INTRODUCTION

IN ADDITION TO CRITICAL, reasonable, and chronological approaches, Lightfoot would maintain an interpretive approach that gave the proper place to tradition and present community. Lightfoot did not form his interpretations independently and he would insist that they should never be. Deriving the literal sense from the Scripture was sometimes a challenge and one needed other interpreters. That modern interpretation was often based on past interpretation was not a profound insight; the church throughout the centuries believed that past tradition was a necessary component for arriving at the literal sense. Even Lightfoot's Protestant Orthodox contemporaries insisted in a ruled reading or an "analogy of faith." John Owen called this the ecclesiastical rule and it included the catholic or universal tradition, the consent of the church fathers, and the writings of any persons holy and learned, whether past or present.[1] Lightfoot would appreciate this rule and definition; one should use the past and present community of faith in the process of interpretation.

Lightfoot, however, went further than a rule of faith. Not only were interpreters to be involved in their past and present community of faith, they should be equally well versed in the traditions of those outside the pale of orthodoxy. John Calvin said: "If we regard the Spirit of God as the sole fountain of truth, we shall neither reject the truth itself, nor despise

---

1. Owen, *Works*, 4:226 cited in Howson, "The Puritan Hermeneutics of John Owen," 372.

it wherever it shall appear, unless we wish to dishonor the Spirit of God."[2] John Lightfoot would whole-heartedly agree; truth often came from unexpected places and he had much to learn from those present and past, Christian and non-Christian.

But, to what degree should we consider these communities authoritative? Should one give equal authority to everything Christians produce and how accepting should one be of Roman Catholics and Jews? Lightfoot approached most of what he read with a reserved openness. He appreciated the Jewish works and the Catholic creeds, but was unafraid to reject their significant problems as he held, unflinchingly, to the Reformed dogmas of the Protestant Orthodox community in which he lived. Each of these communities considerably influenced his exegesis.

His approach is, in many ways, a *via media* between Christianity and Judaism. He rejected the automatic authority of the Catholic Magisterium and rejected the Jews as unenlightened by the Spirit. Furthermore, he felt no compulsion to accept either the interpretations of the Reformers or his contemporaries within Protestant Orthodoxy. Sometimes he carefully considered the variety of opinions, while at other times, he rejected them with seemingly little consideration. He found a way to take what was good from each tradition without compromising either his Christian beliefs or his Jewish interpreters.

While he was not a maverick exegete, and tradition did not bind him too tightly, he was a man under authority. For Lightfoot, though, the main authority was Scripture itself. Still, while Scripture was the main interpreter of Scripture, Lightfoot, appropriated the traditional interpretations of the past, to greater or lesser degrees, along with those scholarly opinions of his contemporaries.

THE SENSUS LITERALIS IS THE ACCEPTED AND AUTHORITATIVE SENSE

A direct relationship exists between *sensus literalis* and authority. Both Judaism and Christianity agree that the literal or plain sense of the text does not necessarily equate to the intentionality of the author; rather, the plain sense relates to the authority it is given. In other words, one could

---

2. Calvin, *Institutes of the Christian Religion*, 2.2.15; see also 2.2.16.

understand the *sensus literalis* as the accepted or authoritative sense, regardless of its "original meaning."[3]

Authoritative Sense in Judaism

In Judaism, Raphael Loewe is the first to suggest an alteration of the traditional meaning of *peshaṭ* from a simple authorial intention to authority, which is based on the community's acceptance. In other words, the plain sense is the accepted communal sense and therefore becomes authoritative, not because it is logically connected to human authorial intent, but because it comes from a generally authoritative teacher and the community has agreed to it. Loewe states that, "the conventional distinction between *peshaṭ* and *derash* must be jettisoned . . . [D]erash is exegesis naturally, or even experimentally propounded without secondary considerations; if it is popularly received, and transmitted into the body of conventional or 'orthodox' opinion, it crystallizes into *peshaṭ*."[4] Therefore, for Loewe, *peshaṭ* is relative. No one ever really understood Judaism's *sensus literalis* as necessarily the most straightforward reading; rather, its literal sense was that which was accepted.

David Weiss Halivni, a specialist in rabbinic literature, agrees: the plain sense is relative. Exegesis is "location bound" or "time bound" as it depends on whether one is from Alexandria or Antioch, or whether one is from the first century or the seventeenth.[5] Granting these kinds of exegesis leads one to insist that meanings differ and yet can still remain authoritative for their time and place. One cannot distinguish the literal sense from the accepted sense. It becomes the literal or plain sense because it was accepted and it thereby became authoritative. The Talmud is a good example of this. Many somewhat contradictory interpretations exist side by side and they are not necessarily tied to authorial intent or a straightforward reading of Scripture. Judaism's *sensus literalis* is whatever is accepted and is thereby authoritative.

---

3. The very concept of "original meaning" is difficult considering the transmission of texts.
4. Loewe, "The 'Plain' Meaning of Scripture in Early Jewish Exegesis," 183.
5. Halivni, *Peshat and Derash*, 3–22.

Authoritative Sense in Christianity

Just as Jewish hermeneutics has allowed progressive changes in meaning as new interpretations are accepted by a new community, so has Christianity. Charles M. Wood speaks to the relativity of the plain sense when he states that it is that which is "normally acknowledged as basic, regardless of whatever other constructions might also properly be put upon the text, . . . [that] sense whose discernment has become second nature to the members of the community."[6] Kathryn Tanner expands on this and Loewe's conclusions in her discussion of the Christian understanding of plain sense:

> The plain sense is a consensus reading, interpretation having distilled into conventional opinion when a certain approach to texts has come to be a community's unselfconscious habit . . . As the immediately apparent sense, produced by a habit of reading in which the members of a community engage without thinking about it, the plain sense is the standard sense of a text. It provides a normative reading, that is, in at least some minimal degree: all other senses, as both new and nonobvious senses, require some additional warrant. In sum, the plain sense is the "familiar, the traditional and hence authoritative meaning" of a text within a community whose conventions for the reading of it have therefore already become relatively sedimented.
>
> The plain sense of scriptural text in specific would consequently be what a participant in the community automatically or naturally takes a text to be saying on its face insofar as he or she has been socialized in a community's conventions for reading that text as scripture.[7]

Furthermore, "[t]he plain sense of a scriptural text in specific would consequently be what a participant in the community automatically or naturally takes a text to be saying on its face insofar as he or she has

---

6. Wood, *The Formation of Christian Understanding*, 43. The question of whether a sacred hermeneutic is necessary is interesting. Wood suggests that we should indeed read the Bible as Scripture, but that this heuristic method does not demand that we *only* read it as Scripture. Wood, "Hermeneutics and the Authority of Scripture," 16. Cf. Garret Green's distinction between saying the text is Scripture and seeing the text as Scripture. Green, "Fictional Narrative and Scriptural Truth," 86–93.

7. Tanner, "Theology and the Plain Sense," 64. The quoted portions in this paragraph come from Loewe, "The 'Plain' Meaning of Scripture in Early Jewish Exegesis," 181. The actual quote is that *peshat* is the "teaching recognized by the public as obviously authoritative, since familiar and traditional."

been socialized in a community's conventions for reading that text as scripture."[8] She continues, "the distinction between what is and is not the plain sense of a text becomes, therefore, a relative distinction between different sorts of communal uses of a text."[9] At the very least, this means that a text derives a specific meaning from the (in this case Christian) interpreting community. Whether or not this is the "original meaning" cannot be determined from this discussion. Nevertheless, we must at least realize that this community's time and place largely helps to determine the *sensus literalis* of Scripture for them.[10]

For the medieval church, the *sensus literalis* was, quite simply, what the Magisterium pronounced. Henri Blocher suggests four different views of the analogy of faith. Only one of these describes, for him, the use by the medieval Roman church.[11] While the medieval church was perhaps not so univocal in its view of tradition and authority, Blocher is largely correct that the focus of this period was the substance of revealed truth as the Magisterium recognized it.

The early, pre-medieval church adopted what H. A. Oberman calls "Tradition 1." This was the standard view early Christians held: that church authority derives from biblical authority.[12] Because the church understood the bigger doctrines that unified Scripture, it insisted that while Scripture was ultimate, the church should still use tradition to counteract heretical distortions and interpretations of Scripture.[13] Tertullian and Irenaeus insisted that the apostolic tradition was infallible because each generation handed it down to the next and it was Christ's faithfully transmitted teaching.[14] Tradition was Scripture. Whether the rule of faith was synonymous with Scripture or whether it was independent of it, as Origen and Clement said, the content, at least, remained basically the same.[15]

---

8. Tanner, "Theology and the Plain Sense," 63.

9. Ibid., 64.

10. In fact, it can be argued the opposite way as well. It is the plain sense that develops the community, establishing the group's identity. Tanner, "Theology and the Plain Sense," 64.

11. Blocher, "'The Analogy of Faith' in the Study of Scripture," 17–38.

12. Oberman, *The Harvest of Medieval Theology*, 365–75.

13. Preus, "The View of the Bible Held by the Church," 359.

14. Tertullian, *Praescr.* 21; Irenaeus, *Haer.* 4, 26.2, cited in Preus, "The View of the Bible Held by the Church," 359.

15. Origen, *Princ.* 3,1,1, cited in Preus, "The View of the Bible Held by the Church," 359.

Oberman's "Tradition 2" begins to overlap with Blocher's view that, at this time, extra-biblical tradition became authoritative as well. Scripture and tradition need not be identical. Jerome had already suggested that the church could speak when it was silent.[16] Even Augustine assumed the authority of extra-scriptural tradition in many matters.[17] By later medievalism, two arguments had made "Tradition 2" normative. First, Jesus had pronounced that the Spirit would lead the church into all truth. Second, logic demanded that if the New Testament determined the spiritual sense of the Old Testament, then the "literal sense of the church"—what the church teaches—should now determine the spiritual sense of the New Testament.[18] The question of biblical hermeneutics had become subsidiary to the question of ecclesiology.

"Tradition 2" may have been normative, but by the fifteenth century, Jean Gerson, the chancellor of the University of Paris, asserted that *sensus literalis* is only what the church, as the official, authoritative interpreter of Holy Writ, declares it to be.[19] There seemed to be a key shift for some to "Tradition 3" where the faith and teaching of the church superseded Scripture and tradition. The Bible no longer expounded the literal (what the text meant) sense; in fact, the Old Testament, and possibly even the New Testament, no longer had a theologically authoritative literal sense of its own.[20] The Bible had only a plain or accepted sense as understood by the church. This move to "Tradition 3" demanded legitimate interpretation only through the more formally authorized interpretations of the Magisterium. While calls periodically resounded to return to "Tradition 1" thinking, it was not until the time of the Reformation that things changed decisively.[21]

Concluding Sensus Literalis

Sensus literalis, community, tradition, and authority each relate directly to one another. As the community accepts new readings, whether they

16. Jerome, *Dialogus contra luciferianos*, 8 in Patrologia Latina 23, cols. 163–64.

17. See Oberman "Scripture and Tradition: Introduction," 56; Muller, *PRRD*, 2:54.

18. Preus, *From Shadow to Promise*, 58, 75–79.

19. Halivni, *Peshat and Derash*, 5.

20. The Old Testament is completely irrelevant theologically and so must have the church expound its spiritual sense.

21. For callbacks to "Tradition 1," consider the work previously mentioned by Paul of Burgos, *Additiones super uturmque prologum*.

are straightforward interpretations or more figurative, they become the "literal sense" of the text and are often crystallized into dogma. *Sensus literalis* is inherently fluid. The New Testament came to be the grid though which one understood the Old Testament and so now, the present-day church could become the grid through which one could understand the New Testament. There is a very real sense in which the traditions of the church continue the authority of Scripture. Lightfoot took this seriously and it would lead him to his own version of a ruled reading that appropriated Jewish and Roman authority, while at the same time rejecting them.

LIGHTFOOT'S APPROPRIATION OF PRE-REFORMATION TRADITION

Rome's Hermeneutics, Theology, and Present State

Appreciation for Catholicism

Lightfoot had mixed opinions regarding the pre-Reformation church. While the Roman Catholic Church was not a true church, some within Rome could be trusted and did indeed belong to Christ. When Rome asked where the church was before Luther, Lightfoot answered without hesitation that "God saw his own, that professed his truth, in the midst of Popery."[22] There has been a true church ever since Christ and there will be to the end of the world.[23] Lightfoot is grateful for much of the past church. He expresses his great delight to be living in a time when he has the books of so many great expositors right at hand. Lightfoot was an avid reader and interacted often with scholars like Pliny, Plutarch, Varro, Gellius, Justin Martyr, Athanasius, Eupolemus, Eupohorus, Eusebius, Josephus, Lyra, Athanasius, Nazianzen, Jerome, Ambrose, Chrysostom, Crantzius, Cyprian, and Epiphanius.[24] He especially loves reading the patristic authors and finds himself in great agreement with Clemens Alexandrinus regarding Septuagintal issues.[25]

Perhaps more than any others, Lightfoot appropriates the work of Augustine for he is "a learned and holy man." He especially appreciates

---

22. Lightfoot, *An Exposition of Three Articles of the Apostles' Creed*, 6:43.

23. Ibid., 40.

24. See Lightfoot, *Miscellanies*, 4:25, 44–46; *Sermons*, "Prudence in Making Vows," 7:155.

25. Lightfoot, *Miscellanies*, 4:32.

Augustine's love of the Hebrew text and Lightfoot quotes his *de civitate Dei* liberally in this regard. He agrees that "that tongue be rather believed, out of which a translation is made into another by interpreters."[26] Their similar love for language evidences itself more when Augustine mentions three Greek books, one Latin and one Syriac, which have Methuselah dying six years before the flood. Lightfoot, of course, is quick to point out that these differences should make us apply ourselves more to the Hebrew text.[27] The vast majority of time Lightfoot quotes Augustine, he does so without comment, as if Augustine's word stands on its own. For instance, he neither confirms nor denies Augustine's understanding that circumcision was on the eighth day "to signify Christ's resurrection who rested the week's end in the grave and rose on the eighth day."[28] Lightfoot even wonders whether Augustine's mistakes are really his mistakes and not the mistakes of others. For instance, Lightfoot expresses his unhappiness with Augustine's allegorization of Abraham's 318 men into a "T" and thus the sign of the cross. Lightfoot insists this "runs both beside the language and the matter."[29] However, his respect for Augustine gives him reason to doubt whether Augustine ever said this to begin with. Lightfoot loved Augustine.

Still, Lightfoot's love of much of the past fathers is nothing compared to those with whom he disagrees. Of course, he dissents with notable heretics as he does when he argues for an "orthodox" hypostatic union against Arius and his followers.[30] But, he also disagrees with the likes of Tertullian, Lactantius, and Jarchi regarding the sons of God in Gen 6. To Lightfoot, these "sons" are the men of Seth's line, and he argues strongly against the "wicked fables" of the Jews and those who follow their interpretations.[31] He disagrees with Theodoret who thought that none of the nations surrounding Canaan spoke Hebrew.[32] In truth though, Lightfoot is not fond of disagreeing with individuals from either the ancient or the

---

26. Lightfoot also quotes from chapter 14, "the truth of things must be fetched out of that tongue, out of which that that we have, is interpreted." Lightfoot, *Miscellanies*, 4:32.

27. Lightfoot, *Miscellanies*, 4:69.

28. Ibid., 37.

29. Ibid., 18–19.

30. Lightfoot, *Horae*, 12:425–7.

31. Lightfoot, *Miscellanies*, 4:12–13.

32. Ibid., 42.

medieval Catholic Church, but when it comes to criticizing the church as a whole, he is among the most hostile opponents.

Problems with Catholicism

For Lightfoot, there was no question that one should generally trust in the councils, synods, convocations, and primitive fathers. The question concerned how far this trust should go. Rome wrongly anathematized all who contradicted the Council of Trent and the holy mother church. Lightfoot believed, however, that the councils and the church often needed contradicting. We should trust and submit to the church only as far as they are true to both Scripture and reason.

Rome had significant problems in submitting to Scripture. First, their presupposition that the Bible is obscure led them to judge it inappropriate for common people because of its style and difficulty.[33] Lightfoot says their real concern is that the laity would read the Bible and discover too much.[34] Not only did they hide the truth of Scripture, they added more to it than should be permitted. The Apocrypha, for Lightfoot, should be rejected as an unreasonable interruption. He poetically illustrates by comparing the two cherubim to the two Testaments. The cherubim on the temple touch the two sides of the house and meet in the middle. The cherubim are the Old and New Testaments and they touch at Malachi, who is the end of prophesying and the beginning of performing. There cannot be a "span between these two plots of holy ground" for they touch one another. "What do the Papists, then, when they put and chop in the Apocrypha, for canonical Scripture, between Malachi and Matthew, law and gospel,—what do they, but make a wall between the seraphins, that they cannot hear each other's cry? What do they, but make a stop between the cherubins, that they cannot touch each other's wing?"[35] The Apocrypha is not a reliable source of truth and hiding the real truth is an abomination.

One could find the real truth in the true Bible. One must measure tradition by it and it alone.

> The Scriptures contain all things needful for faith and life; as that in Isa. viii. 19, 20; "And when they shall say unto you, Seek unto

---

33. Lightfoot, *Sermons*, "Difficulties of Scripture," 7:206–16.
34. Ibid., 214.
35. Lightfoot, *Miscellanies*, 4:51.

> them that have familiar spirits, and unto wizards, that peep, and that mutter; should not a people seek unto their God—to the law and to the testimony. If they speak not according to this word, it is because there is no light in them:"—so may I say also in this case; if they say to you, Seek to councils, fathers, canons, determinations of the church;—"To the law, and to the testimony"; to Scripture and holy writ, that contains every thing you need to inquire after for salvation; what to be believed and what to be done.[36]

Scripture is necessary and the problem with the vast majority of the Roman Catholic Church is that it ignores Scripture and by doing so forfeits the claim to be the true church.

> That church that is built more on traditions and doctrines of men, than on the word of God, is no true church, nor religion. But the church of Rome is built more upon traditions and doctrines of men, than on the word of God. Ergo, the foundation of the true church of God is Scripture: "and are built upon the foundation of the apostles and prophets." But if you look upon what the whole frame of Popery is built, you will find it upon a sand of human tradition: that the pope is head of the church; that he pardons sin; rules over princes; where find you this in Scripture? They are but points of the cursed inventions of men: That priests can sing souls out of purgatory; that the service of God should be in an unknown tongue; that the priests can change the bread into a God; and generally the whole rabble of their Romish religion hath not so much as any one underpinning of scripture-warrant, but all founded upon the rotten trash of human inventions, and self ends.[37]

The church fathers, themselves, would support his Scripture-centered understanding. "I might instance, how the fathers themselves harp upon this string. 'Non quid Augustinus, nec quid Hieronymus, sed quid Scritpura:' 'Not that which Austin or Jerome says, but what the Scriptures say, is truth.' And, 'Non creditor, quia non scribitur;' 'It is not believed, because it is not written.' And, 'Non quid Hieronymus, sed quid Moses, quid Paulus;' 'Not that which Jerome saith, but what Moses, what Paul, say.'"[38]

No man, not even the great men of the early church are permitted to disagree or ignore Scripture. Furthermore, Lightfoot encouraged his readers to distrust anyone who thought otherwise. "Then, is no man,

---

36. Lightfoot, *An Exposition of Three Articles of the Apostles' Creed*, 6:54.
37. Ibid., 45–46.
38. Ibid., 59.

no company of men, to be believed, but as what they say, is agreeable to Scripture? No council, father, church. If they speak not according to Scripture, it is because there is no light in them, and not to be believed."[39] For Lightfoot, a ruled reading meant that Scripture was the sole arbiter of truth, and tradition only deserved trust and submission as it found its foundation in Scripture.

Lightfoot insists that tradition should be submissive not only to Scripture, but to reason as well. Rome fails often in this regard. Concerning the Roman Catholic belief that hell is underground, Lightfoot exclaims, "Upon what ground, who can show? It is neither agreeable to reason, nor at all to Scripture."[40] He then argues the unreasonableness of their claims. First, he contends the absurdity of heaven being empty for four thousand years.[41] Then, "it is an absurd thing to think a thief should be first that went to heaven." Then, "it is an absurd thing, that Abraham, while he lived, should be a friend of God, converse with God, entertain God at his table; and, when he is dead, he is become a mere stranger to God." Finally he says, "it is absurd to think, that holy ones, that served God all day, and should at night receive their wages, should be denied it."[42] Their doctrine goes against all reason. "Such doctrine is that of the Romanists, and such absurdities they make people believe, to build up their purgatory for their profit. Nor are they only thus absurd, but as irreligious in this doctrine."[43] Rome is both unscriptural and unreasonable.

Because of Rome's foundational problem, their theology is tenuous, at best. They use Scripture to support their magisterial presuppositions. They emphasize the light within them for guidance and salvation, while at the same time, they strain the Scriptures and wrest from them anything they think may serve their opinions.[44] These faulty opinions, which contradict Scripture, include: their emphasis on alms as meritorious, their delusion of transubstantiation, and their belief in purgatory.[45] Their un-

39. Ibid.
40. Ibid., 5.
41. Ibid., 5–6.
42. Ibid., 6.
43. Ibid., 7.
44. Lightfoot, *Sermons*, "Creed of the Sadducees," 7:289.
45. For merit in alms see Lightfoot, *Miscellanies*, 4:60. For transubstantiation delusions see Lightfoot, *Sermons*, "Fraud and Violence of Satan," 7:73; Lightfoot, *Rules for a Student of the Holy Scriptures*, 2:15; Lightfoot, *A Few and New Observations upon the*

derstanding of Mary is neither reasonable nor scriptural. He shows how "senseless Popery is" when it turns the greeting of the angel to Mary into a prayer and sometimes a charm.[46] Lightfoot is not so bold as to rebuke the Catholics regarding idol worship, but rather, simply says that their bowing to statues and images, even in memorandum, fails to line up with the command to avoid all appearances of evil. Noting the difference between Matthew's use of two distinct Greek words for "rock" and assuming Jesus' same distinction in Syriac, Lightfoot condemns Rome's belief that Peter was the rock.[47] In his comments on Job 4:18 and 5:2 Lightfoot takes a moment aside from his main point to ridicule the papists for believing that the holy ones here are saints and not angels. His reason for bringing it up is to condemn the greater problem of Rome's acceptance of the invocation of departed saints.[48]

Lightfoot does not take every opportunity he has to condemn Rome, but it is safe to say that he misses very few opportunities. One interesting omission is in his sermon about the disobedient prophet in 1 Kgs 12:24 where the entire point of his message was that one should not trifle with the commands of God. Although there are a dozen places in this sermon to insult Rome in this regard, Lightfoot says nothing.[49] However, this is surely the exception to the rule. Lightfoot usually treats Rome with great hostility and considers them to be outside the faith not only because Rome's exegesis is so often incorrect and unreasonable, but because they often ignore Scripture altogether.

Lightfoot's animosity towards Rome is evident throughout his writings and he finds abundant reason in the Scripture for his feelings towards them. When the book of Revelation mentions the star that fell from heaven, Lightfoot is certain this refers to Rome, since the falling means that they fell from the truth.[50] The millennium taken "determinately" brings us to the deep and dark age of "popery."[51] This is not to suggest that one

---

Book of Genesis, 2:339; Lightfoot, *A Handful of Gleanings out of the Book of Exodus*, 2:374; Strype, "Preliminary Matters to Lightfoot's Genuine Remains," Lightfoot 1:191. For purgatory see Lightfoot, *Sermons*, "The Penitent Thief," 7:275.

46. Lightfoot, *Harmony of the Four Evangelists*, 4:162.
47. Lightfoot, *Horae*, 11:225–26.
48. Lightfoot, *Explanation of Diverse Difficult Places of Holy Scripture*, 5:354.
49. Lightfoot, *Sermons*, "The Disobedient Prophet," 7:167–76.
50. Lightfoot, *Sermons*, "Jannes and Jambres," 7:98.
51. Lightfoot, *Sermons*, "Fraud and Violence of Satan," 7:63–64. It also brings in

should understand the millennium in this way, it is just another opportunity for Lightfoot to condemn Roman Catholicism because it "cozens the world."[52] The false Jerusalem is definitely Rome. He further compares Protestantism's secession from Rome to the Christians of old who came out of Judaism. Since they crucified Christ, they take people back to old Jerusalem and not new.[53] He denounces them for their persecution of the faithful mentioned in Rev 20:7–8.

> Think of this, and of the constant practice of Rome, to seek to destroy those, that will not be of her mind and religion; then guess, who is the Gog and Magog in the text, that takes up persecution and fighting against those, that will not be deceived by Satan, as they themselves are. The design of this day, engageth us to hate Popery, that must be maintained and propagated with blood and force. I shall not dispute, which is the true religion, the Protestant or the Popish. Only set Jacob and Esau before you: whether of the two is more lovely? Popery is rough and rugged; witness the Inquisition, the massacre, the Marian days, and the fifth of November. Think of these, and hate Popery.[54]

Scripture always mentions Rome negatively and this fuels Lightfoot's acrimony.

Lightfoot is so passionately opposed to Rome, that it often affects his own interpretations. He looks for any and every opportunity to affront these heretics. Their very mention in Scripture, or some other text, results in several extra tangential pages and what is often caustic language.[55] In one passage, he altogether ignores the original meaning of the context and uses the words *Mene, mene, tekel upharsin* as an attack against Rome.[56] In one instance discussing the phrase, "Christ descended into Hell," he shows how this article of the creed easily leads to a belief in purgatory.[57] For this reason, he disagrees with the phraseology of the creed in English. Although he takes the phrase apart and references many relevant texts,

---

"Mahometism" which is a convenient way to place Islam and Roman Catholicism together. See *Sermons*, "The First Resurrection," 7:189.

52. Lightfoot, *Sermons*, "The First Resurrection," 7:188.
53. Lightfoot, *Sermons*, "The New Jerusalem," 7:121.
54. Lightfoot, *Sermons*, "Fraud and Violence of Satan," 7:73.
55. Lightfoot, *Sermons*, "Jannes and Jambres," 7:98–101.
56. Lightfoot, *Sermons*, "Elymas the Sorcerer," 7:109.
57. Lightfoot, *An Exposition of Three Articles of the Apostles' Creed*, 6:3–36.

it appears that he has certain presuppositions that he wants to prove before he ever enters into the study. He desires to see the Roman Catholics wrong, and this often drives his exegesis.

Lightfoot's respect for many individuals whom he found scriptural and reasonable in the pre-Reformation church contrasts sharply with his feelings towards the church as a whole. Rome was not a true church and many of its traditions should be ignored. He maintains that "we are in a miserable condition, if, upon the penalty of salvation, we are to believe every tradition, and trash, that foolish or ungodly men would put upon us."[58] Still, they were not always wrong. When Rome was faithful to Scripture and to reason, their counsels, creeds, and traditions were worthy of embrace.

Judaism' Hermeneutics, Theology, and Present State

Just as Lightfoot both despised and appreciated the writings of Rome, so is this true regarding the works of Judaism. There is no doubt that Lightfoot's greatest contribution to biblical studies is his appropriation of Judaica. At the same time, his animosity towards the Jews is evident on nearly every page.

Appreciation for Judaism

Lightfoot's use and knowledge of the rabbis is well known and often mentioned. [59] His *Horae* and each *Harmony* is replete with rabbinical comments about geography and obscure phrases. Moreover, his special knowledge of the midrash and Talmud considerably help in his frequent allusions to the Old Testament. He loved learning from the rabbis. George Bright, one of his biographers, says that the reason Lightfoot was kind to the rabbis was because of their likeminded respect for the Hebrew text.[60]

If Lightfoot showed any sympathy towards the Jews, it was predominantly because they wrote extensively concerning the great doctrine of the coming Messiah. The Jews not only fully acknowledged this doctrine, but also cherished it. They knew that the presence of Elijah would precede the Messiah's coming.[61] They knew he would be born before the destruc-

---

58. Ibid., 60.

59. Pitman, "Preface to the Octavo Edition of Dr. Lightfoot's Works," Lightfoot, 1:xli–xlii.

60. Bright, "Preliminary Matter to Vol. I of the English Folio-Edition," 1:39.

61. Lightfoot, *Horae*, 11:235.

tion of the temple and many looked for it at the time of John the Baptist.[62] It was the people's own opinion that "their redemption by Messias must be upon their repentance."[63] Even rabbinic commentators refer to the Messiah in the same way as the New Testament does. They characterize him as the "Son of David," "the Word," the "Son of God," "My servant," the "Son of Man," the "consolation of Israel," and the "Spirit of the Lord."[64] Lightfoot also likes to remind his readers that the "learned and ancient" rabbis ascribe to the Messiah humility and suffering.[65] Without some knowledge of talmudic writings, he insists, we shall be unable to understand even the fundamentals of Christianity.[66]

PROBLEMS WITH JUDAISM

While Lightfoot gained much understanding from the rabbinic writing, his kindness towards those in an "accursed state" was the exception to the rule.[67] Lightfoot finds problems with the Jewish writing and rejects it as opposed to his ruled reading because it coincided neither with Scripture nor with reason.

When the Jews used Scripture, they did so nonsensically and without basic reason, and Lightfoot despised all such inaccurate glosses, allegories, fables, and fiction. He recognized that much of the Jew's problem,

62. Ibid., 422. Lightfoot, *Harmony of the New Testament*, 3:36 and *Horae*, 12:185.

63. Lightfoot recognizes the dispute among the "gemarists" on this, but quotes two pages of texts concluding that the statement of Jesus and John the Baptist "Repent for the Kingdom of Heaven is at hand," applies itself to them "even upon their own doctrines and conclusions." *Harmony of the Four Evangelists*, 5:154–55.

64. For "Son of David" see Lightfoot, *Harmony of the Four Evangelists*, 5:261; Lightfoot, *Horae*, 11:11; *Horae*, 12:179. For "the Word" see Lightfoot, *Harmony of the Four Evangelists*, 4:118; Lightfoot, *Horae*, 12:230. For the "Son of God" see Lightfoot, *Hebrew and Talmudical Exercitations upon the Acts*, 8:469; Lightfoot, *Horae*, 12:286. For "My Servant" see Lightfoot, *Horae*, 12:287. For the "Son of Man" see Lightfoot, *Harmony of the Four Evangelists*, 5:259; Lightfoot, *Horae*, 12:288. For the "consolation of Israel" see Lightfoot, *Horae*, 12:384. For the "Spirit of the Lord" see Lightfoot, *Horae*, 12:554.

65. Lightfoot, *Harmony of the Four Evangelists*, 5:185; Lightfoot, *Hebrew and Talmudical Exercitations upon the Acts* 8:437–38. The latter Jews would not apply Isa 53 to Christ, "yet the ancient learned of the nation . . . did so apply it as may be perceived by the gloss of the Chaldee paraphrast upon the place, and by a remarkable passage in the Talmud."

66. Pitman, "Preface to the Octavo Edition of Dr. Lightfoot's Works," Lightfoot 1:xlii.

67. It is interesting that the vast majority of negative statements about the Jews take place in his *Horae*. It is also interesting that in the *Horae* he seldom polemicizes against anyone except the Jews.

like Rome's, was one of authority. Their glosses came from the fact that their tradition (oral law) was equal to written law. This, of course, brought about many misinterpretations that Lightfoot understood as wild fancies and errors.[68] They allude to the Old Testament, but often in so doing, they controvert it and create fables about it.[69] Even in their comments and allusions we see that they, "according to their usual vein, do find strange expositions."[70] A rather tame example is Lightfoot's offense over the fact that the Talmud would make Elias one who practiced his devotions in public.[71] They get considerably more unreasonable, however, and Lightfoot is not opposed to listing many of these senseless Jewish errors. For instance, he loves to quote their fable that Jonah was able to see out of the whale's eyes in their travels to Nineveh.[72] Yet, still they increase in foolishness. Some rabbis argue that the garments God gave to Adam were garments of light. Lightfoot thinks this is ludicrous saying that "the Rabbin had writ his critical toys and his foolish pieces of wit upon the law, or some such trifling commentary of his own upon it."[73] The two Shoshbenin at Adam and Eve's wedding were Gabriel and Michael, which is a "ridiculous and trifling story" according to Lightfoot.[74] They hold to unreasonable stories like Og surviving the flood by hanging onto the top of the ark.[75]

For Lightfoot, the senselessness of their stories runs rampant. One example of this senselessness is Moses' seamless coat, which the rabbis gloss further by saying it was made of only one thread. The "senseless" reason for this is so that Moses would avoid suspicion lest he, at any time, should hide any consecrated money within the seams of his coat.[76] They are equally ridiculous in their computations, saying that the Sabbath day journey is two thousand cubits, which is not in Scripture and from which "we may learn from hence the pleasant art they have of working any thing

---

68. Pitman, "Preface to the Octavo Edition of Dr. Lightfoot's Works," Lightfoot 1: xcv.
69. Lightfoot, *Miscellanies*, 4:16.
70. Ibid., 60.
71. Ibid., 4.
72. Ibid., 27.
73. Lightfoot, *Horae*, 11:380.
74. Ibid., 12:243.
75. Lightfoot, *Miscellanies*, 4:68.
76. Lightfoot, *Horae*, 12:201.

out of any thing."[77] They say the breadth of Jacob's ladder was eight thousand parasanae (32,000 miles) and the bulk of each angel was about 8,000 English miles in compass. He calls them "admirable mathematicians these indeed."[78] They often fit numbers to their own case.[79]

On rare occasions, and because of his general animosity, Lightfoot rejects Jewish allegories that might be helpful in interpretation. *Deuteronomy Rabbah* 293.4 says, "The Holy Blessed God said to Moses, As thou has given thy life for Israel in this world,—so, in the ages to come, when I shall bring Elias the prophet amongst them you two shall come together." The idea that Moses and Elias will come together is erroneously deduced from Nah 1:3 which states יְהוָֹה בְּסוּפָה וּבִשְׂעָרָה דַּרְכּוֹ. Since Moses is thrown into the sea (סוּפָה) in Exod 2 and Elias goes up into heaven (בִשְׂעָרָה) in 2 Kgs 2 then they find abundant proof of their statement in Nah 1:3.[80] Instead of considering this as a possible benefit in understanding either what Luke was doing in the text, or what Jesus was doing in the event, Lightfoot instead rejects it as nothing more than fiction. So even when the allegories are potentially helpful, Lightfoot calls them, "devilish witchcrafts," "magical," and "diabolical delusion."[81] The Jews controvert, create fables, give senseless exegesis, and love allegory, which for Lightfoot is a taint on their own posterity and upon the church of Christ.[82]

In addition to their glosses and the allegorical atrocities they add to the text, Lightfoot despises the Jews for their rejection of central Scriptural necessities. Not only do they reject the New Testament, they attempt to discredit it as well. The Jews attempt to deface the truth of Matt 1:5 that says that Rahab was the wife of Salmon. They say instead that she was married to Joshua.[83] Likewise, they try to "disgrace" the gospel of Luke

---

77. Ibid., 220.
78. Ibid., 241.
79. Ibid., 11:17.
80. Ibid., 88.
81. Ibid., 80.
82. Lightfoot, *The Fall of Jerusalem*, 3:404. The allegories come from the Talmud, the Jewish Derushim and Philo Judaeus into the writings of the church fathers "to their great loss of time, and little profiting of the church."
83. Lightfoot, *Harmony of the Four Evangelists*, 4:174.

saying that Jechonias was the natural father of Salathiel, even though we know from Jer 22:30 that this is not the case.[84]

The Jews attempts to discredit the New Testament in minor areas are nothing more than a symptom of their real problem: they refuse to accept Jesus as the Messiah. They do this for two reasons. First, they put tradition "even above the word of God."[85] Second, they are deceived, lost, and unable to come to the truth. Lightfoot beautifully summarizes their present state: they "made void the commands of God and through the commands of men and traditions their minds were poisoned with blasphemy and hatred of the true Messiah, and the pure truth of God."[86]

Despite their obvious excitement over the coming Messiah and the fact that their rules acknowledged that Jesus was that Christ, they still put him to death.[87] They believed in "the Spirit of King Messias," mentioning him in their comments on the Torah as early as Gen 1:2.[88] Yet, they corrupted the stories, purposely blinding themselves to the truth. The Talmud mentions the journey of Jesus into Egypt but even this was "corrupted with venomous malice and blasphemy (as all their writings are)."[89] There is so much blasphemy that Lightfoot even wonders whether he should report it all. His reason for doing so is that the reader might know, "and, with equal indignation, abhor, the snarlings and virulency of these men . . ."[90]

God would reject the Jews and this was a good enough reason to stand in opposition to them. Certainly, Lightfoot admits, the Jews were deceived, but he insists that their deception occurred because of their voluntary blindness.[91] Because of this, God calls Israel "those that are without," a phrase usually used to refer to the heathen as distinct from

84. Ibid., 175.
85. Lightfoot, *Horae*, 11:212.
86. Ibid., 12:441.
87. Ibid., 11:270–71.
88. Ibid., 12:554. Lightfoot also mentions that most resolved that Christ should come in the time of the Roman Empire and near to the destruction of the temple by it. He mentions the Chaldee paraphrast in Isa 11:4 in this regard who says "with the speech of his lips shall Messias slay Romulus the Wicked one." Lightfoot, *Harmony of the Four Evangelists*, 4:190. See also Bright's examples in "Preliminary Matter to vol. I of the English Folio-Edition," Lightfoot 1:21.
89. Lightfoot, *Horae*, 11:43.
90. Ibid., 12:239.
91. Ibid., 11:391–12.

Israel.⁹² Lightfoot also insists that the word "maranatha" refers to Christ's coming to punish the Jews.⁹³ Even before the Jews killed Christ, God had rejected his ancient people.⁹⁴ For this reason, Lightfoot felt compelled to reject them as well.

Their state was so vile that even when Lightfoot might naturally attack others, he chooses, instead, to denounce the Jews. For instance, Lightfoot vehemently opposes the Enthusiasts who despise study. Still, in his discussion of John 14:26 and 16:23, he ignores the Enthusiasts. He does this even though the aforementioned Scripture references clearly teach that the Holy Spirit will reveal all things and will lead them into all truth. Instead, Lightfoot focuses on the proper interpretation, combined with another attack on the Jews who are "under the cheat and imposture of traditions."⁹⁵ Lightfoot seldom has praise for the Jews.

The introduction to his *Harmony of the New Testament* is perhaps Lightfoot's best summary of his use of the Jewish writing and his hatred of the Jews themselves:

> For though it is true, indeed, that there are no greater enemies to Christ, nor greater deniers of the doctrine of the gospel, than the Hebrew writers; yet, as Korah's censers, and the spoils of David's enemies, were dedicated to the sanctuary-service,—so may the records, to be met with in these men, be of most excellent use and improvement to the explication of a world of passages in the New Testament. Nay, multitudes of passages are not possibly to be explained, but from these records.⁹⁶

Lightfoot used the information regarding the culture and dialect as legitimate helps, but ignored no chances to show his great animosity towards the authors.

---

92. Ibid., 391.

93. Ibid., 12:565. Cf. his comments on Mark 9:1 which mentions the kingdom of God coming in power and which Lightfoot believes describes the destruction of the Jews. Lightfoot, *Horae*, 11:404.

94. Lightfoot, *Horae*, 11:304–5. He further says that Paul knew that the far greatest part of the seed of Israel "his brethren and kinsmen according to the flesh," was to be cast-off by God, and "accursed by Christ," for their "disobedience and unbelief." Interestingly, Lightfoot believed that Paul knew this "well enough, from the Scriptures of the Old Testament, whatsoever he knew besides by revelation." Lightfoot, *Sermons*, "St. Paul's Wish to be Accursed," 7:315.

95. Lightfoot, *Horae*, 12:385.

96. Lightfoot, *Harmony of the New Testament*, 3:vii–viii.

Rome and Judaism are the Same

His problem with both the Jews and the Roman church was first, that their traditions were unreasonable and unscriptural and second, that either because of that or prior to that, they had been rejected by God. For Lightfoot, Judaism and Rome were very much the same thing. He considers the Talmud to be equivalent to the Council of Trent regarding authority since "so highly do they, Papist-like, prize the vain traditions of men."[97] Regarding the intercession for the dead, he wonders whether the "Romans Judaize or the Jews Romanize" and he praises God that he has not been shut up in the same darkness as the "Jewish Popery or the Popish Judaism."[98] In addition, justification and salvation are, for both Jews and Catholics, a by-product of works.[99] In these ways, he notes that tradition is not altogether positive and he even quotes Jesus against the Papists, Millenaries, and Jews when he says: "Why do you transgress the commandment of God by your tradition (Matt 15:3)?"[100] He compares them most beautifully in his treatise on the Apostles' Creed. After mentioning all the unbelievable traditions of Rome he says:

> Scripture never knew such base ware; we must go to some other kind of shop for it. And that pedlar, with them, is tradition. When they cannot find authority to warrant them by Scripture, then they have recourse to some tradition. When they have some bastard doctrine or practice, and want Scripture to father it, then they go to some old rotten tradition. Just so did the Jews; and these are so like them, that egg to egg is not more. You know Christ's accusation of those; "This people draweth nigh unto me with their mouth, and honoureth me with their lips, but their heart is far from me. But in vain they do worship me, teaching for doctrines the commandments of men." And the very same quarrel hath he against these. The Jews pretended a thousand traditions of the fathers,—so do these: they equaled them with Scripture,—So do these: they spoiled all religion, and made the word of God of none effect,—and so do these; as if God were a niggard in his word, and did not afford food for salvation, but we must seek it in dunghills.[101]

---

97. Lightfoot, *Miscellanies*, 4:15.
98. Ibid., 57–59.
99. Lightfoot, *Sermons*, "The Penitent Thief," 7:275.
100. Lightfoot, *Explanation of Divers Difficult Places of Holy Scripture*, 5:382–83.
101. Lightfoot, *An Exposition of Three Articles of The Apostles' Creed*, 6:55.

Rome and Judaism are equally flawed in their recourses to tradition and their end state.

Conclusion

Both Rome and Judaism were often unscriptural and unreasonable and Lightfoot had no reservations in making that clear. They were both heavily allegorical and had tendencies towards ridiculous fictions. They even accepted traditions that were blasphemous. Still, this did not mean that one should equally ignore or reject all Jewish and Roman writings. When they pointed to Christ even accidentally, they deserved applause. When they taught, even implicitly and unintentionally, that Scripture was the supreme authority over tradition, they were to be revered. Despite his many differences from the early church fathers, the medieval church teachers, and the rabbis throughout history, Lightfoot would insist that understanding each of them was a necessary tool to reaching the real meaning of a text.

REFORMATION AND PROTESTANT ORTHODOXY ON ECCLESIASTICAL HERMENEUTIC

While tradition was perhaps the most important part of a ruled reading in the medieval period, this changed significantly during the Reformation. The Protestant understanding of authority shifted from an emphasis on tradition to a more Scripture-based authority. The Reformation divines insist that "the authority of inspired scripture could be set above the authority of the holy and catholic, but uninspired, church and its tradition."[102] Reformers like Calvin and Musculus argued against the supreme authority of the church, and Calvin did so by saying that Scripture was self-authenticating because God speaks in it.[103] Scripture had, in a real sense, regained its authority.

What really changed, however, was not the authority of Scripture, but the authority of Scripture as interpreted in a grammatico-historical literal sense. Hans Frei says that "not until the Reformation is the literal [grammatico-historical] sense understood as authoritative—because perspicuous—in its own right, without authorization from the inter-

---

102. Muller, *PRRD*, 2:239.
103. Ibid., 2:78, 61.

pretive tradition."[104] Although not a logically necessary development, this understanding of the grammatico-historical reading became the normative or "plain" reading of the texts and the new Protestant community accepted it.

The Reformers did not altogether ignore the authority of the church in interpretation. In fact, they retained a healthy respect for patristic tradition. Peter Martyr considered the "verdict of the church" to be considerably significant.[105] John Calvin consistently drew on church fathers for support in his formulations. But rather than seeing tradition as ruling in regard to doctrinal matters, Calvin preferred to say that tradition *served* in doctrinal matters.[106] The church remained helpful and provided the proper context for the interpretation of Scripture.[107]

"The language of authority became even more important in the time of the orthodox."[108] They continued to cling to a Scripture-interprets-Scripture understanding of the analogy of faith, insisting that tradition should not become doctrine, but it does maintain authority. In fact, William Whitaker is famous for using patristic tradition to combat tradition as doctrine.[109] Still, tradition did become doctrine. Scripture-based tradition, regardless of whether the language was Scriptural, was not only accepted, it was a necessary part of a proper ruled reading.[110] If the tradition could not withstand the scrutiny of Scripture, one must abandon it. Both the Reformers and the Protestant Orthodox accepted many creeds, articles of faith, catechisms and other such traditions that were reflections of Scripture. Future interpretations of Scripture were to fit in with these statements. Flacius comments: "Every understanding and exposition of Scripture is to be in agreement with the faith . . . For everything that is said concerning Scripture or on the basis of Scripture must be in agreement with all that the catechism declares or that is taught by the articles of

---

104. Frei, "The 'Literal Reading' of Biblical Narrative in the Christian Tradition," 42.
105. Blocher, "The Analogy of Faith," 18.
106. Muller, *PRRD*, 2:74.
107. Ibid., 80.
108. Ibid., 248.
109. William Whittaker, *Disputation de sacra Scriptura*. See also Muller, *PRRD*, 2:107.
110. William Perkins mentions plenty of traditions that the apostles record, which are not mentioned in the Bible and we are permitted to grant because they are not denied in the Bible. William Perkins, *A Reformed Catholike*, 1:580–82.

the faith. Any interpretation differing from that offered in the creeds and confessions is a denial of the true sense of Scripture."[111]

The Protestant Orthodox continued in the same path. Georg Sohnius, a professor at Heidelberg, sums up the desire for creedal agreement in interpretation. "Norma et regula hujus interpretationis est fides et caritas: quarum illa in symbolo apostolrum, haec in decalogu exponitur. Unde apostolos praecipit ut interpretation sit analogia fidei, Rom. Cap. 12, hoc est, cum primis fidei axiomatic et quasi principiis totoque coelestis doctrinae corpore consentiat."[112] Interpretations should agree with first principles and the whole body of heavenly doctrine. Bullinger was more specific when he said: "let it therefore be taken for a point of catholic religion, not to bring in or admit anything in our expositions which others have alleged against the received articles of our faith, contained in the Apostles' Creed and other confessions of the ancient fathers. For saith the apostle: 'In defense of the truth we can say somewhat, but against the truth we are able to say nothing.'"[113] Richard Bernard adds even more: the things that he and the Protestant Orthodox community uniformly held as certain were those "that agree with the principles of Religion, the points of Catechism set down in the Creed, the Lord's Prayer, the Ten commandments, and the doctrine of Sacraments."[114]

The time of formalized confessions did not end with the Apostles' Creed and the early church. With great energy, the community continued to standardize doctrine during the time of Protestant Orthodoxy. The beginning of Protestant Orthodoxy was largely polemical, but by the end, the church formally recognized these now entrenched doctrines. Polemics became secondary as controversial questions were simply shifted to a formal theology and what became a new analogy of faith. Christians maintained their respect for tradition and justified their interpretations

---

111. Illyricus, *Clavis scripturae seu de sermone sacrorum literarum, plurimas generales regulas continentis* II, cited in Kümmel, *The New Testament: The History of the Investigation of its Problems*, 30.

112. Sohnius, *De Verbo Dei*, cited in Ritschl, *Dogmensgeschichte des Protestatismus*, 1:357. Roughly translated: "The norm and rule of this interpretation is faith and love: faith is expounded in the symbol of the apostles, love in the Decalogue. Hence, the apostle prescribes that interpretation be analogous to faith (Rom. 12), that is, that it should agree with the first axioms or principles, so to speak, of faith, as well as with the whole body of heavenly doctrine."

113. Bullinger, *Decades*, I.iii (75-76), cited in Muller, *PRRD*, 2:458.

114. Richard Bernard, *The faithfull shepheard*, 28.

with the Bible alone.[115] Nevertheless, the community still had to decide what was orthodox and what was not. The ecclesiastical hermeneutic was sorely put to the test. As assemblies gathered to discuss new formulations, constant friction existed over what should be included in the statements like the *Westminster Confession of Faith*. The analogy of faith would now include new modern statements of faith and confessions.

As has been seen, Lightfoot was willing to appropriate the best of the past traditions (as they were true to Scripture) and use them to understand Scripture more fully. Still, while using the best of Rome and Judaism, he was part of the Protestant Orthodox community and was greatly indebted to the Reformers. It was this community that compelled him towards new formulations of the faith that would become a new analogy of faith for later interpreters.

LIGHTFOOT'S RECENT HERITAGE AND PRESENT COMMUNITY

Reformers and Especially Beza

As F. F. Bruce has stated and we have confirmed, Lightfoot stood out among his contemporaries as an independent thinker who did not shrink back from exegetical creativity.[116] While Lightfoot's exegetical creativity made conflict with his colleagues inevitable, this was not his intention. Lightfoot preferred to see himself in a long line of worthy interpreters. He considered himself among the orthodox scholars of the past and present and disliked going against the opinions of the church fathers. He would never ignore the teachings of the past, nor of holy and learned men of the present. He respected the men at the Westminster Assembly and was more than usually courteous and generous in his interactions with them. Although disagreeing with great men like this caused him pain, this did not deter him from doing so. He did not seek after popularity and was quick to condemn many groups and individuals with mocking and scornful speech.

Lightfoot loved the writings of Calvin and Luther and quoted them with some regularity and always courteously. He quoted no one, however, as often or with as much enthusiasm, as he did Beza. His respect for Beza's

---

115. Muller, *PRRD*, 2:466.

116. Bruce, "History of New Testament Study," *New Testament Interpretation*, 34–37 cited in Dockery, *Christian Scripture: An Evangelical Perspective on Inspiration, Authority and Interpretation*, 133.

translation, which was side by side with the Greek and the Vulgate, is evident throughout his writings. While not often, Lightfoot does periodically express his explicit agreement with Beza, like when he opposed the Vulgate's translation of τὰ ἐνόντα in Luke 11:41.[117] The vast majority of the time however, he simply quotes Beza and moves on. After all, it is unnecessary to comment when there is such vast agreement.

While agreement may have been the default, Lightfoot was the premier linguistic scholar of his day and took many opportunities to disagree even with heroes like Beza. Most of these differences are superficial in areas such as translation and spelling. Working on Matt 27:33, Beza says that Golgotha has been misspelled. Lightfoot says that the "good man censures amiss," and then argues the normative omission of letters in the Syriac.[118] He further criticizes Beza for ignoring the difference between shoes and sandals in Mark 10:10.[119] His disagreements are generally of little theological relevance.

Despite his vast agreement with Beza and his general animosity towards Rome and Judaism, he did not play favorites. Regarding John 13:1, he disagrees with both the Vulgate and Beza, who add the word "day" to "now before the feast . . ."[120] Some translation issues result from faulty assumptions and hermeneutics. For instance, Lightfoot agrees with the Vulgate's translation of Matt 16:15 over against Beza's translation.[121] The problem is that Beza has mistranslated because he did not assume that verses 15 and 16 must cohere. Even though they seem independent, incoherent, and unclear, "there is no reason, why we may not suppose a connexion."[122] Lightfoot favored Rome over the Reformers.

Sometimes, he prefers Jewish views to those of the Reformers. For instance, Beza argued that Mark 3:17 was corrupt and tried to change the spelling of Boanerges to Benerges. Lightfoot commends Hugh Broughton who disagrees with Beza in favor of the Jewish rendering. Lightfoot says, "the Jews themselves will defend our gospel."[123]

117. Lightfoot, *Horae*, 12:116.
118. Ibid., 11:348.
119. Ibid., 176–77.
120. Ibid., 12:372–73.
121. Ibid., 156.
122. Ibid.
123. Ibid., 11:386–88.

Beza's translation is sometimes weak because he does not consider the whole Scripture when he translates a single passage. For instance, Beza translates the feast in Mark 15:6 (Κατὰ δὲ ἑορτὴν ἀπέλυεν) as plural, saying it should be "*Singulis festis*" (at each of the feasts). This cannot be plural, Lightfoot says, because John 18:39 says that they released the prisoner on the Passover and this action does not suit well the other feasts. After all, the other feasts do not commemorate the release of the people out of Egypt.[124] In addition, Lightfoot is often unhappy with Beza for being skeptical of the text when he is unable to explain it.[125] What appears to be standard for Lightfoot is that one is only able to explain the text, as it is, with the right information. Beza and others are too quick to question what is there in front of them. This does not mean that Lightfoot never emends the text or questions it, as we have already seen in our discussion on text criticism; it just means that he is critical of others who jump too fast to a corrupt text solution. Beza stands in a worthy tradition and is helpful and revered, but Lightfoot is not willing to ignore, or even to downplay his mistakes.

Lightfoot is a direct heir of the Reformation doctrines and holds staunchly to them, but this does not mean that he accepts all interpretations without study. He praises Calvin, Luther, and Beza, but is also willing to disagree with them. He stands for what he sees as truth, even if his disagreement with the Reformers means he must side with Rome or Judaism. Still, most of the disagreements are minor textual nuances and never are dogmatics at issue.

Among His Contemporaries, Especially in the Westminster Assembly

Lightfoot was a thinker, and, as such, remained open-minded towards anything that was not blatantly opposed to his analogy of faith. One can see this open-minded attitude in his exposition of 2 Sam 19:29. Here he "crave[s] leave to refuse the common and very generally-received exposition and interpretation of these words of David, that tends not a little to his crimination and reproach."[126] His open-mindedness really shows through, however, when he is willing to consider a ghost story by Isabel Billinger as truthful. Strype suggests that Lightfoot believed her story

124. Ibid., 443.
125. Ibid., 178–79.
126. Lightfoot, *Sermons*, "A Sermon Preached upon 2 Sam. XIX. 29," 7:203.

that a spirit came to her with information regarding her killers.[127] While Lightfoot is perhaps more uncertain than Strype lets on, Lightfoot does say in response "whether it be true or false" showing that he at least entertains the possibility of a dead spirit communicating with man.[128] Lightfoot was open and did not reject things without good reason.

Interestingly, Lightfoot did not appreciate others who strayed from commonly held beliefs, but he himself was open, creative, and consistently disagreed with well-established opinions.[129] For instance, his views on the book of Revelation were in the minority in his community.[130] His was such a marginal position that Lightfoot almost refused to deal with the book, saying that he could not go along with the "common stating of times and matters there."[131] He did not see himself as an innovator, and yet, he disagreed with many of his colleagues.[132] He argued for general admission to the sacraments, and the legitimacy of feasting on the Sabbath, and against the idea that a wedding should be merely a civil matter.[133] Regarding the article of the creed, "He descended into Hell," he argued against the idea that Jesus simply continued under the power of death, saying that the meaning was too short.[134] He contended against some of the divines that only public officers (pastors) were to read the Scripture in public.[135] He disagreed with a gentleman named Gibson over Matthias's second-class apostolic status, saying that Christ ordained him as well in

---

127. See the story in Strype, "Preliminary Matter to Lightfoot's Genuine Remains," Lightfoot, 1:175–80. This includes a letter from Mr. Thomas Blackwell on the same subject. Strype suggests Lightfoot believed this story on page 180.

128. Strype, "Preliminary Matter to Lightfoot's Genuine Remains," Lightfoot 1:175.

129. Dr. Morgan says this of him and it is recorded by Pitman in his "Preface to the Octavo Edition," Lightfoot 1:xvi.

130. Although, for equal animosity see the writings of Increase Mather, the president of Harvard College, Cambridge and especially *A Dissertation Concerning the Future Conversion of the Jewish Nation*, 9.

131. Lightfoot, *Harmony, Chronicle and Order of the New Testament*, 3:vii.

132. Strype, *Appendix to Author's Life*, Lightfoot 1:168.

133. For general admission to sacraments see Strype, *Appendix to Author's Life*, Lightfoot 1:75–78. For feasting on the Sabbath see Strype, *Appendix to Author's Life*, Lightfoot 1:78. For weddings not being merely civil see Strype, *Appendix to Author's Life*, Lightfoot 1:78.

134. Lightfoot, *An Exposition of Three Articles of the Apostles' Creed*, 6:2–36, esp. 3–17 and 24–25. For his rebuke of Rome regarding this see 2:4. Strype, *Appendix to Author's Life*, Lightfoot 1:79.

135. Strype, *Preliminary Matter to Lightfoot's Genuine Remains*, Lightfoot 1:150.

the casting of lots.¹³⁶ He disagreed with "ruling elders" being confirmed from among the laity.¹³⁷ Lightfoot had an opinion on everything and was never shy about revealing it.

This was especially true in the Westminster Assembly. One of only a few Erastians there, he often found himself arguing with Independents like Mr. Goodwin and Mr. Nye. His debates are long and detailed, including discussions regarding ordination, deacons, excommunication, and the number of congregations the church in Jerusalem had.¹³⁸ Lightfoot was generally well respected but many disliked him because they were dissatisfied with his views on the LXX, chronology, the utter rejection of the Jews, the keys to the Kingdom and the idea that binding and loosing had not to do with discipline but doctrine.¹³⁹

Many of his differences were with friends and over trivial matters, and in such situations he was an avid promoter of peace. However, he esteemed morality and doctrine as more important than peace and unity. He considered himself a defender of orthodoxy and of sound teaching. He fought diligently against the antinomians, the perfectionists, and the millenaries.¹⁴⁰ Regarding the law and the antinomians, he insists that some of the law still exists.¹⁴¹ He condemns the perfectionists as arrogant and ignorant and goes on to discuss their major problem as a misunderstanding of the difference between perfection and holiness.¹⁴² The millenaries, he insisted, were thinking just like the judaizing Jews. Lightfoot found it ridiculous that the millenaries thought that commonly understood expressions like the millennium of Rev 20:5 were to be understood in

---

136. Ibid., 151.

137. Ibid., 151–55.

138. Ordination: Strype, *Preliminary Matter to Lightfoot's Genuine Remains*, Lightfoot 1:150. See also Lightfoot, *Harmony and Chronicle of the New Testament*, 3:67; Lightfoot, *Harmony of the Four Evangelists,* 5:21. Deacons: Strype, *Preliminary Matter*, Lightfoot 1:155; See also Lightfoot, *Harmony and Chronicle of the New Testament*, 3:189 and 258. Excommunication: Strype, *Preliminary Matter*, Lightfoot 1:157, See also Lightfoot, *Exercitations upon the First Epistle to the Corinthians*, 12:466–76.

139. Strype, *Preliminary Matter*, 1:165–67. We have already mentioned his position on the LXX and chronology and will discuss more on the utter rejection of the Jews. For his discussion on the keys of the kingdom see Lightfoot, *Harmony of the New Testament*, 3:99 and Lightfoot, *Horae*, 11:226.

140. Strype, *Appendix to Author's Life*, Lightfoot, 1:169–73.

141. Lightfoot, *Horae*, 11:225–31, especially p. 230; cf. 246.

142. Lightfoot, *Meditations Upon Some Abstruser Points of Divinity*, 5:361–65.

the literal sense of the Jews.[143] He argues that they wrongly believe in a restoration, not to a former estate, but to such a one as never was before.[144] He also stands against the heresies of Anabaptism and Socinianism.[145]

Some scholars who disagreed with Lightfoot exaggerated minor matter to make them appear to be matters of orthodoxy. When others suggested that his views were somehow unorthodox, he was quite vocal and his strong personality showed through. This is most evident in Lightfoot's *A Battle with a Wasp's Nest*, which is a response to Joseph Heming's inflammatory pamphlet entitled "Judas Excommunicated." In the pamphlet Heming condemns Lightfoot saying, "Mr. Lightfoot has gone against manifest light of truth, the whole current or stream of orthodox, godly and learned expositors, common sense, etc."[146] Lightfoot's response shows him to be unhappy that so much time must be wasted on what he would consider a trivial matter, instead of on "teaching the sound and saving doctrines of salvation."[147] He calmly, but solidly rebukes Heming for his tone and time wasted, but then spends forty six pages defending his conclusions using reasonable arguments and mentioning scholars of his time who agree with his opinions and method of exegesis. While the original disagreement was largely unimportant, Lightfoot could not allow anyone to think him non-scriptural, lacking in reason, or outside the stream of orthodoxy. He was fully committed to Scripture, reason, and tradition and everyone had to know it.

He was usually quite convinced of his opinion, but he maintained plenty of areas of uncertainty in which he yielded, either in person or in print. He was generally humble and consistently referred to others as superior to him. For instance, Lightfoot provides several reasons why biblical authors might give the Son of Man epithet only to Jesus, but

143. Lightfoot, *Sermons*, "The First Resurrection," 7:189.

144. Lightfoot, *Meditations Upon Some Abstruser Points of Divinity*, 5:381; *Sermons*, "Prudence in Making Vows," 7:165; Pitman, "Preface to the Octavo Edition," Lightfoot 1:xiv.

145. Pitman, "Preface to the Octavo Edition," Lightfoot, 1:xvii. See also Lightfoot, *Sermons*, "A Sermon Preached at St. Mary's Cambridge, Oct. 7, 1655" 6:391; *Sermons*, "Creed of the Sadducees," 7:289.

146. Joseph Heming, "Judas Excommunicated," 11 cited in Lightfoot, *A Battle With A Wasp's Nest*, 1:422. This article is under the name of Peter Lightfoot, but the preceding page quotes Orme's "Bibliotheca Biblica" which suggests that this is by John Lightfoot. Lightfoot, *A Battle With A Wasp's Nest*, 1:372.

147. Lightfoot, *A Battle With A Wasp's Nest*, 1:378.

Lightfoot's own opinion, he says, is far inferior to the opinion of others.[148] In his preface to *The Harmony of the Four Evangelists*, he says that he had decided not to do the work because another had already begun it, who was a far better artist than he was.[149] Lightfoot eventually did publish his work in this area after his far more "learned and worthy friend" encouraged him to do so.[150] He is willing to receive instruction from the "more learned" and he often presents his case saying that the answer is for the learned to decide.[151] He never assumes he has the last word in anything. He praises fellow colleagues with some regularity in his writings and dialogues with many whom he respects. Among others, he especially praises the brilliance of men like John Buxtorff, Edmund Castell, Brian Walton, Sir Thomas Brograve, Matthew Poole, Huntington, Barrow, Pockock, Marshal, Sir Rowland Cotton, and Hugh Broughton.

Lightfoot is clearly indebted to the Reformed and Protestant Orthodox community. After all, they took seriously both a grammatico-historical literal sense and the traditions of the past. His letters and his willingness to be involved in the Westminster Assembly show a desire to understand the interpretations of his contemporaries. He purposely puts his views out to the test. Nevertheless, he did not back down easily, from either friend or opponent. He disagreed with Beza consistently and with numerous colleagues in the Westminster Assembly. In fact, the vast majority of his writing and his speaking was to form a contrarian position. After all, there was little reason to add his expertise to things that others did well and all the reason in the world to contribute "his service towards the correcting of supposed abuses in religion."[152]

CONCLUSION

Many scholars now maintain that the "literal sense" of Scripture has become the accepted community sense. If approval and agreement exists, then it is the *sensus literalis*. This remained true in the Protestant

---

148. Lightfoot, *Miscellanies*, 4:13.

149. Lightfoot, "To the Reader" of *The Harmony of the Four Evangelists*, 5:viii–ix.

150. Ibid., ix.

151. See Lightfoot, *Horae*, 11:133 where he says that he has never found mention of a literal trumpet in almsgiving and so questions whether Matt 6:2 should be understood according to the letter. See also Lightfoot, *Horae*, 11:355 where he discusses Mary Magdalene and the view of the Talmud regarding her as "a plaiter of hair."

152. Strype, "Preliminary Matter to Lightfoot's Genuine Remains," Lightfoot 1:168.

hermeneutic, but in order for it to reach Protestant agreement, one had to deduce it by way of the grammatico-historical method. Even things that theologians once approved, one should reconsider on the basis of the authority of Scripture.

Lightfoot accepts the authority of tradition in his analogy of faith, providing it is scriptural and reasonable. One should interpret Scripture in light of other Scripture and in light of dogmatic formulations found in the creeds and confessions. Lightfoot both appreciates and despises Roman Catholicism and the rabbis. They have helpful insights, but they lack enlightenment from the Spirit, and so Lightfoot often treats them with hostility. He insists on being a part of the major theological discussions of his time and considers the arguments of colleagues and opponents. Although humble, he does not yield easily to those who disagree. He readily questioned his colleagues in the Westminster Assembly, the Reformers like Beza, and even his contemporaries' understanding of the Apostles' Creed. Lightfoot is not compelled by, nor is he willing to ignore the expositions and insights of the past and present, regardless of their source. Lightfoot, like Muller says of Protestant Orthodoxy in general, "intended to state theology in and for [his] own time, and in a manner suitable to the institutional and intentionally catholic Protestant church, which now claimed all that was good in the tradition of the church for Protestantism."[153] For Lightfoot, though, this applied not only to the orthodox church, but also to all traditions. Lightfoot deemed the worthwhile Catholic and Jewish traditions acceptable as interpretational guides for arriving at the most literal sense. When it came to community and authority, he had found a *via media* between Judaism and Christianity.

---

153. Muller, *PRRD*, 2:96.

7

Lightfoot's Figurative and Christological Approach

INTRODUCTION

LIGHTFOOT BELIEVED THAT THE *sensus literalis* of Scripture could best be derived by holding some things that seemed to conflict as nevertheless non-negotiable. The most significant was that the Bible had both human and divine origins. One must not ignore the humanity of the text in one's attempt to revere its sacredness. Because men wrote it for humanity, it spoke to human issues: it spoke of history and geography, it used human logic and language, and it could be understood by using basic grammatical-historical rules.

At the same time, its divinity meant that it was not susceptible to error; the original text was perfect in all of its details and intention. This meant that the message was far more than a human message; it had special status and only enlightened eyes could understand the deeper message. This deeper message was especially important when it came to the Old Testament. After all, without a heightened meaning, both Christians and Jews struggled to find relevance in the Old Testament. For Lightfoot, the meaning was obvious. The Old Testament existed to point to Jesus. Lightfoot was unflinching in the practice of this christological rule, but his methodology for deriving this meaning was far from uniform. He often speaks of the fanciful ideas of others who invent meanings by over-spiritualizing and using allegories, all the while struggling with these same tendencies himself.

This chapter will show that, while Lightfoot appreciates the grammatico-historical exegesis of his forebears, and even denounces Jewish and early Christian spiritualization, he himself is not able to avoid similar hermeneutical problems. We will look first at the contrast between the Jews and Christians regarding how to understand the Old Testament and specifically how Lightfoot saw both of these groups. Next, the bulk of this chapter will analyze Lightfoot's own works concerning how the Old Testament corresponds to the New. In doing this, we will show that Lightfoot was a big proponent of typology as inherent in *sensus literalis*, but his lack of formal typological rules often propelled him into what he himself condemned.

THE RELEVANCE OF THE OLD TESTAMENT

Lightfoot believed that the Old Testament was relevant for every age. This is because its original design was to give spiritual light to Israel by speaking of important Christian doctrines and, most importantly, the advent and work of Christ.[1] Of course, he was openly critical of the Jews because they, in their darkness, missed it:

> And how God made spiritual and heavenly promises before the law, these and other places do abundantly testify; Luke i. 70, 71, &c; "as he spake by the mouth of his holy prophets, which have been since the world began," &c.—Tit. i. 2: "In hope of eternal life, which God, that cannot lie, promised before the world began."—and that one for all, John i. 4; "In Christ was life." In him came the promise of life and grace, even from the beginning: and that life was the light, that holy men looked and walked after: and that light shone in darkness of the types of the law, and in the darkness of the obscurity of the prophecies: "and the darkness comprehended it not."[2]

They could find everything that they needed in the Old Testament; the doctrines were all there. Only the blindness of the readers prevented them from understanding.

> These very doctrines, that Christ is speaking of to him, are so copiously taught in the Old Testament, that a student and expounder of the Old Testament, such as Nicodemus took himself to be, might deservedly be blamed, and did fall under a most just reproof, when

---

1. It had always been one of the primary ministerial tasks "to prove the doctrine of the gospel, and the person, and the actions and the sufferings of Christ, out of the Old Testament." Lightfoot, *Horae*, 12:539.
2. Lightfoot, *Sermons*, "The Blessing of Long Life," 7:395.

> he proved so ignorant of them, and unseen in them, as he showed he was. How regeneration is taught in Ezek. xi. 19, and Psal. li, and other like texts; and how a new birth by baptism and the Spirit is taught in Ezek. xxxvi. 25, 25,—he and the rest of his nation might have learned, but they had eyes and saw not, &c. It was not the deficiency of the doctrines, but it was the blindness of the doctors, that was the cause, that they were so ignorant of them.[3]

Lightfoot believed the Old Testament was relevant for his day; its promises stretched much further than its own time. The blessing of long life, for instance, in Exod 20:12 "had, wrapped up in it, a farther promise of life eternal. And so had the other temporal promises that were given them."[4] These promises are hidden because "men are not so sensible of things spiritual, as they be of bodily; have not the feeling of things that concern life eternal, as they have of this life." The "Jewish church" was simply not old enough to understand "spiritual dispensations in their abstract simplicity," so God gave them such "carnal ordinances, according as they were able to bear them."[5] So, for Lightfoot, the Old Testament concerned the eternal and specifically the things of Christ, but these were not always immediately obvious.

Lightfoot knew well the teachings of the church regarding Jesus and the Old Testament. Of course, the scholars of the church were christological in their exegesis, but even they struggled with how that worked in the Old Testament. Justin Martyr believed that the Old Testament was a specifically Christian book, belonging to the church even more than to the synagogue: for it witnessed to Christ and his glory.[6] The medieval church generally believed as Augustine: that the Old Testament was, in itself, unedifying to the Christian (did not uphold the rules of faith and charity) and, therefore, it was also insignificant, unless understood figuratively.[7] Hugh of St. Victor saw the Old Testament as having no doctrinal significance, and that it became theological and therefore relevant only at the advent of Christ. James Preus, after providing examples of the understanding of Peter Lombard, summarizes his beliefs (and with him, much of medieval thought): "Here again is a clear example of the literal sense of

---

3. Lightfoot, *Harmony of the Four Evangelists*, 5:44–45.
4. Lightfoot, *Sermons*, "The Blessing of Long Life," 7:396.
5. Ibid., 397.
6. Martyr, *1 Apol.* 32, 2.
7. Preus, *From Shadow to Promise*, 11–23.

the New Testament providing the spiritual understanding of the Old; the New Testament 'spirit' (that is, true meaning) is patent in its letter. The New Testament contains the normative literal correction and perfection of the unedifying OT letter."[8]

Despite some dissidence regarding the use of the Old Testament, evidenced by the Manichean and Marcionite heresies, the plain (accepted) sense was an interpretation of the Old Testament that had Christ as its center or goal.[9] Their christological understanding of the Old Testament kept them from the normative juristic exegesis and helped them to stay clear of what they saw as the wooden and fanciful interpretation of their Jewish contemporaries.[10] This christological approach continued throughout church history and the Reformers confirmed its use.[11] Luther says that "Christ is the sum and truth of Scripture" and "the entire Scripture points only to Christ."[12] The second generation Reformers looked to clarify the Old Testament by trying to find its fulfillment in the New, and specifically in Christ.[13] This understanding continued in Protestant Orthodoxy and is aptly summarized by Zanchi who said that the scope or center "toward which all the scriptures tend . . . is Jesus Christ."[14] Regardless of whether one sees the Old Testament/New Testament relationship as shadow and reality, prophecy and fulfillment, or metaphorical type and literal antitype, the Old Testament is retained as something in need of a final consummation. Moreover, one could find this consummation, first and foremost, in Christ.[15]

---

8. Ibid., 39.

9. Greene-McCreight, *Ad Litteram*, 3. I might add whether the interpretation is designated as typology, allegory, tropology, or any other figurative reading, it is not the method that was important to the authors; rather, it was Christ as the goal.

10. Cf. Preus, "The View of the Bible Held by the Church," 361.

11. See Preus, *From Shadow to Promise*. He has several more in-depth questions to answer, but at least argues the consistency of Christ as the hermeneutical key to the Old Testament ("the *telos* of the law and the prophets" [p. 4]). Specifically consider Paul of Burgos who although surrounded by a community that accepted the church as the authority on the literal sense, said that Christ alone establishes the *sensus literalis*. See Luther's commentaries on Genesis, Deuteronomy, Psalms, and Isaiah as examples of reformation confirmation.

12. Luther, *D. Martin Luthers Werke, Kirtische Gesamtausgabe*, 3: 620; 2:73.

13. Muller, *PRRD*, 2:323–24.

14. Zanchius, *In Mosen et universa Biblia, Prolegomena*, in *Opera*, VIII, col. 16, cited in Muller, *PRRD*, 2:105.

15. Frei, "The 'Literal Reading' of Biblical Narrative in the Christian Tradition," 42.

If the entire Old Testament was about eternal matters and Christ, then how should one read it to see these things most clearly? Is the Old Testament a book of prophecies, allegories, or types? While Lightfoot has no specific instruction regarding how one can find Christ in the *sensus literalis* of Scripture, we can determine much by examining his own exegesis of specific passages, as well as his comments about others.

ALLEGORY

Lightfoot is Anti-Allegory

Allegory, generally understood as an interpretation that ignores the historical meaning in favor of a higher spiritual meaning, was an often-used method of biblical interpretation, both for the Jews and for the church. Philo and the Derushim were full of mystical exposition and Lightfoot was sad to see how this had crept into the church as well. Perhaps we can attribute its acceptance to Paul's use of *allegoroumena* in Gal 4:22–24. Whatever the case, allegory was often accepted as a way to reach the meaning behind the text.

Jews Wrongly Allegorical

While Lightfoot believed that the Bible was divine and pointed to spiritual things, he did not think all methods for arriving at a christological understanding were equal. In fact, one could fairly say that Lightfoot despised allegory. Of course, not only did he oppose allegory, he blamed the Jews for introducing it to the church to begin with: "A second taint we mentioned, that these primitive Jews set not only upon their own posterity, but too much also upon the church of Christ, was the turning of the Scriptures all into allegory."[16] From where does the Christian allegorical problem get its base? From the Jews and especially Philo, who are more "ingenious than they are solid when it comes to exegesis."[17] "So it is easily to be known from whence it comes, by any that reads Philo Judaeus, and the Jewish Derushim. The Talmuds, indeed, are, for the most part, upon disputes; but sometimes, they bring in how such or such a doctor did 'darash' [mystically expound] such or such a place of Scripture: and then, you have directly such stuff as this. Philo, in his discourse concerning the

---

16. Lightfoot, *The Harmony, Chronicle, and Order of the New Testament*, 3:404.
17. Ibid.

Therapeutae, or Essenes, relateth, that they had used this mystical exposition of old."[18]

Lightfoot has very little appreciation for Philo's "quaintness of style and writing." He dislikes his explaining "divinity by philosophy, or rather, forcing philosophy out of divinity," resulting in "spoiling the one and not much mending the other."[19] However, his biggest concern was with Philo's use of allegory, "which did not only obscure the clear text, but also much soil the theology of succeeding times . . . His manner . . . rather seemeth to draw the subject, whereon he writeth, wither his fancy pleaseth, than to follow it, wither the nature and inclination of it doth incline."[20]

This is an important exegetical rule for Lightfoot: taking from Scripture according to its nature and inclination. Allegory, however, is exactly the opposite of this. It is based on "fancy" and "whatsoever cometh to his hand." The problem with allegory is that the Scripture becomes a tool in the hand of the "interpreter" to do with as he will. Philo was so confident and convinced that his allegory resulted in wonderful "mysteries" that he actually felt he could change Scripture to make it fit in with his new understandings.[21] His soul actually had "raptures" and "taught him strange, profound, and unknown speculations." For instance, Lightfoot says that Philo was very unmannerly and uncivil with Joseph and that he cared so much for his allegory, that he actually wrongly censures a great patriarch.[22] Lightfoot also believes that this mystical understanding leads to impiety. "[H]is allegories make him impious; and he counteth the story of Paradise to be but foolery, if it be taken literal."[23] Philo was certainly the most significant allegorical interpreter, but mystical exposition was rampant throughout the Jewish writings.

The "ridiculous" allegories of the Jews are nothing more than "fiction." One should not consider allegories, like the witch of Endor raising Moses with Samuel, and Moses not dying, as plausible because of their faulty allegorical hermeneutics.[24] For Lightfoot, allegories might also in-

18. Ibid.
19. Lightfoot, *Commentary on the Acts,* 8:245.
20. Ibid.
21. Ibid.: "sometimes he checketh the Scripture, if it speak not as he would have it, as p. 100."
22. Lightfoot, *Commentary on the Acts,* 8:247.
23. Ibid.
24. Samuel and the witch of Endor is found in *Lev. Rab.* 195:3. Moses not dying can

clude illegitimate exaggeration, like those who state that at the Red Sea, even the infants sang in the wombs of their mothers.[25] "This is it" says Lightfoot, "for such as these to allegorize the Holy Scriptures."[26] This tendency to "allegorize" was a terrible blight on the Jews.

Church Wrongly Allegorical

It made sense to Lightfoot that the Jews would have "strange and mysterious" allegorizing; but that the church would waste time on such things was unforgivable. Perhaps the most significant Christian allegorist was Origen. He often denied the historical reality of the events mentioned in the Old Testament outright, insisting that "they who do not believe that there are allegories in the writings do not understand the law."[27] In his *Principia* he insists, "when the Scripture history could not otherwise be accommodated to the explanation of spiritual things, matters have been asserted which did not take place, nay, which could not have taken place; and others again, which though they might have occurred, yet never actually did so."[28] He said that to believe that God literally clothed Adam and Eve in animal skins was ridiculous. God gave these stories not for the historical benefit, but for the spiritual benefit only.[29]

Although the Latin church was more sparing in its allegorical interpretation, they were not without their figurative understandings.[30] Both the Western and Eastern churches frequently arrived at typical meanings, but did so without rule or limit.[31] The church seemed free to do as they wished, provided they saw the Old Testament as a prophecy, a type, a figure, or a symbol of something in the New. Augustine believed that "to those who rightly understand it, the Old Testament is a prophecy of the

---

be found in *Pesiq. Rab. Kah.* 93:1. These stories are mentioned and ridiculed in Lightfoot, *Horae*, 12:88.

25. Lightfoot, *Horae*, 12:26–27.
26. Ibid., 88.
27. Origen, *On First Principles*, 4:2, 280.
28. Origen, *Princ. Lib. iv. c.* 15 ed. Delarue, cited in Fairbairn, *The Typology of Scripture*, 1:3.
29. *Opera*, vol. ii, 29; *Princ. Lib. iv. c.* 16, cited in Fairbairn, *The Typology of Scripture*, 1:3.
30. Fairbairn, *The Typology of Scripture*, 1:7.
31. Ibid.

New."³² The medieval church never questioned that there was a figurative meaning for the Old Testament. The real question was whether, for instance, Adam in Eden, foreshadowed Christ in a literal sense or spiritual sense. This question of literal or spiritual sense of the text would be a primary discussion at the Council of Constance, which met from 1414–18.³³

Lightfoot knew well that allegory "was used by divers of the fathers, to their great loss of time, and little profiting of the church" and this was unacceptable.³⁴ He consistently criticized the church's wrong desire to "soar in high places." For instance, in his *Miscellanies* he states: "Whosoever desires to be taken up with allegories about this piece of God's service, Flaviacensis will furnish him; and if he will not do, the fathers are copious enough, and, it may be, too much, this way."³⁵ Commenting on the book of Acts he again bemoans allegorical practice:

> How too many of the fathers in the primitive church followed him in this vein, it is too well known, to the loss of too much time, both in their writing and in our reading. Whether it were, because he [Philo] was the first, that wrote upon the Bible, or rather, because he was the first, that wrote in this strain, whose writings came unto their hands,—that brought him into credit with Christian writers; he was so far followed by too many, that while they would explain Scripture, they did but intricate it, and hazarded to lose the truth of the story, under the cloud of the allegory.³⁶

Allegory simply did not reveal the heightened, spiritual meaning as many of the church fathers insisted; rather, Lightfoot thought, it hid the truth of the story and was therefore unacceptable.

LIGHTFOOT INTERPRETED FIGURATIVELY

While Lightfoot spoke ill of many of the more fanciful expositions, he himself was still a proponent of spiritual meaning. One can and should understand some things literally while necessarily understanding other things more spiritually. For instance, John 4:35 includes both literal and spiritual meanings. "In the former part of the words, 'Say ye not, there

---

32. *Faust.* 15.2 Translated by Stothert.
33. Miner, *Literary Uses of Typology: from the late Middle Ages to the Present*, 370.
34. Lightfoot, *The Harmony, Chronicle, and Order of the New Testament*, 3:404.
35. Lightfoot, *Miscellanies*, 4:25.
36. Lightfoot, *Commentary on the Acts*, 8:246.

are four months, and then cometh harvest,' he speaketh literally of their harvest of corn: but in the latter, 'the fields are already white to harvest,' he speaketh, parabolically or spiritually, of the multitudes of people, both among Jews and Gentiles, that were ready to be reaped and gathered by the gospel."[37]

The Old Testament also includes things that one must interpret spiritually. Hosea 2:20–23 ("I will answer the heavens, and they shall answer the earth, and the earth shall answer the grain, the wine and the oil, and they shall answer Jezreel"; ESV) has "a divine and spiritual sense and purpose." One should also understand Amos 9:13–14, which speaks of the ploughman overtaking the reaper, in such a divine and spiritual way.[38] Isaiah 11:6–7 refers neither to a current literal wolf dwelling with the lamb or leopard lying down with a kid, nor to a future universal peace. Lightfoot insists this is an allusion to the ark where the animals do not harm one another. Isaiah, however, used this passage to describe "the power of the gospel in the Christian church."[39]

> So it is in the church, and so is it by the power of religion: those humours and passions of men, which before have been bloody, cruel, proud, self-willed, dissentious, and rebellious,—if once the powerful operation of religion get in among them, it quells these rebels, quenches these firebrands, reduces these extravagants, and, like the dispossessed in the gospel, make him to sit calmly and quietly, and in his right mind, whom none might come within the compass of before, without a danger.[40]

For Lightfoot, spiritual interpretation was not the same as allegorical interpretation.

FIGURATIVE INTERPRETATION IN REFORMATION AND PROTESTANT ORTHODOXY

If mystical exposition was not automatically against the rules, then where were the lines to be drawn? What was legitimate and what was not? What Lightfoot called allegory was obviously out of bounds in theory and he reprimanded others who allegorized as such.

37. Ibid.
38. Lightfoot, *Harmony of the Four Evangelists*, 5:102.
39. Lightfoot, *Sermons*, "Elias Redivivus," 6:157.
40. Ibid.

But, how did Lightfoot justify his own heightened interpretation? The answer appears to be by defining his correspondences between the Old and New Testaments as typology. While Lightfoot never speaks explicitly about a typological rule, or even what he means by "typology," the words "type" and "figure" appear throughout his writings. Before we seek to understand what he means by these ideas, it would e helpful to look at typology as those prior to and during Lightfoot's life might have understood it.

By 1480, the word "type" had begun to appear in writings, but at least Robert Henryson's usage had more to do with the parabolic character of fables, than with any historical correspondence.[41] While the Reformers distanced themselves from much of medieval exegesis, they continued to embrace hermeneutical methods that emphasized the movement from promise or shadow in the Old Testament, to fulfillment or reality in the New Testament. They attempted to be different from their medieval counterparts and fell into allegorizing and typology comparatively seldom. Still, they did not set aside a typological understanding of the old to the new covenant. Luther certainly held to a christological reading of the Old Testament, in addition to his tropological understanding.[42] Zwingli is known for his christological and typological interpretations and recognized that the literal was bound up with these types and figures. God, Zwingli said, directed the text beyond its ancient context toward a contemporary meaning.[43] Calvin refused Luther's christological exegesis, although it would be hard to see him as a strict grammatico-historical exegete either. He suggested that "Old Testament references to the 'last day,' the 'day of the Lord,' and the 'restoration of Israel' can, in the pre-exilic prophets, refer to the return of Israel from Babylon, to the coming of Christ and the new age inaugurated by him and, by extension, to the life of the present-day church."[44] Rather than see Calvin against christological readings altogether, we should understand Calvin as opposing christological readings that ignored the historical reference.[45] He clearly used

---

41. Miner, *Literary Uses of Typology*, 378.

42. See Luther's *Lectures on Genesis*, in *Luther's Works*, vols. 1–8. See especially vol. 6, 221–26, where Jacob's grief is an example of the church of distress and consolation.

43. Muller, *PRRD*, 2:68–69.

44. Muller, "The Hermeneutic of Promise and Fulfillment in Calvin's Exegesis," 78.

45. Even this is perhaps overstated. Cf. Puckett, *John Calvin's Exegesis of the Old Testament*, 110–13.

typology, but it is fair to say that none of the Reformers "attempted to construct a well-defined and properly grounded typological system."[46] As time continued, however, Protestant Orthodoxy felt responsible to codify the beliefs of the Reformation. Characteristically assuming a relationship between promise and fulfillment in the Old and New Testaments, they insisted on "establishing rules for the right identification and understanding of the types and figures, as distinct from the imposition of typology on the text."[47]

In 1607, with the Reformation beliefs firmly entrenched, Samuel Hieron discussed a more strict typology where "the people of Israel were a type of God's people; Canaan a type of heaven."[48] His consistent use of the word "type" did not immediately clarify anything. Writers failed to distinguish their application of types, even in a theological context. Sometimes, it described an emblem, a hieroglyphic, a heraldic device, a historical painting, or simply a symbol representing something else.[49] Confusion of terminology certainly continued in the seventeenth century and beyond. The interpretive manuals of Glasius, Weemse, Taylor, Guild, Whitaker, and many others helped bring some unity and clarity to their Christology. While this continuity and agreement was primarily in regard to a single sense, the considerable works on christological readings in Early Orthodoxy all discussed the correct reading of types and figures.[50] John Owen insisted that in order to understand the seeming contradictions of the Old Testament, one had to practice legitimate interpretation and this included a sound understanding of the scriptural employment of figures and types.[51]

Rivetus stood strongly with Calvin, arguing against the use of typological interpretations in the Old Testament, on the ground that they endangered the historical sense of the text. Yet, he did allow for a typological interpretation of select messianic psalms.[52] Whitaker said that only one

---

46. Fairbairn, *The Typology of Scripture*, 1:9.

47. Muller, *PRRD*, 2:120; 2:453.

48. Miner, *Literary Uses of Typology*, 307.

49. Korshin, "The Development of Abstracted Typology in England, 1650–1820," 148–49.

50. Muller, *PRRD*, 451–52.

51. Owen, *A Defense of Sacred Scripture against Modern Fanaticism*, in *Biblical Theology*, 814.

52. Muller, *PRRD*, 2:118.

sense existed, although one could not find it simply in the words. We are to proceed from the sign to the thing signified and in this bring out no new sense, only new light that the sign had concealed.[53] Perkins insisted on only one sense, but that "not onely the bare historie, but also that which is thereby signified, is the full sense of the Historical-grammatical."[54] These, as well as Gisbertus Voetius, Thomas Cartwright, and Daniel Chamier, clung to this literal historical sense and so were less inclined to find Jesus in every word.[55] Others still held to a historical sense, but were considerably freer in their christological discoveries. One can trace the most significant advances here to the Coccleian school.

The Dutch theologian, Johannes Cocceius, perhaps best know for his federal covenant theology, is also well known for his ability to find Christ everywhere in the Old Testament. In fact, his typology undergirds his federalistic interpretation. His federalism abrogated the Old Testament covenant of works, and for that reason, much of the Old Testament was only worthwhile when understood to be figures and types that the New Testament superseded.[56] While he failed to outline his figurative methodology, we can glean much from his commentaries. Fairbairn says that Cocceius "conceived that *every* event in Old Testament history, which had a formal resemblance to something under the New Testament, was to be regarded as typical."[57] And yet, he strongly believed in a single literal historical sense of Scripture.

It is perhaps too strong to say, as Fairbairn did, that Glass, Cocceius, Witsius, and Vitringa have no essential differences in their understanding of typology.[58] Vitringa, for example, refuted his mentor's mystical interpretations and was critical of his "uncontrolled and fanciful allegory, which he thought denigrated the literal sense of the Old Testament."[59] In fact, Vitringa was more interested in what he called the *implementum*

---

53. Whitaker, *Disputation on the Holy Scripture against the Papists*, iv.1: 404–5.

54. Perkins, *A Commentarie or Exposition, upon the five first chapters of the Epistle to the Galatians*, 346.

55. Muller, *PRRD*, 2:97.

56. Contemporaries of his, like Witsius, comment on defects in the Old Testament mode of revelation while Rijsen and Leigh argue that the dispensation or economy of the Old Testament is superseded but not the teaching. See Muller, *PRRD*, 2:362–64.

57. Fairbairn, *The Typology of Scripture*, 1:10.

58. Ibid., 11.

59. Childs, "Hermeneutical Reflections on C. Vitringa," 90.

prophetiae literale and the *themata collecta comparanda cum historia*—the fulfillment of prophecy. Vitringa found it largely unnecessary to have multiple fulfillments; rather, he insisted that Christ alone often fulfills it. Some historical fulfillment always takes place, and sometimes more than one, but once Vitringa discovers the fulfillment, then he is open to allegorical interpretation. He remains under the influence of Cocceius to the extent that he strives to see a history of prophecies unfolding, which he links in seemingly arbitrary stages.[60] He also does allow some element of a typological sense to enter at the edges of his historical verification.[61]

It is in this context of terminological confusion and a highly dominant christological methodology that we find John Lightfoot. He sees the importance of some kind of spiritual reading. It certainly had significance for the Jewish people when it was written, while at the same time, it pointed to something higher of a later time. The Old Testament was, after all, types and shadows that needed to reach their fulfillment.

> Look upon the religion of the Jews: that was all but types and shadows: Moses's face veiled,—Israel in the cloud, all divinity and religion under mysteries and figures. The tabernacle was filled with a cloud, as soon as it was set, and all the ordinance given out of it, cloudy and shadows. Hereupon the gospel is called "the truth" because it unriddled those mysterious hieroglyphics, unveiled the face of Moses, and showed the substance and body, which those veils and shadows did enfold. Thereupon it is, that the evangelist makes that most pertinent opposition, "The law was given by Moses." The moral law was given by Moses, the ministration of condemnation, as the apostle calls it, "but grace came by Jesus Christ" against condemnation. The ceremonial law was given by Moses, a ministration of types and shadows; but truth came by Jesus Christ, "substantiating and resolving all."[62]

The Old Testament law is full of shadows, clouds, hieroglyphics, veils, and types, which God gave to prepare the people for the truth of Jesus. Its truths were obscured in that they were merely pictures of the reality to come. The apostle John speaks directly to the way in which truth in the person of Jesus comes—first through promise, then through types, then through proclamation. In Lightfoot's comments on John 1:5, he says,

---

60. Ibid., 94.
61. Ibid., 96.
62. Lightfoot, *Sermons*, "Jannes and Jambres," 7:93–94.

> This light of promise and life by Christ, "shined in the darkness" of all the cloudy types and shadows under the law, and obscurity of the prophets. And those dark things "comprehended it not," i.e., did not so cloud and suppress it, but it would break out; nor yet so comprehended it, but that there was an absolute necessity there should a greater light appear. I do so much the rather incline to such a paraphrase upon this place, because I observe the evangelist here treateth of the ways and means, by which Christ made himself known to the world, before his great manifestation in the flesh; first in the promise of life, ver. 4; next by types and prophecies; and lastly, by John the Baptist.[63]

Its obscurity is only temporary and it will break free and it will be understood. Jesus is the one to which all these types point.

What did Lightfoot understand by using words such as type, shadow, and figure? Lightfoot could find correspondences in every paragraph of Scripture, but it is not always easy to understand his terminology and how the correspondences fit together. It almost seems that "typology" is nothing more than clever allegory that he instigates. Before we turn to prophecy and the two formal types, it is helpful to consider briefly the accepted modern terminology.

Unfortunately, scholars still fail to agree on the definition of typology, much less, whether any version of it is even legitimate. Even so, Fairbairn has succeeded in bringing many together under Bishop Marsh's excellent definition. He argues that for something to be typological one must first hold that "in the character, action, or institution which is denominated the type, there must be a resemblance in form or spirit to what answers to it under the gospel; and secondly that it must not be any character action, or institution occurring in Old Testament Scripture, but such only as had their ordination of God and were designed by him to foreshadow and prepare for the better things of the gospel."[64] The type must not only resemble the later antitype, but the author must have designed it to do just that. Of course, as many scholars have noted, it is not always easy to determine if God designed something of one time to typify something of another time. Still, with this more modern definition in mind, we will examine Lightfoot's typology and see, for him, how the Old Testament and the New Testament correspond. In order to do that, we must first ex-

---

63. Lightfoot, *Horae*, 12:231.
64. Marsh, *Lectures*, 371 cited in Fairbairn, *The Typology of Scripture*, 1:46.

amine the distinction, if there is one, between prophecy and other forms of correspondence.

PROPHECY AND TYPOLOGY

One significant thing to note about Lightfoot's Old and New Testament correspondences is that Lightfoot seldom makes any distinction in terminology. He uses "types," "figures," predictions," "resemblances," and other words in an overlapping fashion. Because of this, it is often impossible to distinguish one from the other. That there actually is overlapping between prophecy and type is readily apparent as all type "necessarily possesses something of prophetical character and differs in form rather than in nature from what is usually designated prophecy."[65] This has been recognized since the early church. Even Augustine says that "the Old Testament, when rightly understood, is one great prophecy of the New."[66] The word "prophecy" is nothing more than a pointer to the future with no universally agreed upon distinctions in form. Fairbairn agrees, saying, "this is strictly true even in regard to those parts of ancient scripture which, in their direct and immediate bearing, partake least of the prophetical."[67]

> The one images or prefigures, while the other foretells, coming realities. In the one case representative acts or symbols, in the other verbal delineations, serve the purpose of indicating beforehand what God was designed to accomplish for His people in the approaching future. The difference is not such as to affect the essential nature of the two subjects, as alike connecting together the Old and the New in God's dispensations. In distinctness and precision, however, simple prophecy has greatly the advantage over information conveyed by type.[68]

Prophecy is verbal foretelling, and simply easier to determine. Type contains prefiguring acts or symbols and leaves far more room for fantasy. This does not mean that type is any less legitimate or significant. Fairbairn

---

65. Fairbairn, *The Typology of Scripture*, 1:106.

66. Vetus testamentum recte intelligentibus prophetia est Novi Testamenti (contra Faust. Lib. xv. 2) And again: Ille apparatus veteris Tesamenti in generationibus, factis, etc., parturiebat esse venturum (*ib*. lib. xix. 31). Cited in Fairbairn, *The Typology of Scripture*, 1:72.

67. Fairbairn, *The Typology of Scripture*, 1:72.

68. Ibid., 106.

Lightfoot's Figurative and Christological Approach 175

continues, "Still the relation between the type and antitype, when pursued through all its ramifications, may produce as deep a conviction of design and preordained connection, as can be derived from simple prophecy and its fulfillment, though, from the nature of things, the evidence in the latter case must always be more obvious and palpable than in the former."[69] Therefore, while types contain true correspondence, they are simply not as apparent or concrete as a prophecy.

Lightfoot, however, seems hardly to distinguish the two at all. One can find, perhaps the best example of his terminological ambiguity, in his comments on Matt 2 and its relationship to Hos 11. Here, he mixes resembling, prefiguring, and prophesying:

> The two allegations produced here out of the Old Testament, this ["Out of Egypt I have called my son"], and that out of Jeremiah, "In Rama was a voice heard,"—are of that fulness, that they speak of two things a piece, and may very fitly be applied unto them both, and show that the one did *resemble* or *prefigure* the other: as this text of Hosea, aimeth both at the bringing of the church of Israel, in old Time,—and the head of that church, at this time out of Egypt.[70]

The text of Hosea aims to refer to both the church in Israel at that time and to the head of the church (Jesus) at this later time to which Matthew refers. They speak of two things: the historical event recorded in Hosea prefigured or resembled the one recorded in Matthew. Even here, prefiguring and resembling are more or less the same and they seem to be "speaking" of two things, implying a prophetic motif. Lightfoot makes the idea that it is prophecy even clearer as he continues to Matt 2:18, which refers back to Jeremiah.

> Now observe the fulness of this Scripture, as it is uttered by the prophet, and as it is applied by the evangelist. It was fulfilled in one kind, in the time of Jeremiah himself, and then was the lamentation and weeping in Ramah itself: for hither did Nebuzar-adan bring his prisoners, after he had destroyed Jerusalem, and there did he dispose of them, to the sword, or to captivity, as seemed good unto himself. And imagine what lamentation and crying was then in that city, when so many were doomed there, either to be slain in that place, or to go to Babel, never to see their own land

69. Ibid.
70. Lightfoot, *Harmony of the Four Evangelists*, 4:231. Emphasis in italics mine.

again. Then was the cry in Ramah, and it was heard no doubt to Beth-lehem. But now the prophecy is fulfilled in another kind, when Herod destroyeth so many children in Beth-lehem, and in the suburbs and borders belonging to it: and now the cry is in Beth-lehem, and it is heard to Ramah.[71]

Here, he speaks of fulfillment and prophecy. Something can be a prophecy, a "prefiguration," a resemblance, or even all of these at the same time, of something that will be fulfilled in the future.

His blurring tendency is not because of a lack of understanding. Num 24:24 is a prophecy of Balaam about Chitim afflicting Eber and Ashur and it seems that Lightfoot understands that this is a prophecy. "This prophecy was fulfilled, when the power of Rome first set her foot upon the neck of the Hebrews by the conquest of Pompey: but, especially, when she tyrannized over Christ, the chief child of Eber, even before and at his birth, as in this story; but chiefly, in condemning him to death, as in the story of his passion."[72] This prophecy has several fulfillments. Chittim, for Lightfoot, is Rome and Balaam's curse is ultimately on Rome for crucifying Christ.[73] Lightfoot understands well that prophecy includes a divine revelation that one could otherwise not know. It is more than a mere resemblance and sometimes more than prefiguring. He says, in his *Exercitations upon the First Epistle to the Corinthians*, that while prophecy can mean three different things, it does indeed include "to foretell and teach something from divine revelation." "In those times, there were some, who, being inspired with a spirit of revelation, either foretold things to come; as Agabus did a famine, Acts xi. 28,—and Paul's bonds, Acts xxi. 10: or revealed the mind of God to the church, concerning the doing or the not doing this or that thing; as, Acts xiii. 2, by the prophets of Antioch, they separate Paul and Barnabas, &c."[74] God revealed things to Agabus and to the church differently than the way Scripture sometimes foresees or typifies the future. There are different ways that God reveals the future.

His distinction about revelation of the future, while never overt, is more evident in his comments on Pss 88–89, psalms written long before Moses by the inspired duo Heman and Ethan. To answer to the objection

---

71. Ibid., 232.
72. Ibid., 190.
73. Lightfoot, *Rules for a Student of the Holy Scriptures*, 2:33.
74. Lightfoot, *Exercitations upon the First Epistle to the Corinthians*, 12:543.

that David is mentioned by name in these psalms, Lightfoot suggests first that "this might be done prophetically; as Samuel is thought to be named by Moses, Ps xcix. 6: for that Psalm, according to a rule of the Hebrews, is held to have been made by him."[75] This is only one possibility however and on the second, Lightfoot spends considerably more time.

The second possibility is that of a normal prophetic gift that God gives to inspired writers of Scripture. Here, his views become considerably jumbled. The Old Testament recording prophecy is not at all strange. Still, Lightfoot seems to see both a separation in his mind as to what this looks like and yet at the same time a tremendous overlap. We know already that, for Lightfoot, Scripture is in itself divine, having been revealed by God himself. In fact, prophecy is the gift God endued on people who wrote the Scripture. "It will be found in Scripture, that when some holy men, endued with the Spirit of God, have left pieces of writings behind them, indited by the Spirit—others, that have lived in after-times, endued with the same gift of prophecy, have taken those ancient pieces in hand, and have flourished upon them, as present, past, or future occasions did require."[76] The prophecy of the past may become a new prophecy for a new time, set, as Lightfoot says, "to a higher key." In fact, this same psalm, which prophesied David, is all about singing of the delivery from Egypt. But, in order for it to fit into a new temple context, a newly inspired writer takes it, sets it to a "higher key; namely, that whereas he treated only of the bodily deliverance from Egypt, it is wound up so high as to reach the spiritual delivery by Christ."[77] There were two possible answers to the problem in these psalms. The first was simply that the human authors predicted, through the power of God, that David would one day be king. The other possibility is that divinely inspired editors came later and, noticing the original intention, added David's name to the text in order to further point the readers to the coming of a greater messianic king. Both of these answers are in some sense prophetic or typological.

He distinguishes, and yet connects prediction and figure in his comments on the skins given to Adam and Eve. "For, that sacrifice was from the beginning, may be observed from that, that Christ is called, 'the Lamb slain from the beginning of the world': and that, not only in prediction,

---

75. Lightfoot, *A Handful of Gleanings out of the Book of Exodus*, 2:356.
76. Ibid.
77. Ibid., 357.

or that it was determined and foretold by God, that he would be slain; but in figure, that sacrifice was offered from the beginning of the world which did presignify his killing and offering-up."[78] While one may struggle with this paragraph, it seems that Lightfoot is distinguishing between two things that point to the same thing. There is both a prediction of the Christ (presumably in Gen 3:15, although Lightfoot is not specific) and a picture of Christ, which is found both in the sacrifice and the Sabbath day. One is explicit at the time and the other John's proclamation only makes obvious.

Even baptism is both an antitype fulfillment and a prophetic fulfillment.

> For as it is undoubted, that John brought those that were to be baptized, into the river,—so is it almost as little to be doubted, that when they were there, he threw and sprinkled the water upon them, both to answer the types of sprinkling, that had preceded in the way, and the predictions thereof, that were given by the prophets, Ezek. xxxvi. 25; understood by Jerome of baptism, Epist. lxxxiii. So [Acts viii. 38] the eunuch first goeth into the water, and then Philip baptizeth him.[79]

Lightfoot is able to deduce from Old Testament passages what it is that John the Baptist actually did when he baptized people. He must have at least sprinkled the people because Ezekiel prophesied that he would do this. Furthermore, there were types that appeared in the Old Testament (probably the priesthood sprinkling of blood although Lightfoot says nothing about this) that would lead to the same conclusion. The point here, again, is that Lightfoot does see some kind of distinction between type and prophecy, although he does not formally note the distinction.

This discussion warrants one final extended example of Lightfoot's use of prophecy and typology from a sermon on Dan 12 entitled "Wait the Time of God."

> So Jacob foreseeing, in Gen. xlix. 17, the great deliverance of Israel from the Philistines, by Samson, of the tribe of Dan, that "he should be as a serpent by the way, and an adder in the path, that bites the horse-heels, that he throws his rider": so he caught the heels of the Philistines' horse, the posts of the house on which they were mounted and overthrew house [sic] and riders, even

---

78. Lightfoot, *Sermons* "The Sabbath Hallowed," 7:382.
79. Lightfoot, *Harmony of the Four Evangelists* 4:274.

three thousand:—I say, Jacob, foreseeing this, presently cries out, ver. 18, "O Lord, I have waited for thy salvation." His eyes look beyond that deliverance of Samson, to the deliverance or salvation of Christ; and, in the sight of that type, his belief of that greater matter signified is confirmed. So in this very thing we are speaking of: till Christ came, God very frequently acquainted his people, beforehand, of what times were to come upon them,—what miseries,—what deliverances,—what oppressions,—what deliverance.[80]

Jacob foresaw that Samson would deliver Israel and cries out to God that he has waited for his salvation. But even in seeing that future event, Jacob is able to look beyond that event to Christ. Samson, therefore, is the fulfillment of the prediction, but is also a type of Christ who is to come. While the distinction is not easily apparent, it is nevertheless real.

For Lightfoot, the same Bible contains both God's predictions of future events and God's pictures or types of future events. For instance, in Gen 12, in a heathen town God promises or predicts to Abraham that the Christ will come. That aspect of it being a heathen town is not a prediction, but is, for Lightfoot, a significant historical correspondence. This setting points to a future Messianic concern for the heathen themselves.[81] Lightfoot insists that Dan 9:21 is a prophecy that foretells Jesus' death to the very hour 490 years later.[82] In addition, in the same section, he mentions many wonderful harmonies that are not obvious predictions: David was to reign exactly as long in Jerusalem as Christ, the son of David lived here upon earth, "thirty-two years and a half."[83] Is this meant to be a prediction or a type or something else altogether? The same question comes up when Lightfoot draws a typological connection between Antiochus' "desolating of religion for three years and one half" and Jesus ministry on Earth of the same amount of time.[84] One finds the answer to what Lightfoot is doing in his ending proclamation that God is a "wonderful numberer of times." God has apparently planned history in exactly this way for a reason, and we, as readers should notice these hints from the literature. This is exactly what modern typology is: literature designed to have historical correspondence from one time to another.

80. Lightfoot, *Sermons*, "Wait the Time of God," 7:221–22.
81. Lightfoot, *Rules for a Student of the Holy Scriptures*, 2:16.
82. Lightfoot, *Sermons* "Wait the Time of God," 7:224.
83. Ibid.
84. Ibid., 225.

While never intentional and seldom clear, Lightfoot does distinguish between prophecy/promise and figure/type. He would probably define typology as more directly connected to the action and object of a narrative and without direct proclamation about its future fulfillment. Prophecy, on the other hand, is associated with direct revelation coming to and from a character in the narrative. Unfortunately, Lightfoot never sought to organize his thinking on paper. Because of this, he often leaves his readers in a terminological quandary. As we move from prophetic labels to more "figure" and "type" labels, we will note that he still fails to clarify completely his understanding of "typology."

TWO FORMAL TYPES

While we do not know the extent to which Lightfoot was aware of the work of Johannes Cocceius, they were contemporaries who would certainly find, in each other, great similarity of thought. Cocceius made a distinction between two equally valid types. Innate types are those that Scripture itself has expressly asserted to possess a typical character. Inferred types are those not proclaimed to be types in Scripture, but on probable grounds, interpreters could infer as conformable to the analogy of faith, and the practice of the inspired writers regarding similar examples.[85] One could justify finding both innate and inferred types, but inferred types often looked too much like the interpretations of the Catholics, the Jews, and even the early Christians. Fairbairn aptly summarizes this school of thought: there was something "vague and loose" in this system, "which left ample scope for the indulgence of a luxuriant fancy."[86] Some deemed a mere resemblance, however accidental or trifling, sufficient to legitimize a correspondence:[87]

> That the Cocceian mode of handling the typical matter of ancient Scripture so readily admitted of the introduction of trifling, far-fetched, and even altogether false analogies, was one of its capital defects. It had no essential principles of fixed rules by which to guide its interpretation—set up no proper landmarks along the field of inquiry—left room on every hand for arbitrariness and caprice to enter. It was this, perhaps, more than any thing else,

---

85. Fairbairn, *The Typology of Scripture*, 1:11. He cites the following as examples: Glass, *Philologia Sac.* 2.1.2.4; Vitringa, *Obs. Sac.* vol. 2., 6.20; Witsius, *De Oeconom.* 4.6.

86. Fairbairn, *The Typology of Scripture*, 1:11.

87. Ibid., 11.

Lightfoot's Figurative and Christological Approach 181

which tended to bring typical interpretations into disrepute, and disposed men, in proportion as the exact and critical study of scripture came to be cultivated, to regard the subject of its typology as hopelessly involved in conjecture and uncertainty.[88]

What is true of Cocceius and his students was also true of Lightfoot. His desire to find Christ everywhere, and his belief that Scripture itself was indeed divine, gave him permission to turn any correspondence into a justified and intentional typology, whether innately found in the text or only inferred.

Before examining his typology, it is perhaps helpful to show that Lightfoot did see a difference between types and allusions. He often made connections between the Old and New Testaments to enhance the poetry and literary quality of his writing, especially when it came to his sermons. There is no reason to suggest that he saw a type or antitype in every connection. For instance, in a sermon on communing with our own hearts, he states: "As a golden thread was to be twisted with every twine and thread of the ephod and breast-plate, or it was not rightly made; so if this action of communing with our own hearts be not entwisted with every one of our actions, we can neither undergo any thing, nor perform any thing, as becomes us to do."[89] Even in a sermon on the blood of the covenant, an easy place to find antitypes, Lightfoot may also simply allude to Old Testament ideas. "As the pillar of fire was darkness to the Egyptians, but light to Israel—so his obedience was destruction to the devil, and satisfaction to God."[90] There is no reason to assume automatically that Lightfoot believes any of these to be actual types. There will certainly be room for debate regarding his intention in a few places, but I have purposely tried to choose examples where he uses either the word type, or where it seems more evident that there is an actual one-to-one correspondence.

Lightfoot did not categorize, or, in any other way, discuss rules for typology, but it is helpful to look at examples by using Fairbairn's distinction of ritual and historical. Even within these two main categories, Lightfoot demonstrated interest in numerous things in order to find his many types: geography, chronology, names, and really anything that brings a resemblance to mind.

---

88. Fairbairn, *The Typology of Scripture*, 1:13–14.
89. Lightfoot, *Sermons*, "Commune with Your Own Heart," 6:108.
90. Lightfoot, *Sermons*, "The Blood of the Covenant," 7:236.

Ritual Types

One can find the most common "preparatory training" of the church in ritual types.[91] And, it is in the category of ritual types that Lightfoot holds strongest to the idea of innate types. For Lightfoot, God designed the law to reach into the future. Four types of laws existed: moral, commemorative, evangelical, and typical. The Sabbath law partook in all parts of the law, but it is the typical that chiefly concerns us here. They include sacrifices, priesthood, purifications, and sprinkling of blood, all of which were to "signify good things to come and to have their accomplishing in Christ."[92] It is helpful to examine a few of what many at that time agreed be types, and see how Lightfoot deals with them.

That the Sabbath is a very important type can be shown either in Scripture (innate) or simply deduced without proof texts (inferred). For instance, Lightfoot uses Heb 4:3: "Where the apostle signifies, that the Sabbath hinted another rest, to wit, God's eternal rest, different from that rest, when God ceased from the works of creation. The sabbath typifies the end:—viz. eternal rest: and the means:—viz. to rest in Christ. One end was to Adam in innocency,—both, to us."[93] So, while Law has a variety of functions, God designed many of these varieties to serve as a picture of something else. The Sabbath law is a picture of our present and future rest in Christ. In fact, the old Jewish Sabbath, which looked back to the first creation, also pointed forward to the resurrection. This is the whole reason the Sabbath day was changed—Christ's death fulfilled it. In this case, in the *Horae*, Lightfoot is commenting on Matt 28:1, which contains the line: "in the end of the Sabbath."

> The old Sabbath was a memory of the first creation. The new Sabbath is in memory of the new creation. Jesus resurrection is the beginning of the new creation and kingdom and so fitly begins on Sunday. When the promise was fulfilled that the serpent would be bruised in the resurrection of Christ, and that was fulfilled which was typified and represented in the old Sabbath, namely, the finishing of a new creation,—the Sabbath could not but justly be transferred to that day on which these things were done.[94]

---

91. Fairbairn, *The Typology of Scripture*, 1:48.
92. Lightfoot, *Sermons*, "The Sabbath Hallowed," 7:380.
93. Ibid., 383.
94. Lightfoot, *Horae*, 11:359.

Lightfoot's Figurative and Christological Approach

He says that the old Sabbath typified the resurrection of Christ, but cites no textual support, nor does he show us how he arrived at this conclusion. Rather, Lightfoot had a logical and reasonable answer to the dilemma and Lightfoot needed no textual proofs.

Not only did the Sabbath point to Jesus, but many other rituals did as well. Lightfoot noted the sacrificial system most often. "The first thing to die in the world is a sacrifice, or Christ in a figure."[95] "For an outward sign and seal of this his faith, and for a farther and more lively expression of the same, God teacheth him the rite of sacrifice, to lay Christ dying before his eyes in a visible figure: . . . and thus the first thing that dieth in the world, is Christ in a figure."[96] While he does not seek to back up this typology with any verses in these locations, he does not lack proof texts and uses them freely throughout his writings. The most obvious is John 1:29 when John the Baptist says that Jesus is the Lamb of God who takes away the sins of the world. In Lightfoot's comments on this verse, he begins by putting forth the command that when one sacrifices an animal, he should lay his hand upon its head. The purpose of this is to transfer his sins to the offering. This is most obvious in the scapegoat in Lev 16:22, but Lightfoot quotes several other Leviticus passages as warrant. He then argues in 1 Pet 2:24 that Christ has "'borne our sins in his own body on the tree,' as the offering on the altar was wont to do.—'He was made by God a sin for us,' 2 Cor. V. 21; that is, חטאת, 'a sacrifice for sin.'"[97] They performed this same ritual during the daily sacrifice. With this walk through his reasoning, Lightfoot has shown us his understanding of an innate type.

One can most easily see the fulfillment of sacrifice in those passages that speak about the Lord's Supper and the Passover Lamb. In comments on Luke 22:19, Lightfoot explains the antitype that one finds in "this is my body." This phrase contains a reference to the body of the paschal lamb:

> For the Jews use this very phrase concerning it: "They bring in a table spread, on which are bitter herbs with other herbs, unleavened bread חרוסת pottage, כבש של הפסח וגופו and the body of the paschal lamb." And a little after: "He eateth כל מגופו של פסח ואו of the body of the Passover." From whence our Saviour's meaning may be well enough discerned; viz. That by the same

---

95. Lightfoot, *Harmony of the Old Testament*, 2:74.
96. Lightfoot, *A Few and New Observations upon the Book of Genesis,* 2:336.
97. Lightfoot, *Horae*, 12:236.

> signification that the paschal lamb was my body hitherto,—from henceforward let this bread be my body.[98]

Because this is an innate type, its correspondence is certain. Lightfoot apparently sees no problem with this despite the fact that he recognizes that the next phrase, "which is broken for you," does not fit very well. It does not fit because the paschal lamb was not to be broken. However, it does fit with the daily sacrifice, which the one who sacrificed was to break and cut up the sacrifice. "And yet" he says, "they are both of them the body of Christ, in a figure." And still, both the Passover lamb and the daily sacrifice agree regarding their antitype despite the several ways that they differ. One was for all of Israel, and one just for a family; one for the atonement of sin, the other not so; one was burned, the other eaten. "Yet in this they agree, that, under both, the body of our Saviour was figured and shadowed out, though in a different notion."[99]

He also takes this opportunity to read back into the Old Testament the reason why one could not eat the lamb raw. The Jews could not eat it raw to make it obvious to Rome that transubstantiation is but a dream. For, if the body was the actual body of Christ, then the type that pointed to it would fit far better if the law permitted it to be eaten raw.[100]

The Passover is a main theme for Lightfoot and with his few innate types mentioned in other writings, he is able to make further, more detailed correspondences, even though completely inferred:

> At the Passover, the beginning of the year is changed;—so, at Christ's Passover, the beginning of the week is changed.[101]

> The Passover was either of a lamb, to signify Christ's innocency; or of a kid, to signify his likeness to sinful flesh: As Lyranus.[102]

> The Passover slain at even; his blood to be sprinkled with a bunch of hyssop; he was to be roasted with fire;—so, Christ slain at even; Christ's blood sprinkled; . . . so, Christ tried with fire of affliction.[103]

---

98. Ibid., 192.
99. Ibid.
100. Lightfoot, *A Handful of Gleanings out of the Book of Exodus*, 2:374.
101. Lightfoot, *Miscellanies*, 4:38.
102. Ibid.
103. Ibid.

> These parts were to be roasted,—his head; his legs; his inward parts;—so, was Christ tortured: his head with thorns; his hands and feet with nails; his inwards, with a spear.[104]

> At the death of a lamb;—Egypt is destroyed; Israel delivered;—so, by the death of a Lamb, hell is destroyed; mankind delivered.[105]

He has made a comparison between an Old Testament year and a New Testament week. He has created possible meanings for lambs and kids and compared them, in one case, to Jesus innocence, but then a similar figure instead symbolizes Jesus' likeness to sinful flesh. He compares the roasting and burning of a lamb to the affliction and torture, a kind of metaphorical burning of Jesus. Finally, he compares the destruction of a country to the metaphorical (only destroyed in the sense that Christians do not have to go there) destruction of hell.

One of the best passages on how Jesus fulfills the Passover and the Feast of Tabernacles is found in his *Horae* on the book of Matthew:

> He fulfilled the typical equity of the Passover and Pentecost, when, at the Passover, he offered himself for a passover,—at Pentecost, he bestowed the Holy Ghost from heaven, as at that time the law had been given from heaven. At that time, the first-fruits of the Spirit were given by him (Rom. viii. 23), when the first-fruits of corn had been wont to be given, Levit. xxiii. 17. It had been a wonder, if he had honoured the third solemnity,—namely, the feast of Tabernacles,—with no antitype.[106]

Then, after detailing the exact timing of everything, he ends speaking of how in the Feast of Tabernacles, "God dwelt in the midst of them." He states, "how aptly typical an aspect they respect the incarnation, when God dwelt among men in human flesh, is plain enough."[107]

Types include not only rituals of sacrifice, Passover, and other feasts, but the tabernacle, in its every detail, also, pointed to Christ. Moses was in divine contemplation on the mountain and saw Christ "as he was to be showed to the Jews, till the time of reformation should come, under the figures of a tabernacle and a priest. The sight of which taught him Christ

---

104. Ibid.
105. Ibid., 39.
106. Lightfoot, *Horae*, 11:34.
107. Ibid.

to the full, in his natures and offices."[108] This was something designed to be a picture in all its details. Each piece of furniture represented something later or more spiritual. The ark, mercy seat, and oracle are all representative of when God would speak to his people by his own Son.[109] In the tabernacle, there were crowns that represented the offices of law, priesthood, and kingdom. One of those "crowns" was the Ark of the Covenant, which the Jews gilded in gold because Christ was pure from sin.[110] It had no feet, in order to be a figure of Christ abasing himself upon the earth. We know the mercy seat is Christ, since the two cherubim bow to it and look at it as all angels bow to Christ and the New and Old Testament look to him as well. In addition, in the same way the mercy seat covers the law, Jesus covers the law that it plead not against his people to condemn them. Each piece points to Jesus: the table of showbread, the golden candlestick, the altars of incense and burnt offerings, the laver of water, and the clothes of the high priest. Each of these symbolized Jesus in some way, either in some small facet of the detail, or in the wider scope. For Lightfoot though, none of these required a solid New Testament connection.

Prefiguring Christ went even further than the furniture and clothing; it extended even to the construction of the tabernacle. Lightfoot insisted that even the strong place where the planks of the tabernacle came together at the corner pointed to Christ as the strength of the church.[111] The bars that ran from one end to the other of the tabernacle "fitly resemble" Christ who is "conveyed throughout the whole of Scripture."[112] Lightfoot once again offers no attempt to connect this to the New Testament, only a mild correspondence. Because the connections are not always readily apparent, Lightfoot is not always clear regarding the antitype. The curtains in the tabernacle, for instance, are certainly a type: "The looping together of the curtains . . . with a golden tie, doth sweetly resemble the uniting of the two natures in Christ, divinity and humanity, into one person,— which two natures were not confounded, as curtains sewed together, but were sweetly knit together by golden and ineffable union."[113] So, while the

---

108. Lightfoot, *Rules for a Student of the Holy Scriptures*, 2:27–28.
109. Lightfoot, *Harmony of the Old Testament*, 2:120.
110. Lightfoot, *Rules for a Student of the Holy Scriptures*, 2:28.
111. Lightfoot, *A Handful of Gleanings out of the Book of Exodus*, 2:393. It is unclear whether this is a formal type or simply an additional application that is helpful.
112. Lightfoot, *A Handful of Gleanings out of the Book of Exodus*, 2:393.
113. Ibid., 394–95.

curtain tie could refer to the two natures in Christ, Lightfoot's very next sentence suggests another possibility: "this might also fully signify the two churches of Jews and Gentiles, knit together by Christ, that so they make but one spiritual tabernacle."[114] There are often many possibilities.

The ritual of circumcision points to Christ, because, as Augustine recognized, parents circumcise their children on the eighth day, just as Christ rested the weeks end in the grave and rose on the eighth day. Lightfoot seems to accept Augustine's reference, while in the very next sentence, he speaks of Rabbi Eliezer as fantastically expounding Jonah 1:16. Lightfoot censures the rabbi for his view that the mariner's sacrifices, in the story of Jonah, included their own circumcision, because both involved blood. For Lightfoot, this is fantastic, but Augustine's correspondence is perfectly warranted despite the fact that neither of them had justification from the text.

Sometimes Lightfoot seems to have Scriptural warrant for a type, but in the end, it appears that Lightfoot's reasoning, rather than Scripture itself, leads to his discovery. In his comments on John 19:34, where blood and water flow from the pierced side of Christ, Lightfoot suggests strongly that there must be some kind of mystery here, which is beyond nature. After all, the Arabic version of the Erpenian edition adds that the soldier pierced Jesus specifically in his right side. This addition was to show that this was an amazing miracle. If God had meant nothing more than a natural flow of blood and water as a result of the piercing, then the soldier would have pierced him on his left side where this resultant flow would have been expected. But since he was pierced on the right side, there was obviously more significance than one might think. But this simple addition by the Erpenian edition is not enough for Lightfoot. After all, our common sense would hardly allow us to imagine that John would confirm this three times without it pointing to something more. There is certainly something significant here, but while most scholars see the blood and water as referring forward to the sacraments, Lightfoot looks back. He insists that this is an antitype of the Old Testament ratification of the covenant, which was by blood and water. Lightfoot admits that we see nothing in the Old Testament that suggests water was involved, but Heb 9:19's confirmation is more than enough for him. "The antitype of which is clearly exhibited in this ratification of the new Testament: and hence it

114. Ibid., 395.

is, that the evangelist, by so vehement asseverations, confirms the truth of this passage,—because it so plainly answers the type, and gives such assurance of the fulfilling it."[115] So, because Hebrews mentions blood and water in the Old Testament ratification process, Lightfoot is able to find that practice in the Old Testament and then move forward to the antitype in the book of John. The real connection, however, is not scriptural at all. The text in Hebrews simply makes possible a correspondence; the real "reason" this is an antitype is because John mentions something three times ("vehement asseverations"), because it seems obvious ("plainly answers the type"), and because Jesus' pierced side would be a good fulfillment of the Old Testament concept of sacrifice.

I do not stand in judgment of his Old Testament/New Testament correspondences. His belief was simple and profound. There was nothing arbitrary in employing the things of the flesh, under a preparatory dispensation, to the higher realities of God's everlasting kingdom. God created the material world to put forth divine truth. Lightfoot bases his understanding of the figurative language of the Bible on this understanding of nature.[116] He believes this and feels no need to justify his correspondences with an explicit typological acknowledgement in the Scriptural text. He justifies them because he found a correspondence and because this is a divine book which demands a heightened meaning from physical ritual acts. This becomes even clearer as we move from ritual type to historical types.

Historical Types

Not only did rituals point to a higher plane, but many circumstances and events in history did as well. If God had created the world to speak about the future and created one dispensation to "prophesy" about another one, then it only made sense that all of history, and not just ritual worship, was preparatory for what was to come. As we examine Lightfoot's use of historical types and whether they were inferred or innate, let us keep in mind two of Lightfoot's fundamental beliefs in this regard.

---

115. Lightfoot, *Horae*, 12:422.

116. See Fairbairn introduction to his third chapter for a summary of why typology is justified. I have borrowed the language for these last few lines largely from this chapter. Fairbairn, *The Typology of Scripture*, 1:62–63.

First, while Jesus was the antitype to manifold Old Testament types, He and the whole Trinity in fact were not absent from the Old Testament. The angel that wrestles with Jacob is not merely a picture of Jesus, he is the actual Jesus.[117] On another occasion, we find that the Trinity itself, "in visible form appears to Abraham, and determines the time of the birth of the promised seed."[118] Then, the Holy Spirit and Jesus both go down to Sodom, but God the Father stays with Abraham to continue to listen to his prayers.[119] When Jude 9 speaks of the burial of Moses by Michael, Lightfoot assumes that Michael and Christ are one and the same. He mentions this at least twice and in both his *Harmony of the Old Testament* and his *Rules to a Student,* he is slightly confusing. In the first, he states: "and how he was buried by the Lord,—that is, by Michael, or Christ, who was to bury Moses's ceremonies."[120] In the latter, Lightfoot mentions only Christ, and not Moses, but still he adds the phrase, "who was to bury his ceremonies."[121] These passages seem to suggest that Christ was actually there, and to perform a physical task, but that it would take on spiritual dimensions later.

Second, in connection with this confusion that is sure to come, one must remember the inexactness of this whole process. Fairbairn aptly summarizes: "It is possible, indeed, that the connection here between the past and the future might be somewhat more varied and fluctuating, and in several respects less close and exact, than in the case of regulated system of symbolical instruction and worship, appointed to last till it was superseded by the better things of the New dispensation."[122] With this clarification and warning in place, let us look to Lightfoot's use of historical "typology."

People of the Old Testament may have either prefigured another Old Testament persona, a New Testament persona (most often Jesus), or even both, in differing circumstances. For this reason, the prefiguring type was not usually the person himself, but the person in a particular circumstance. For instance, in one place, Moses is "like a second Noah" in that

---

117. Lightfoot, *Harmony of the Old Testament,* 2:99.
118. Lightfoot, *Rules for a Student of the Holy Scriptures,* 2:17.
119. Lightfoot, *Harmony of the Old Testament,* 2:91.
120. Ibid., 138.
121. Lightfoot, *Rules for a Student of the Holy Scriptures,* 2:34.
122. Fairbairn, *The Typology of Scripture,* 1:63.

God preserves both of them in an ark.[123] However, Noah is also like Jesus in his second coming in that Noah ended the world through the flood and Jesus in his coming again in clouds of glory.[124] At the same time, in a place that many commentators find correspondence between Noah and Jesus, Lightfoot sees a very different meaning. In Gen 5:29, Noah is called a comforter, but it is not as a figure of the comfort that comes in redemption. Rather, it is because "in him liberty should be given to the world, to eat flesh."[125] There are not even any comments that move the reader to the Old Testament liberty of eating all foods that Christ brought about in the inauguration of his kingdom.

Typology is readily apparent when it comes to the figure of Isaac and Lightfoot finds both innate and inferred correspondences. Of course, the near sacrifice of Isaac was typological. Both Isaac and the ram are types of Jesus, but in Lightfoot's *Rules for a Student*, he mentions no text to justify the connection; he simply assumes it. He says, "Isaac and the ram, a true type of Christ's two natures; the one only suffering, and the other not; yet that that suffered not, giving validity and value to that that suffered."[126] It seems that he considers death, in general, to be a close enough correspondence to warrant a typology. Even Abel's death was Christ in figure; Lightfoot buttresses this with the Jewish understanding that when Cain killed his brother, he made wounds in his hands and feet.[127] One can see Isaac's connection to Jesus even before Isaac's actual birth: "Isaac, in his mother's womb, taken by Abimilech, as Christ, in Mary's womb, taxed by Caesar."[128] This shows itself even more apparent in the case in Isaac's birth. Because it was a supernatural birth, we know that Abraham foresaw the supernatural birth of Christ, and rejoiced. Moreover, giving Isaac a name that meant laughter went far beyond Abraham's joy in a newborn baby. Lightfoot ties this into John 8:56 saying that Abraham's joy was in Christ for "Your father Abraham rejoiced to see my day; and he saw it, and was glad."[129]

123. Lightfoot, *Harmony of the Old Testament*, 2:111.
124. Lightfoot, *Sermons*, "The Great Assize," 6:354.
125. Lightfoot, *A Few and New Observations Upon the Book of Genesis*, 2:339.
126. Lightfoot, *Rules for a Student of Holy Scriptures*, 2:18.
127. Lightfoot, *Sermons* "Cain Described," 7:343.
128. Lightfoot, *Rules for a Student of Holy Scriptures*, 2:17–18.
129. Lightfoot, *Harmony of the Old Testament*, 2:91. See also *Rules for a Student*, 2:18 where he says "Abraham seeth the day of Christ, and rejoiceth; and, in token, calleth his son's name Isaac, 'laughter.'"

Lightfoot considers deliverance important, as he sees most people who deliver Israel as Christ in figure. Joshua is perhaps the most obvious one, as his very name in the Old Testament and the LXX is Jesus. It is not just his name, however, that makes him a type; rather, it is the fact that Joshua brings rest just as Jesus will bring eternal rest.[130] Lightfoot sees both he and Jehoshua as great deliverers and therefore both point directly to Jesus. "These were two renowned ones before:—the one whereof brought the people into Canaan, after the death of Moses; and the other brought them thither out of Babel; and so both were lively figures of our Jesus, that bringeth his people to the heavenly Canaan."[131]

Lightfoot often understands Moses, the premier deliverer, as a type of Christ, but strangely, not in his function as a deliverer. In his birth, he is a type of Christ. "In this doth Moses typify Christ;—that his true father is unknown to the Egyptians, and he reputed the son of Pharaoh; as the true father of Christ unknown to the Jews, and he reputed the son of Joseph.[132] His miracles show that he is a type of Christ. These, "which were the first done by any prophet in the world, did more especially refer to the miracles of 'that great Prophet, that should come into the world,' by whose power these miracles were done by Moses at this time."[133] When we get to the actual deliverance, however, Lightfoot never has Moses pointing to Jesus. Still, despite this, Israel's deliverance from Egypt itself can be considered typological—"namely, that whereas he [the divine penman] treated only of the bodily deliverance from Egypt, it is wound up so high as to reach the spiritual delivery by Christ."[134]

Despite no explicit Old Testament connection to Jesus, Lightfoot finds typology both in Solomon's majesty and in his wisdom:

> His wisdom, power, peace, and magnificence, exceeding all kings upon earth, did make him not only renowned among all people, but also, in these, he became a type of Christ. Thus high in all eminences and perfections that earth could afford, did the Lord exalt him; and yet afterward suffered him foully to fall, that he like Adam in happiness, might exemplify, that no earthly felicity can

---

130. Lightfoot, *Harmony of the Old Testament*, 2:112.
131. Lightfoot, *Harmony of the Four Evangelists*, 4:163.
132. Lightfoot, *Harmony of the Old Testament*, 2:112.
133. Lightfoot, *A Handful of Gleanings out of the Book of Exodus*, 2:361.
134. Ibid., 357.

be durable; and that here is nothing to be trusted to, but all things vanity, but the kingdom that is not of this world.[135]

While wisdom seems a key aspect of the next connection, that which connects it most easily is nothing more than a chronological similarity. Ignatius' *Epistle ad Magnes* mentions that Solomon showed his wisdom in deciding the controversy between the two harlots at age twelve. Jesus also was twelve years old in the temple showing his wisdom. In this case, the Old Testament text does not even give us the important detail to make the connection; Lightfoot assumes it based on a letter of Ignatius. Even if he could maintain his chronological connection, it is nothing more than a similarity of age. This chronological typology is rampant in Lightfoot's work.

The literature contains many historical correspondences that all revolve around similar timing or numbers: Jesus redeemed on the sixth day just as the fall had been on the sixth day. Christ rested on the seventh day in the grave, just as God did on the seventh day. God likely created Adam on the third hour and had Jesus crucified at the same time. Adam probably fell at the sixth hour, for that was the time of eating, and John 19:14 says it was the sixth hour when Jesus was condemned to be crucified. At the ninth hour (the cool of the day), God promised a redeemer and at the ninth hour, that redeemer breathed his last breath.[136] The creation is a figure of Christ's redemption because the timing of each is the same. "For it was just at that time of the year, when John began to baptize, which was the beginning of the gospel; and it was at that time of the year, when our Saviour suffered and fulfilled that which this prefigured,—viz. our redemption."[137] In Josh 2, the two spies who went out for three days picture Jesus because Jesus was also buried for three days.[138] However, in Josh 5, Lightfoot comments that there were three days of soreness due to circumcision, but he includes no corresponding comments linking that to the burial of Christ.[139] The entire story of Job points to Jesus, but primarily because Job had exactly three friends with him: "Job had three

---

135. Lightfoot, *Harmony of the Old Testament*, 2:202.

136. Each of these connections is made in Lightfoot's sermon entitled "The Sabbath Hallowed," 7:376–78.

137. Lightfoot, *A Handful of Gleanings out of the Book of Exodus*, 2:374.

138. "Here are the three days, just so counted, as the three days of our Saviour's burial." Lightfoot, *Harmony of the Old Testament*, 2:139.

139. Lightfoot, *Harmony of the Old Testament*, 2:139.

with him, when he is changed by affliction;—so Christ hath three with him, when he is changed in transfiguration: which three, as they were by Christ, when Moses and Elias, law and prophecy, told him, in the mount, 'of his departing, which he should accomplish at Jerusalem';—so these three were with him, when he began to accomplish these things."[140]

Additionally, Jesus began his ministry at the age of thirty just as the priests of the Old Testament began their ministry at thirty: "Our Saviour's age, at his entrance into his ministry, answereth to this type."[141] It seems that Lightfoot finds connections that are more than just interesting. If the numbers are the same, or even close in some circumstances, he considers them types.

Not only numbers and specific individuals, but historical types also include objects, ideas and states of being from the Old Testament that are designed to prefigure Christ. For instance, the skins that Adam and Eve wear are, in themselves, pointers to Jesus, although mostly because they were given through sacrifice.[142] The entire concept of barrenness turning to fruitfulness evidenced in Rebekah and Sarah was as a harbinger, to provide room for the belief of Christ's supernatural birth.[143] The firstborn children, so commonly mentioned in the Old Testament, all point to Christ, "that in him was fulfilled what was typified by the first-born under the law, who was as King, priest, and prophet, in the family, and 'holy to the Lord.'"[144] Even the ladder from Jacob's vision is "a type of Christ incarnate, which brings heaven and earth together, in his two natures, and in his reconciliation."[145] It is a type, even though Lightfoot fails to mention John 1:51, a passage commonly understood to allude to Jacob's ladder. When we glance at his comments on John 1:51 in the *Horae*, we find an outright denial of any connection. He states, "there are those, that, in this place, observe an allusion to Jacob's ladder."[146] He then goes on to explain it as having no correspondence.

---

140. Lightfoot, *Miscellanies*, 4:76.
141. Lightfoot, *Harmony of the Old Testament*, 2:124. Luke 3:23 makes this apparent.
142. Lightfoot, *Sermons*, "Faith of Adam," 7:335.
143. Lightfoot, *Rules for a Student of the Holy Scriptures*, 2:18.
144. Lightfoot, *Harmony of the Four Evangelists*, 4:194.
145. Lightfoot, *Harmony of the Old Testament*, 2:97.
146. Lightfoot, *Horae*, 12:240.

In the same way that Lightfoot ignores the hermeneutical relevance of Jacob's ladder, so also does he ignore the relevance of the rock that is Christ in 1 Cor 10:4. He mentions the rock four times in his writing, and on each of those occasions, he prefers to discuss the reality of the pools and the drinking situation. He insists that the rock was real, that it did not move, and that Moses did not strike a literal Jesus. Yet, he never attempts to explain how Jesus is the antitype for this rock.[147]

OTHER OLD AND NEW TESTAMENT CONNECTIONS

While Jesus is the most common antitype to Old Testament individuals, rituals and events, Lightfoot, at times, finds other connections. He makes most of these connections to the church. In his *Rules for a Student*, Lightfoot states: "Leah and Rachel are figures of the two churches; the church of the Jews under the law, and the church of the gentiles under the gospel: the younger the more beautiful, and more in the thoughts of Christ, when he came in the form of a servant: but the other, like Leah, first embraced and taken to wife."[148] This is true also of his comments about the black daughter of Pharaoh that Solomon took as his wife. Song of Solomon 1:5–6 refers to her in "the first and literal acceptation," but one should also understand this spiritually, "as applied to the church."[149]

While relatively limited, Lightfoot did find parallel passages that did not connect directly to the church or to Jesus. He notes that Peter parallels the ruin of the old world with the ruin of Jerusalem in 1 Pet 3:19–21. Jude tells us that Jesus, although preaching throughout all times under the law, preached also during the time of Noah. Lightfoot things Jude mentions this in order to make this parallel more apparent that "the present state of the Jews was like theirs in the times of Noah."[150] The destruction of the city of Jericho is a "figure of the subduing of the strong holds of Satan, among the heathens, by the power of the Gospel."[151] The sons of Jacob, in the Deut 33 blessing, obviously refer to the tribes. However, Deut mentions them in a specific order, not in conjunction to their birth order, so as to signify a more spiritual relevance. The author mentions Judah before Levi

---

147. Ibid., 422 and 525; Lightfoot, *A Handful of Gleanings out of the Book of Exodus*, 2:381; Lightfoot, *Rules for a Student of the Holy Scriptures*, 2:25.

148. Lightfoot, *Rules for a Student of the Holy Scriptures*, 2:98.

149. Lightfoot, *A Few and New Observations upon the Book of Genesis*, 2:339.

150. Lightfoot, *Horae*, 11:305.

151. Lightfoot, *Harmony of the Old Testament*, 2:138.

to show that the kingdom's dignity surpasses that of the priesthood, for Christ is the promised king from that tribe. By placing Benjamin before Joseph, he intended to signify that Jerusalem is greater than Samaria.[152] None of these examples point directly to Christ.

Genesis, Malachi, Matthew, and Peter each speak to the practice and significance of baptism. When Matthew says to fly from the wrath to come, he is referring to the last words of Malachi, "lest I smite the earth with a curse." The command to fly from that is to partake in the waters of baptism, for it is that which signs and fences one from the curse.[153] To show this, Lightfoot uses 1 Pet 3:20–21, which actually uses the word avnti,tupon. He says, "in that matter as Noah and his sons were, by water, delivered from the flood, 'so also baptism now, the antitype of that type, saveth us,' from the deluge of divine indignation, which, in a short time, is to overflow the Jewish nation."[154] Therefore, baptism is the antitype of the flood. While Lightfoot finds the vast majority of his antitypes in Christ, he also includes the church with some regularity as well as other things from time to time.

CONCLUSION

While I have dismissed many relevant examples for the sake of brevity, I believe these represent a fair sampling of Lightfoot's use of figures, types, allusions, and prophecies. He recognizes the distinctions in prophecy and typology, but would also suggest that typology is a form of prophecy. When he is making comments on the New Testament, he is quick to find connections to the Old Testament. He does this most often in the area of ritual types; nevertheless, he uses both types with great regularity. Even with such regular use, Lightfoot feels no need to have explicit Scriptural support for his connections. In response to the anachronistic question by Bishop Marsh, "Must not, therefore, the silence of New Testament in the case of any supposed type, be an argument against the existence of that type?," he would answer in the negative.[155] He despises allegory and yet seems to appropriate it often. This is because he would probably define allegory as a correspondence that it too fanciful for him to accept. There is not necessarily a formal difference between allegory and type.

152. Ibid.
153. Lightfoot, *Horae*, 11:77.
154. Ibid.
155. Bishop Marsh, *Lectures*, 392, cited in Fairbairn, *The Typology of Scripture*, 1:61.

8

Summary of Findings

Determining the plain sense of a divinely inspired, human-authored text was fraught with difficulties. Does the Holy Spirit play a significant or even necessary role in interpretation? Does divine illumination guarantee the correct interpretation in every instance? And if it is a human text, are not some scientific rules necessary in order to understand? If so, whose rules should be followed and how intensely? How should one understand the Bible, and who and what should help in its interpretation?

For John Lightfoot, a divinely authored text meant the necessity of the Holy Spirit's illumination in understanding. This was of paramount importance. The Jews were blinded and because they were in darkness, they missed the entire point of the Old Testament. This blindness led to ridiculous interpretations and these in turn kept them from the truth. Rome was also sadly lacking in understanding and largely for the same reason as the Jews. Both insisted that salvation was a by-product of works and this "Jewish Popery or Popish Judaism" kept them from seeing the grace of the gospel. God, he insisted, would utterly reject the Jews. But neither Rome nor Judaism rightly understood the gospel, and without this preliminary understanding, they could not hope to understand rightly the divine text. They needed the Holy Spirit's illumination for understanding, and God did not grant it to them.

Suggesting that some could not grasp the true meaning of Scripture without the Holy Spirit did not mean that having the Holy Spirit guaranteed the correct understanding. Although Lightfoot was less caustic with those in his own tradition, he would not agree that all Protestant Christian interpretation was equal. He did not hesitate to disagree even with the previous generations' reformed interpretations. Beza, who generally deserved praise, also made mistakes that resulted in faulty interpretations. Even his contemporaries in the Westminster Assembly made significant hermeneutical errors on the sacraments, on the Apostles' Creed, and on polity, among other things. While Lightfoot was generally courteous, he could not abide some people, like Mr. Heming, a man whom he would normally find great agreement. For these reasons, we see that Lightfoot believed that Holy Spirit was both necessary for understanding Scripture, and at the same time, was not sufficient to arrive at the proper meaning of the text.

In order to grasp the *sensus literalis* of the text, one needed to follow certain basic rules. The first rule comes directly from the fact that the Holy Spirit is not sufficient and insists that rational thinking is necessary. Few interpreters of his time would have disagreed, although some were leaning in the other dangerous direction. Some suggested that rational thinking was the ground of certainty and that one should either ignore divine illumination, or at least put it into the background. In agreement with most of Rome, Judaism, and Protestant Orthodoxy, Lightfoot vigorously opposed the early tenets of rationalism while still insisting that reason was essential for understanding and for teaching. Lightfoot tried to find the via media between philosophical rationalism and the mysterious illumination of the Holy Spirit.

Reading slowly and critically was another rule perhaps largely influenced by the Jewish writings he incessantly read. The Hebrew MT was without error in every detail. Scribes faithfully preserved it through rigid care and the watchful eye of the Holy Spirit. Because of this, every stroke in the text carried great importance. Slightly larger than normal letters and wandering strokes of the pen were fraught with significance and one had to consider each carefully in order to glean the Holy Spirit's purposes. Lightfoot was on the cusp of modern textual criticism and maintained regular dialogue with Cappel and Buxtorff. He even questioned the authorship of certain biblical books, due to findings that did not fit with traditional understandings. Nevertheless, despite his keen grammatical and textual eye, he was not willing to compromise on matters of dogma. On matters of Christian faith, he was unmoving and feared many of the advances that seemed to be leading to a compromised Bible. In this area too, he was able to find a *via media* between a more modern critical approach and faithfulness to the Holy Spirit's inerrant text.

One of Lightfoot's great distinctions is the amount of time that he spent on issues of historical chronology. Scripture's perfection meant that *everything* in the Bible was accurate—from the detailed land descriptions to the genealogies of the patriarchs and the reigns of the kings. The Old Testament chronology was extremely wooden, while the New Testament, which one should continue to take "literally," was more open to numerical representations. Regardless of the small qualification, Lightfoot believed that all of the Scripture was historical and God had designed it to give the accurate times of historical events. In fact, all students of Scripture must take the time to create charts that portray all of the events from the creation of the world in 3928 BC to the end of the New Testament. Again, this fundamentalist tendency regarding dating was necessary, in Lightfoot's mind, if the text was inspired by the "numberer of times" Himself.

The fourth essential to understanding Scripture was reading within a community of faith. After all, interpretations became authoritative over time, resulting in traditions of dogma that had become firmly entrenched. It was unwise to ignore these traditions and not give them due consideration. The midrash, Mishna, and Targumim contained numerous worthy insights. Even Catholicism had a strong exegetical history in many areas. The Reformers, while not scholastic in their approach, had successfully broken free from the errors of Rome, and so Lightfoot owed them a great debt. Some traditions, however, were not worthy of maintaining. While Lightfoot's contemporaries may have thought he went too far in appropriating the rabbinic writings, the Jews themselves would not have seen it that way. For them, Lightfoot's interpretations would have fallen right in line with those of his Protestant Orthodox contemporaries—unmistakably Christian and anti-Jew. There was no question for Lightfoot: the medieval interpretations of Rome and the Jews often demanded opposition. Scripture was the best interpreter of Scripture, not tradition. Even the Reformers sometimes lacked accuracy and it was up to the individual exegete to determine his understanding of the analogy of faith and to what extent he would use it. The interpreter, empowered by the Holy Spirit and taking into consideration the beliefs and methods of those in the past and present, should try to arrive at an interpretation that retained a proper understanding of the dual authorship of Scripture.

Perhaps more than any of his other rules, the rule of christological reading, did not lend to a *via media* between Judaism and Christianity. By this rule, the Jews were completely rejected, for they did not see what their Scripture so prominently displayed. The Old Testament was explicit in its prophecies, the vast majority of which concerned the Messiah, whom they, in their darkness, missed. However, it was not only explicit prophecies that pointed to the Jesus of the New Testament, so also did every page of Scripture, in one sense of another. Lightfoot was not consistent in his terminology but certainly, the Old Testament contained figures, resemblances, and types that were designed to be fulfilled in the New Testament and even beyond. Types were a form of prophecy and one could find them everywhere, regardless of whether the New Testament made the explicit connection or not. Of course, Lightfoot insisted that one avoid allegory at all cost, although even he was unable to maintain consistency. In this, he unintentionally accepted the methods of much of the rabbis and early church fathers who were overly enamored with "fantastical" connections.

The tension in Lightfoot's writings stems from two primary factors: the dual authorship of the Scripture and the cacophony of interpretive voices on which he reflected. On the one hand, Lightfoot insisted that exegesis must do justice to the particulars of the text in their historical context—Christian interpreters were not always successful in this area. On the other hand, Lightfoot maintained the unity of the text and the uniformity of Scripture's message as a witness to Jesus Christ; Jewish interpreters always failed in this. God inspired the Bible, but Lightfoot insisted that reason, critical methodology, and detailed numerical analysis were necessary for arriving at the literal sense. While tension existed between these two, Lightfoot felt no compulsion to choose one over the other.

Bibliography

Anderson, Bernard W. *Understanding the Old Testament.* 3rd ed. Englewood Cliffs: Prentice-Hall, 1975.
Aquinas, Thomas. *Summa Theologiae.* New York: Benziger, 1948.
Archer, Gleason L., and Gregory Chirichigno. *Old Testament Quotations in the New Testament.* Chicago: Moody, 1983.
Asselt, Willem J. van, and Eef Dekker, eds. *Reformation and Scholasticism: An Ecumenical Enterprise.* Grand Rapids: Baker, 2001.
Astruc, Jean. *Conjectures sur les memoires originaux: don't il paroit que Moyses'est servi pour composer le liver de la Genese: avec des remarques qui appuient ou qui ecaircissent ces conjectures.* Brussels: Fricx, 1753.
Augustine. *City of God.* New York: Dutton, 1945.
———. *On Christian Doctrine.* Translated by D. W. Robertson. New York: Liberal Arts, 1958.
Barker, William S. *Puritan Profiles.* Fearn, UK: Mentor, 1996.
Barr, James. *Fundamentalism.* Philadelphia: Westminster, 1978.
———. "Literality." *Faith and Philosophy* 6 (1989) 412–28.
———. *Old and New in Interpretation.* New York: Harper & Row, 1966.
———. "Why the World was Created in 4004 B.C.: Archbishop Ussher and Biblical Chronology." *The John Rylands University Library* 67.2 (1985) 575–608.
Bartling, V. A. "Christ's Use of the Old Testament with Special Reference to the Pentateuch." *Concordia Theological Monthly* 36 (1965) 567–76.
Beale, G. K. "Did Jesus and His Followers Preach the Right Doctrine from the Wrong Texts? An Examination of the Presuppositions of Jesus and the Apostles' Exegetical Method." *Themelios* 14.3 (1989) 89–96.
Beegle, Dewey. *Scripture, Tradition, and Infallibility.* Grand Rapids: Eerdmans, 1973.
Bernard, Richard. *The faithfull shepheard, or The shepheards faithfulnesse : wherein is . . . set forth the excellencie and necessitie of the ministerie; a ministers properties and dutie; his entrance into this function and charge; how to begin fitly to instruct his people; catechising and preaching; and a good plaine order and method therein.* London: Arnold Hatfield for Iohn Bill, 1607.
Bland, Kalman P. "Issues in Sixteenth-century Jewish Exegesis." In *The Bible in the Sixteenth Century*, edited by David Steinmetz, 50–67. Durham, NC: Duke University Press, 1990.
Blocher, Henri. "The Analogy of Faith." *Scottish Bulletin of Evangelical Theology* 5 (1987) 17–38.
Bock, Darrell. "Evangelicals and the Use of the Old Testament in the New." *Bibliotheca Sacra* 142 (1985) 209–23; 306–19.

Bowker, J. *The Targums and Rabbinic Literature: An Introduction to Jewish Interpretation of Scripture*. Cambridge: Cambridge University Press, 1969.

Box, G. H. "Hebrew in the Reformation . . . and After." In *The Legacy of Israel*, edited by Edwin Robert Bevan and C. J. Singer, 315–76. Oxford: Clarendon, 1927.

Bratcher, Robert. *Old Testament Quotations in the New Testament*. London: United Bible Societies, 1961.

Braude, William G. *Pesikta Rabbati*. 2 vols. New Haven, CT: Yale University Press, 1968.

Braude, William G., and Israel J. Kapstein. *Pĕsikta Dĕ-Rab Kahăna*. Philadelphia: Jewish Publication Society of America, 1975.

Briggs, Charles Augustus. *The Higher Criticism of the Hexateuch*. New York: Scribner's Sons, 1897.

Bromiley, Geoffrey W. "The Church Fathers and Holy Scripture." In *Scripture and Truth*, edited by D. A. Carson and John D. Woodbridge, 199–224. Grand Rapids: Zondervan, 1983.

Brown, Raymond Edward. "The *Sensus Plenior* of Sacred Scripture." PhD diss., St. Mary's University, 1955.

Bruce, F. F. "History of New Testament Study." In *New Testament Interpretation*, edited by I. H. Marshall, 21–59. Exeter, UK: Paternoster, 1975.

Bullinger, Heinreich. *Fiftie godlie and learned sermons divided into five decades, conteyning the chiefe and principall pointes of Christian religion, written in three severall tomes or sections*. London: Henry Middleton for Ralphe Newberrie, 1577.

Burnett, Stephen George. "The Christian Hebraism of Johann Buxtorff (1564–1629)." Ph.D. diss., University of Wisconsin, Madison, 1990.

Burrows, Millar. *An Outline of Biblical Theology*. Philadelphia: Westminster, 1946.

Callahan, James. *The Clarity of Scripture*. Downers Grove, IL: InterVarsity, 2001.

Calvin, John. *Institutes of the Christian Religion*. Edited by John T. McNeill. Translated by Ford Lewis Battles. Philadelphia: Westminster, 1960.

Cano, Melchior. *De locis theoligicis libri duodecimo*. n.p.: Coloniae Agrippinae, 1585.

Cappel, Louis, *Commentarii et notæ criticæ in Vetus Testamentum, Jacobi Cappelli Observationes in eosdem lobros. Ludovici Cappelli Arcanum punctationis Revelatum*. Amsterdam: Blaeu, 1689.

Caro, Rabbi Yizhak. *Sefer Toledoth Yizhak*. 1877. Facsimile reprint. Jerusalem: Makor, 1978.

Carruthers, Samuel William. *The Everyday Work of the Westminster Assembly*. Philadelphia: The Presbyterian Historical Society (of America) and The Presbyterian Historical Society of England, 1943.

Carson, D. A., and H. G. M. Williamson, eds. *It is Written: Scripture Citing Scripture*. Cambridge: Cambridge University Press, 1988.

Cassian, John. *Conlationes XXIV*. Vienna: Filivm, 1886.

Chadwick, H. "The Bible in the Greek Fathers." In *The Church's Use of the Bible*, edited by D. H. Nineham, 25–39. London: SPCK, 1963.

Childs, Brevard. *The Book of Exodus*. Old Testament Library. Louisville: Westminster, 1974.

———. "Hermeneutical Reflections on C. Vitringa, Eighteenth-Century Interpreter of Isaiah." In *In Search of True Wisdom Essays in Old Testament: Interpretation in Honour of Ronald E. Clements*, edited by Edward Ball, 89–98. Sheffield, UK: Sheffield Academic, 1999.

---. "The Sensus Literalis of Scripture: An Ancient and Modern Problem." In *Beiträge zur Alttestamentlichen Theologie*, edited by Herbert Donner, Robert Hanhart, and Rudolf Smend, 80–93. Gottingen: Vandenhoeck & Ruprecht, 1977.
Clark(e), Adam. *Bibliographical Dictionary*. 1802–6. Reprint, Metuchen, NJ: Cordasco, 1971.
Cohen, Charles. "Two Biblical Models of Conversion: An Example of Puritan Hermeneutics." *Church History* 58.2 (1989) 182–96.
Cohen, Hermann. *Religion of Reason: Out of the Sources of Judaism*. New York: Ungar, 1972.
Constantin, C. "Rationalisme." In *Dictionnaire de théologie catholique*, vol. 13, edited by Alfred Vacant, E. Mangenot, Emile Amann, 2. Paris: Letouzey et Ane, 1899–1950.
Cotter, Anthony. "The Obscurity of Scripture." *Catholic Biblical Quarterly* 9.4 (1947) 453–64.
Coughenour, Robert A. "The Shape and Vehicle of Puritan Hermeneutics." *Reformed Review* 30 (1976) 23–34.
Danby, Herbert. *The Mishnah: Translated from the Hebrew with Introduction and Brief Explanatory Notes*. Oxford: Clarendon, 1933.
Davidson, Edward H. "John Cotton's Biblical Exegesis: Method and Purpose." *Early American Literature* 17.2 (Fall 1982) 119–38.
Davis, Thomas M. "Exegetical Traditions of Puritan Typology." *Early American Literature* 5.1 (1970) 11–50.
De Sola Pool, David. "Hebrew Learning Among the Puritans of New England Prior to 1700." In *Publications of the American Jewish Historical Society"* XX, 31–83. n.p.: American Jewish Historical Society, 1911.
De Spinoza, Benedict. *A Theologico-Politcal Treatise*. Translated by R. H. M. Elwes. New York: Dover, 1951.
Dockery, David S. *Christian Scripture: An Evangelical Perspective on Inspiration, Authority and Interpretation*. Nashville, TN: Broadman & Holman, 1995.
Dodd, C. H. *According to the Scriptures*. New York: Scribner's Sons, 1953.
---. *The Old Testament in the New*. Philadelphia: Fortress, 1965.
Doeve, J. W. *Jewish Hermeneutics in the New Testament*. Assen: Van Gorcum, 1954.
---. *Jewish Hermeneutics in the Synoptic Gospels and Acts*. Assen: Van Corcum, 1954.
Donner, H., Robert Hanhart, and Rudolf Smend, eds. *Beiträge zur Alttestamentlichen Theologie*. Gottingen: Vandenhoeck & Ruprecht, 1977.
Edgar, S. L. "Respect for Context in Quotations from the Old Testament." *New Testament Studies* 9 (1961–62) 55–62.
Ellis, E. Earle. "Biblical Interpretation in the New Testament Church" In *Mikra: Text, Translation, Reading, and Interpretation of the Hebrew Bible in Ancient Judaism and Early Christianity*, edited by Martin Jan Mulder, 691–726. Philadelphia: Fortress, 1988.
---. *The Old Testament in Early Christianity*. Grand Rapids: Baker, 1991.
---. *Prophecy and Hermeneutics in Early Christianity*. Grand Rapids: Eerdmans, 1978.
Epstein, I., ed. *Hebrew-English Edition of the Babylonian Talmud*. Translated by M. Simon. London: Soncino, 1960–.
---. Soncino Classics Collection on CD-ROM. Version 3.0.8, n.p., 1996.
Ericson, Norman. "The NT Use of the OT: A Kerygmatic Approach." *Journal of the Evangelical Theological Society* 30.3 (1987) 337–42.

Etheridge, J. W. *The Targums of Onkelos and Jonathan Ben Uzziel on the Pentateuch*. New York: KTAV, 1968.

Evans, Craig. "The Function of the Old Testament in the New." In *Introducing New Testament Interpretation*, edited by Scot McKnight, 163–99. Grand Rapids: Baker, 1989.

Fairbairn, Patrick. *Hermeneutical Manual: or, Introduction to the Exegetical Study of the Scriptures of the New Testament*. Philadelphia: Smith and English, 1859.

———. *Typology of Scripture*. Vol. 1. New York: Funk & Wagnalls, 1911.

Farrar, Frederic. W. *History of Interpretation*. New York: Dutton, 1886.

Feinberg, Stanley P. "Thomas Goodwin's Scriptural Hermeneutics and the Dissolution of Puritan Unity." *The Journal of Religious History* 10.1 (1978) 32–49.

Filson, Floyd V. "The Unity of the Old and the New Testaments: A Bibliographic Survey." *Interpretation* 5.2 (1951) 134–52.

Fishbane, Michael. *Biblical Interpretation in Ancient Israel*. Oxford: Clarendon, 1985.

———. *Biblical Myth and Rabbinic Mythmaking*. Oxford: Oxford University Press, 2003.

Fitzmyer, J. A. "The Use of Explicit Old Testament Quotations in Qumran Literature and in the New Testament." *New Testament Studies* 7 (1960–61) 297–333.

Fowl, Stephen E., and Gregory Jones, "Practicing the Rule of Christ." In *Virtues and Practices in the Christian Tradition: Christian Ethics after MacIntyre*, edited by Nancey C. Murphy, Brad J. Kallenberg, and Mark Thiessen Nation, 111–31. Harrisburg, PA: Trinity, 1997.

Freedman, H. and Maurice Simon, eds. *Midrash Rabbah*. 10 vols. London: Soncino, 1977.

Frei, Hans. "The 'Literal Reading' of Biblical Narrative in the Christian Tradition: Does It Stretch or Will It Break?" In *The Bible and the Narrative Tradition*, edited by Frank McConnell, 36–77. New York: Oxford University Press, 1986.

Friedlander, G. *Pirke de-Rabbi Eliezer*, 4th ed. New York: Sepher-Hermon, 1981.

Froehlich, Karlfried, "'Always to Keep the Literal Sense in Holy Scripture Means to Kill One's Soul': The State of Biblical Hermeneutics at the Beginning of the Fifteenth Century." In *Literary Uses of Typology*, edited by Earl Miner, 20–48. Princeton: Princeton University Press, 1977.

———, ed. and trans. *Biblical Interpretation in the Early Church*. Philadelphia: Fortress, 1984.

Fulke, William. *A Defense of the Sincere and True Translations of the Holy Scriptures in the English Tongue, against the Cavils of Gregory Martin*. 1583. Reprint. Cambridge: The Parker Society, 1843.

Gane, Erwin R. "Exegetical Methods of Some Puritan Preachers." *Andrews University Seminary Studies* 19.1 (1981) 21–36.

Gaster, Moses. *The Ma`aseh Book* I. Philadelphia: The Jewish Publication Society of America, 1934.

Gerhardsson, Birger. *Memory and Manuscript: Oral Tradition and Written Transmission in Rabbinic Judaism and Early Christianity*. Uppsala: Gleerup, 1961.

Geiger, A. "Das Verhältnis des naturlichen Schrfitsinnes zur talmudischen Schriftdeutung." In *Wissenschaftliche Zeitschrift für jüdische Theologie*. Vol. 5, 234–59. Leipzig: Levysohn, 1844.

Ginzberg, Louis. *The Legends of the Jews*. 15th ed. 7 vols. Translated by Henrietta Szold. Philadelphia: Jewish Publication Society of America, 1910.

Goldin, Judah. *The Fathers according to Rabbi Nathan*. New Haven, CT: Yale University Press, 1955.

Goodenough, Erwin Ramsdell. *An Introduction to Philo Judaeus*. New Haven, CT: Yale University Press, 1940.

Gould, Stephen Jay. "Fall in the House of Ussher: How Foolish was the Archbishop's Precise Date for Creation?" *Natural History* (1993) 12, 14–16, 18–21.

Green, Garrett. "Fictional Narrative and Scriptural Truth." In *Scriptural Authority and Narrative Interpretation*, edited by Garrett Green, 86–93. Philadelphia: Fortress, 1987.

Green, William Henry. "Primeval Chronology." *Bibliotheca Sacra* 47.186 (1890) 285–303.

Greene-McCreight, Kathryn. *Ad Litteram: How Augustine, Calvin, and Barth Read the "Plain Sense" of Genesis 1–3*. New York: Lang, 1999.

———. "Literal Sense." In *Dictionary for Theological Interpretation of the Bible*, edited by Kevin J. Vanhoozer, Craig G. Bartholomew, and N. T. Wright, 455–56. Grand Rapids: Baker Academic, 2005.

Grogan, G. W. "The New Testament Interpretation of the Old Testament: A Comparative Study." *Tyndale Bulletin* 18 (1967) 54–76.

Halivni, David Weiss. *Peshat and Derash*. Oxford: Oxford University Press, 1991.

Ham, Ken. "Do the Days Really Matter." No Pages. Cited 17 June 2008. Online: http://www.icr.org/article/689/.

Hamilton, Thomas. "John Lightfoot." In *Dictionary of National Biography*, vol. 11, edited by Leslie Stephen and Sidney Lee, 1108–10. London: Oxford University Press, 1949.

Hanson, Anthony T. *The New Testament Interpretation of Scripture*. London: SPCK, 1980.

Hayes, John H., and Frederick C. Prussner. *Old Testament Theology: Its History and Development*. Atlanta: John Knox, 1985.

Heatherington, William M. *History of the Westminster Assembly*. New York: 1843.

Henry, Matthew. *Matthew Henry's Commentary on the Whole Bible wherein each Chapter is summed up in its contents: the sacred text inserted at large in distinct paragraphs; each paragraph reduced to its proper heads: the sense given, and largely illustrated with practical remarks and observations*. 6 vols. McLean, VA: MacDonald, n.d.

Higgins, A. J. B. *The Christian Significance of the Old Testament*. London: Independent, 1949.

Hodge, Charles. *Systematic Theology*. 3 vols. 1871–73. Reprint. Grand Rapids: Eerdmans, 1993.

Hooker, Morna D. "Beyond the Things that are Written? St. Paul's Use of Scripture." *New Testament Studies* 27 (1981) 295–309.

Howson, Barry H. "The Puritan Hermeneutic of John Owen: A Recommendation." *Westminster Theological Journal* 63 (2001) 351–76.

Hyman, A. *Torah Ha-kethubah va-Hamessurah: A Reference Book of the Scriptural Passages Quoted in Talmudic, Midrashic and Early Rabbinic Literature*. Tel-Aviv: Dvir, 1979.

Illyricus, Matthias Flacius. *Clavis Scripturae, seu, De sermone sacrorum literarum, plurimas generales regulas continentis*. 2 vols. Basel: Per Ioannem Oporinum, & Eusebium Episcopium, 1567.

Irenaeus. *Adversus Haereses*. Translated by Dominic Unger. New York: Paulist, 1992.

Johnson, S. Lewis. *The Use of the Old Testament in the New*. Grand Rapids: Zondervan, 1980.

Josephus. *Works of Josephus*. Translated by William Whiston. 4 vols. Grand Rapids: Baker, 1974.

Kamin, Sarah. "Rashi's Exegetical Categorization: With Respect to the Distinction between Peshat and Derash." *Immanuel* 11 (Fall 1980) 16–32.

Key, Newton E. "John Lightfoot." In *Oxford Dictionary of National Biography*, vol. 33, edited by H. C. G. Matthew and Brian Harrison, 753–56. London: Oxford University Press, 2004.

Klein, Michael L. *The Fragment-Targums of the Pentateuch according to their Extant Sources. Volume I. Texts, Indices and Introductory Essays*. Rome: Biblical Institute, 1980.

———. *The Fragment-Targums of the Pentateuch according to their Extant Sources. Volume II. Translation*. Rome: Biblical Institute, 1980.

Knox, W. L. "Philo's Use of the Old Testament." *Journal of Theological Studies* 41 (1940) 30–34.

Kornfeld, Nachum Y., and Abraham B. Walzer. *Sefer Hayashar: The Book of the Generations of Adam*. Hoboken, NJ: KTAV, 1993.

Korshin, Paul. "The Development of Abstracted Typology in England, 1650–1820." In *Literary Uses of Typology: From the Late Middle Ages to the Present*, edited by Earl K. Miner, 147–203. Princeton: Princeton University Press, 1977.

Kugel, James L. and Rowan A. Greer. *Early Biblical Interpretation*. Library of Early Christianity; Philadelphia: Westminster, 1986.

Kümmel, Werner Georg. *The New Testament: The History of the Investigation of its Problems*. Translated by S. McLean Gilmour and Howard C. Kee. Nashville, TN: Abingdon, 1972.

Lampe, G. W. H. *Essays on Typology*. Chatham, UK: Mackay, 1957.

Laplanche, Francois. *L'Écriture, le sacré et l'historie: érudits et politiques protestants devant la Bible en France au XVIIe siècle*. Amsterdam: APA-Holland University Press, 1986.

Lauterbach, Jacob Z. *Mekilta de-Rabbi Ishmael*. 3 vols. Philadelphia: The Jewish Publication Society of America, 1933.

———. "Peshat." In *Jewish Encyclopedia: A Descriptive Record of the History, Religion, Literature, and Customs of the Jewish People from the Earliest Times to the Present Day*, vol. 9, edited by Isidiore Singer, 652–53. New York: Funk and Wagnalls, 1901–6.

Lea, Thomas D. "The Hermeneutics of the Puritans." *Journal of the Evangelical Theological Society* 39.2 (1996) 271–84.

LeDeaut, R. "Targumic Literature and New Testament Interpretation." *Biblical Theology Bulletin* 4 (1974) 243–89.

Leigh, Edward. *A Systeme or Body of Divinity Consisting of Ten Books, Wherein the Fundamentals and Main Grounds or Religion are Opened*. London: A.M. for William Lee, 1662.

"Life of Lightfoot." In *Biographia Britannica, or the Lives of the Most Eminent Persons who have Flourished in Great Britain and Ireland*, vol. 5, 2931–36 London: Innys, 1747–66.

Lightfoot, John. *The Whole Works of Rev. John Lightfoot*. Edited by John Rogers Pitman. 13 vols. London: Dove, 1822–25.

Lindars, Barnabas. *New Testament Apologetic: The Doctrinal Significance of the Old Testament Quotations*. Philadelphia: Westminster, 1962.

———. "The Place of the Old Testament in the Formation of New Testament Theology." *New Testament Studies* 23 (1977) 59–66.

Loewe, Raphael. "Jewish Scholarship in England." *Transactions—Jewish Historical Society of England* (1960) 125–48.

———. "The 'Plain' Meaning of Scripture in Early Jewish Exegesis." *Papers of the Institute of Jewish Studies London* I (1964) 140–85.

Longenecker, Richard. *Biblical Exegesis in the Apostolic Period*. Grand Rapids: Eerdmans, 1975.

———. "Can We Reproduce the Exegesis of the New Testament?" *Tyndale Bulletin* 21 (1970) 3–38.

———. "'Who is the Prophet Talking About?' Some Reflections on the New Testament's Use of the Old." *Themelios* 13.1 (1988) 4–8.

Loonstra, Bert. "Scholasticism and Hermeneutics." In *Reformation and Scholasticism*, edited by Willem J. van Asselt and Eef Dekker, 295–306. Grand Rapids: Baker, 2001.

Luther, Martin. *D. Lectures on Genesis*. 8 vols. *Luther's Works*. St. Louis, MO: Concordia, 1955.

———. *Martin Luthers Werke; Kirtische Gesamtausgabe*. Weimar: Böhlau, 1883.

Maccovius, Johannes. *Loci communes theologici: Ex omnibus ejus, quae extant, collegiis, thesibus, per locos comm. disputatis, manuscripts antiquis, recentioribus, undiquaeaue sollicite conquisitis, collecti, digesti, aucti, indice capitum, rereumque locupletati*. Amsterdam: 1658.

Maddox, Mickey. "Recovering the Riches of Pre-modern Exegesis." *Modern Reformation* 8 (July 1999) 16–20.

Marsh, George Perkins. *Lectures on the English Language*. New York: Scriber, 1860.

Martyr, Justin. *The First and Second Apologies*. New York: Paulist, 1997.

Mather, Increase. *A Dissertation Concerning the Future Conversion of the Jewish Nation* London: R. Tookey for Nath. Hillier, 1709.

McCasland, S. V. "Matthew Twists the Scripture." *Journal of Biblical Literature* 80 (1961) 143–48.

McCartney, Dan. "The New Testament's Use of the Old Testament." In *Inerrancy & Hermeneutics*, edited by Harvie Conn, 101–16. Grand Rapids: Baker, 1988.

McKenzie, John L. "The Transformation of the Old Testament Messianism." In *Studies in Salvation History*, edited by C. Luke Salm, 96–113. Ebglewood Cliffs, NJ: Prentice-Hall, 1964.

McNamara, Martin. *The New Testament and the Palestinian Targum to the Pentateuch*. Rome: Pontifical Biblical Institute, 1966.

McNeill, John T. *The History and Character of Calvinism*. New York: Oxford University Press, 1954.

Mead, R. T. "A Dissenting Opinion about Respect for Context in Old Testament Quotations." *New Testament Studies* 10 (1962–63) 279–89.

Metzger, B. M. "The Formulas Introducing Quotations of Scripture in the New Testament and in the Midrash." In *Historical and Literary Studies: Pagan, Jewish, and Christian*, edited by B. M. Metzger, 52–63. Leiden: Brill, 1968.

Mielziner, M. *Introduction to the Talmud*. New York: Bloch, 1925.

Miller, M. P. "Targum, Midrash, and the Use of the Old Testament in the New Testament." *Journal for the Study of Judaism* 2 (1971) 29–82.

Miller, Perry, and Thomas H. Johnson. *The Puritans*. New York: Harper & Row, 1969.

Miner, Earl K. *Literary Uses of Typology: From the Late Middle Ages to the Present*. Princeton: Princeton University Press, 1977.

Mitchell, Alexander. *The Westminster Assembly—Its History and Standards*. London: Nisbet, 1883.

Mitchell, Fraser. *English Pulpit Oratory from Andrewes to Tillotson: A Study of its Literary Aspects*. New York: Russel & Russel, 1962.

Montefiore, C. G. "The Old Testament and Judaism." In *Record and Revelation*, edited by Henry Wheeler Robinson, 427–57. New York: Oxford University Press, 1938.

Moo, Douglas. "The Problem of *Sensus Plenior*." In *Hermeneutics, Authority, and Canon*, edited by D. A. Carson and John D. Woodbridge, 179–211. Grand Rapids: Zondervan, 1986.

Moule, C. F. D. "Fulfillment Words in the New Testament: Use and Abuse." *New Testament Studies* 14 (1967–68) 293–320.

Mulder, Martin Jan. *Mikra: Text, Translation, Reading, and Interpretation of the Hebrew Bible in Ancient Judaism and Early Christianity*. Assen: Van Gorcum, 1988.

Muller, Richard A. *After Calvin: Studies in the Development of a Theological Tradition*. New York: Oxford University Press, 2003.

———. "Calvin and the Calvinists: Assessing Continuities and Discontinuities between the Reformation and Orthodoxy." Parts 1 and 2. *Calvin Theological Journal* 30 (1995) 345–75; 31 (1996) 125–60.

———. "The Hermeneutic of Promise and Fulfillment in Calvin's Exegesis of the Old Testament Prophecies of the Kingdom." In *The Bible in the Sixteenth Century*, edited by David Steinmetz, 68–82. Durham, NC: Duke University Press, 1990.

———. *Historical Handbook of Major Biblical Interpreters*. Edited by Donald K. McKim. Downers Grove, IL: InterVarsity, 1998.

———. *Post-Reformation Reformed Dogmatics: The Rise and Development of Reformed Orthodoxy, ca. 1520 to ca. 1725*. 2nd ed. 2 vols. Grand Rapids: Baker, 2003.

———. "Scholasticism and Orthodoxy in the Reformed Tradition: An Attempt at Definition." Inaugural Address at the Calvin Seminary Chapel, Grand Rapids, 7 Sept. 1995.

Mullinger, James B. *Cambridge Characteristics in the Seventeenth Century*. London, 1867.

Neal, Daniel. *History of the Puritans or, Protestant Nonconformists; from the Reformation in 1517 to the Revolution in 1688*. 3 vols. 1837. Reprint. Minneapolis: Klock & Klock, 1979.

Neil, Stephen, and Tom Wright. *The Interpretation of the New Testament: 1861–1986*. Oxford: Oxford University Press, 1988.

Neusner, Jacob. *The Idea of History in Rabbinic Judaism*. Leiden: Brill, 2003.

———. *Invitation to Midrash: The Workings of Rabbinic Interpretation. A Teaching Book*. San Francisco: Harper & Row, 1989.

———. *The Talmudic Anthology in Three Volumes, II*. Frankfurt: Lang, 1995.

———. *The Tosefta: Translated from the Hebrew with a New Introduction*. Peabody, MA: Hendrickson, 2002.

Newton, Isaac. *The Chronology of Ancient Kingdoms Amended*. London: printed for J. Tonson, 1728.

Nicole, Roger. "The New Testament Use of the Old Testament." In *Revelation and the Bible*, edited by C. F. H. Henry, 135–51. Grand Rapids: Baker, 1958.

North, J. D. "Chronology and the Age of the World." In *Cosmology, History, and Theology*, edited by Wolfgang Yourgrau and Allen duPont Breck, 307–33. New York: Plenum, 1977.

Numbers, Ronald L. "'The Most Important Biblical Discovery of Our Time': William Henry Green and the Demise of Ussher's Chronology." *Church History* 69 (2000) 257–76.

Oberman, Heiko. A. *Forerunners of the Reformation: The Shape of Late Medieval Thought*. New York: Holt, Rinehart, and Winston, 1966.

———. *The Harvest of Medieval Theology: Gabriel Biel and Late Medieval Nominalis*. Rev. ed. Grand Rapids: Eerdmans, 1967.
Origen. *Contra Celsum*. Translated by Henry Chadwick. Cambridge: Cambridge University Press, 1953.
———. *On First Principles*. Translated by G. W. Butterworth. Gloucester, MA: Smith, 1973.
Owen, John. *Biblical Theology*. Translated by Stephen P. Westcott. Pittsburgh: Soli Deo Gloria, 1994.
———. *The Works of John Owen*. 16 vols. Edited by William H. Goold. London: Banner of Truth, 1965.
Packer. J. I. "Infallible Scripture and the Role of Hermeneutics." In *Scripture and Truth*, edited by D. A. Carson and J. D. Woodbridge, 325–56. Grand Rapids: Zondervan, 1983.
———. *The Quest for Godliness*. Wheaton, IL: Crossway, 1990.
Patte, Daniel. *Early Jewish Hermeneutics in Palestine*. Missoula, MT: Scholars, 1975.
Perkins, William. *A Commentarie or Exposition, upon the Five First Chapters of the Epistle to the Galatians*. Cambridge: Legatt, 1604.
———. *The Whole Works of that Famous and Worthy Minister of Christ in the Universitie of Cambridge, M. William Perkins, in three volumes*. London: Legatt, 1631.
Polman, A. D. R. *The Word of God according to St. Augustine*. Translated by A. J. Pomerans. Grand Rapids: Eerdmans, 1961.
Poole, Matthew. *A Commentary on the Holy Bible*. Peabody, MA: Hendrickson, 1985.
———. *Synopsis Criticorum*. 5 vols. London: 1669.
Preus, J. S. *From Shadow to Promise*. Cambridge, MA: Belknap, 1969.
Preus, Robert D. "The View of the Bible Held by the Church: The Early Church through Luther." In *Inerrancy*, edited by Norman L. Geisler, 357–84. Grand Rapids: Zondervan, 1980.
Poythress, V. S. "Divine Meaning of Scripture." *Westminster Theological Journal* 48 (1986) 241–79.
Puckett, David. *John Calvin's Exegesis of the Old Testament*. Louisville: Westminster/John Knox, 1995.
"Rationalism," In *Oxford Dictionary of the Jewish Religion*, edited by R. J. Zwi Werblowsky and Geoffrey Wigoder, 573–74. New York: Oxford University Press, 1997.
Renfrew, C. *Before Civilization: The Radiocarbon Revolution and Prehistoric Europe* Harmondsworth, UK: Penguin, 1976.
Richardson, Alan. *The Bible in the Age of Science*. Philadelphia: Westminster, 1961.
Ritschl, Otto. *Dogmensgeschichte des Protestatismus*. Vol. 1. Leipzig: Hinrichs, 1908.
Rogers, Jack Bartlett. "The Church Doctrine of Biblical Authority." Pages 15–46 In *Biblical Authority*, edited by Jack Rogers, 15–46. Waco, TX: Word, 1977.
Rogers, Jack Bartlett, and Donald K. McKim. *Interpretation and Authority of Scripture*. San Francisco: Harper & Row, 1979.
Rooden, Peter T. van. *Theology, Biblical Scholarship and Rabbinical Studies in the Seventeenth Century: Constantijn L'Empereur (1591–1648), Professor of Hebrew and Theology at Leiden*. Translated by J. C. Grayson. Leiden: Brill, 1989.
Ross, Hugh. *Creation and Time*. Colorado Springs: Navpress, 1994.
Rowley, H. H. "The Fulfillment of the Old Testament in the New." In *The Re-Discovery of the Old Testament*, 202–15. Philadelphia: Westminster, 1946.

Rupp, E. G., and Philip S. Watson, eds. and trans. *Luther and Erasmus: Free Will and Salvation*. Library of Christian Classics. Philadelphia: Westminster, 1969.

Ryken, Leland. *Worldly Saints: The Puritans as they Really Were*. Grand Rapids: Zondervan: 1986.

Sabourin, Leopold. *The Bible and the Christ: The Unity of the Two Testaments*. New York: Alba, 1980.

Sailhamer, John. "The Canonical Approach to the Old Testament: It's Effect on Understanding Prophecy." *Journal of the Evangelical Theological Society* 30.3 (1987) 307–15.

Schaff, Philip. *The Creeds of Christendom*. 3 vols. Grand Rapids, Baker, 1966.

Schertz, C. E. "Christian Hebraism in 17th Century England as Reflected in the Works of John Lightfoot." PhD diss., New York University, 1977.

Schper, Abraham. "Christian Hebraists in Sixteenth Century England." PhD diss., University of London, 1944.

Shires, H. M. *Finding the Old Testament in the New*. Philadelphia: Westminster, 1974.

Silva, Moises. *Has the Church Misread the Bible?* Grand Rapids: Zondervan, 1987.

Skinner, Quentin. "Meaning and Understanding in the History of Ideas." *History and Theory* 9.1 (1969) 3–53.

Smalley, Beryl. *The Study of the Bible in the Middle Ages*. Notre Dame, IN: University of Notre Dame Press, 1964.

Smith, Robert W. "James Ussher: Biblical Chronicler." *Anglican Theological Review* 41.2 (1959) 84–94.

Sohnius, Georgius. *Continens Scripta Auctoris Methodica: Quae Sund Haec: I. De verbo Dei & ejus tractatione libri duo*. Herbornae Nassoviorum: Corvin, 1609.

Spicq, Ceslas. *Esquisse d'une histoire de l'Exégèse Latine au Moyen Age*. Paris: Vrin, 1944.

Strack, Hermann L. *Introduction to the Talmud and Midrash*. Philadelphia: Jewish Publication Society of America, 1931.

Strack, H. L., and P. Billerbeck. *Kommentar Zum Neuen Testament Aus Talmud und Midrash*. 4 vols. Munich: Beck, 1922–28.

Steinmetz, David C. "The Superiority of Pre-Critical Exegesis." *Theology Today* 37.1 (1980) 27–38.

Steinmetz, David, Richard Muller, and John L. Thompson, eds. *Biblical Interpretation in the Era of the Reformation: Essays Presented to David C. Steinmetz in Honor of his Sixtieth Birthday*. Grand Rapids: Eerdmans, 1996.

Strouse, Thomas M. "A Review of and Observations about Peter Whitfield's A Dissertation on the Hebrew Vowel-Points." No Pages. Cited 7 June 2006. Online: http://www.deanburgonsociety.org/CriticalTexts/witfields.htm.

Surberg, Raymond F. *Introduction to the Intertestamental Period*. St. Louis, MO: Concordia, 1975.

Tanner, Kathryn E. "Theology and the Plain Sense." In *Scriptural Authority and Narrative Interpretation*, edited by Garrett Green, 59–78. Philadelphia: Fortress, 1987.

Targum Neofiti 1: Deuteronomy: Translated, with Apparatus and Notes. Translated by Martin McNamara. The Aramaic Bible 5a. Collegeville, MN: Liturgical, 1994.

Targum Neofiti 1: Numbers; Targum Pseudo-Jonathan: Numbers. Translated by Martin McNamara and Ernest G. Clark. The Aramaic Bible 4. Collegeville, MN: Liturgical, 1994.

Targum Neofiti 1 and Pseudo-Jonathan: Exodus: Translated, with Apparatus and Notes. Translated by Martin McNamara. The Aramaic Bible 2. Collegeville, MN: Liturgical, 1994.

The Targum Onquelos to Deuteronomy: Translated, with Apparatus and Notes. Translated by Bernard Grossfeld. The Aramaic Bible 9. Wilmington, DE: Glazier, 1988.

The Targum Onquelos to Exodus: Translated, with Apparatus and Notes. Translated by Bernard Grossfeld. The Aramaic Bible 7. Wilmington, DE: Glazier, 1988.

The Targum Onquelos to Leviticus and Numbers: Translated, with Apparatus and Notes. Translated by Bernard Grossfeld. The Aramaic Bible 8. Wilmington, DE: Glazier, 1988.

Targum Pseudo-Jonathan: Deuteronomy: Translated with Notes. Translated by Ernest G. Clarke. The Aramaic Bible 5b. Collegeville, MN: Liturgical, 1998.

Targum Pseudo-Jonathan: Exodus: Translated with Notes. Translated by M. Maher. The Aramaic Bible 2. Collegeville, MN: Liturgical, 1994.

Tate, J. *Plato and Allegorical Interpretation.* Oxford: Oxford University Press, 1929.

Tasker, R. V. G. *The Old Testament in the New Testament.* Philadelphia: Westminster, 1947.

Taylor, Charles. "John Lightfoot." Page 84 in vol. 8 In *The Jewish Encyclopedia: A Descriptive Record of the History, Religion, Literature, and Customs of the Jewish People from the Earliest Times to the Present Day*, vol. 84, edited by Isidiore Singer, 84. New York: Funk and Wagnalls, 1901–6.

Trueman, Carl R. "John Owen's *Dissertation of Divine Justice*: An Exercise in Christocentric Scholasticism." *Calvin Theological Journal* 33.1 (1998) 87–103.

———. "Rage, Rage against the Dying of the Light." *Westminster Theological Journal* 70 (2008) 1–18.

Turrettinus, Franciscus. *Institutes of Elenctic Theology.* Edited by James T. Ennison, Jr. Translated by George Musgrave Giger. 3 vols. Phillipsburg, NJ: Presbyterian and Reformed, 1992–97.

Van Dixhoorn, Chad. "Appendix A, Lightfoot's Journal." In *Reforming the Reformation: Theological Debate at the Westminster Assembly 1643–1652.* Vol. 2. PhD diss., Cambridge University, 2004.

Waal, Van D., ed. *The Relationship between the Old and New Testament.* South Africa: NTSSA, 1981.

Ward, John. *The Borough of Stoke upon Trent in the Commencement of the Reign of Queen Victoria.* London: Lewis, 1843.

Warfield, B. B. "Editorial Notes." *Bible Student* 8 (1903) 241–52.

———. "On the Antiquity and Unity of the Human Race." *Princeton Theological Review* 9 (1911) 1–25

Weingreen, Jacob. "Exposition in the Old Testament and in Rabbinic Literature." In *Promise and Fulfillment*, edited by F. F. Bruce, 187–201. Edinburgh: T. & T. Clark, 1963.

Weiss, H. *Dor dor ve-dorshav: hu sefer divre ha-yamim le-Torah she-ba'al peh 'im korot sofreha ve-sifreha.* Vilna, Lithuania: Goldenberg, 1911.

Welton, D. M. *John Lightfoot, the English Hebraist.* Leipzig: Ackerman and Glasser, 1878.

Whitaker, William. *A Disputation on Holy Scripture, against the Papists, especially Bellarmine and Stapleton.* Translated and edited by William Fitzgerald. Cambridge: Cambridge University Press, 1849.

White, Andrew Dickson. *A History of the Warfare of Science with Theology in Christendom.* New York: Appleton, 1896.

Whitfield, Peter. *A Dissertation on the Hebrew Vowel-Points: Shewing that they are an Original and Essential Part of the Language.* Liverpool, UK: Whitfield, 1748.

Wilcox, Max. "On Investigating the Use of the Old Testament in the New Testament." In *Text and Interpretation*, edited by E. Best and R. Wilson, 231–43. Cambridge: Cambridge University Press, 1979.

Wood, Charles M. *The Formation of Christian Understanding: An Essay in Theological Hermeneutics.* Philadelphia: Westminster, 1981.

———. "Hermeneutics and the Authority of Scripture." In *Scriptural Authority and Narrative Interpretation*, edited by Garrett Green, 3–20. Philadelphia: Fortress, 1987.

Wright, G. E. *God Who Acts: Biblical Theology as Recital.* London: SCM, 1952.

Zanchius, Jerome. *Operum theologicorum.* 8 vols. Geneva: Sumptibus Samuelis Crispini, 1617.

Author Index

Anderson, Bernard W., 201
Aquinas, Thomas, 21, 45, 201
Archer, Gleason L., 201
Asselt, Willem J. van, 52–53, 201, 207
Astruc, Jean, 70, 74, 201
Augustine, 21, 28, 44, 76, 135–36, 166–67, 174, 201

Barker, William S., 201
Barr, James, 39–42, 72, 111, 115, 117, 127, 201
Bartling, V. A., 201
Beale, G. K., 201
Beegle, Dewey, 201
Bernard, Richard, 151, 201
Bland, Kalman P., 53–54, 65, 201
Blocher, Henri, 133–34, 150, 201
Bock, Darrell, 201
Bowker, J., 202
Box, G. H., 202
Bratcher, Robert, 202
Braude, William G., 202
Briggs, Charles Augustus, 74, 202
Bromiley, Geoffrey W., 21, 202
Brown, Raymond Edward, 21, 45, 202
Bruce, F. F., 152, 202, 211
Bullinger, Heinreich, 29, 151, 202
Burnett, Stephen George, 202
Burrows, Millar, 35, 202

Callahan, James, 27, 202
Calvin, John, 10, 29, 31, 46, 53, 101, 129, 149, 150, 152, 154, 169, 170, 202

Cano, Melchior, 79, 202
Cappel, Louis, 4, 6, 74, 84, 86–87, 91, 109, 197, 202
Caro, Rabbi Yizhak, 55, 202
Carruthers, Samuel William, 202
Carson, D. A., 202, 208–9
Cassian, John, 44, 202
Chadwick, H., 202, 209
Childs, Brevard, 39, 41, 44–46, 72, 171, 202
Clark(e), Adam, 12, 203
Cohen, Charles, 2, 203
Cohen, Hermann, 54, 203
Constantin, C., 50, 203
Cotter, Anthony, 34, 203
Coughenour, Robert A., 2, 203

Danby, Herbert, 203
Davidson, Edward H., 64, 112, 203
Davis, Thomas M., 2, 203
De Sola Pool, David, 11, 203
De Spinoza, Benedict, 6–7, 42, 48, 203
Dockery, David S., 152, 203
Dodd, C. H., 203
Doeve, J. W., 203
Donner, H., 203, 204

Edgar, S. L., 203
Ellis, E. Earle, 203
Epstein, I., ed., 40, 86, 124, 203
Ericson, Norman, 204
Etheridge, J. W., 204
Evans, Craig, 204

Author Index

Fairbairn, Patrick, 166, 170–74, 180–82, 188–89, 195, 204
Farrar, Frederic. W., 7, 28, 30, 204
Feinberg, Stanley P., 2, 204
Filson, Floyd V., 35, 204
Fishbane, Michael, 204
Fitzmyer, J. A., 204
Fowl, Stephen E., 16, 204
Freedman, H., 204
Frei, Hans, 20, 44–46, 149–50, 163, 204
Friedlander, G., 204
Froehlich, Karlfried, 20, 36, 44, 204
Fulke, William, 71, 204

Gane, Erwin R., 2, 204
Gaster, Moses, 204
Gerhardsson, Birger, 204
Geiger, A., 42, 204
Ginzberg, Louis, 204
Goldin, Judah, 204
Goodenough, Erwin Ramsdell, 205
Gould, Stephen Jay, 126–27, 205
Green, Garrett, 132, 205, 210, 212
Green, William Henry, 125, 205, 208
Greene-McCreight, Kathryn, 45–46, 163, 205
Grogan, G. W., 205

Halivni, David Weiss, 40–42, 47, 131, 134, 205
Ham, Ken, 127, 205
Hamilton, Thomas, 8, 12, 205
Hanson, Anthony T., 205
Hayes, John H., 6, 205
Heatherington, William M., 205
Henry, Matthew, 74–75, 205
Higgins, A. J. B., 205
Hodge, Charles, 125–26, 205
Hooker, Morna D., 205
Howson, Barry H., 2, 129, 205
Hyman, A., 205

Illyricus, Matthias Flacius, 21, 29, 70, 150–51, 205
Irenaeus, 107, 133, 205

Johnson, S. Lewis, 205
Josephus, 62, 98–99, 116, 135, 205

Kamin, Sarah, 42, 205
Key, Newton E., 8, 206
Klein, Michael L., 206
Knox, W. L., 206
Kornfeld, Nachum Y., 206
Korshin, Paul, 170, 206
Kugel, James L., 206
Kümmel, Werner Georg, 151, 206

Lampe, G. W. H., 206
Laplanche, Francois, 74, 84, 206
Lauterbach, Jacob Z., 40, 43, 206
Lea, Thomas D., 2, 206
LeDeaut, R., 206
Leigh, Edward, 57, 171, 206
Lindars, Barnabas, 206
Loewe, Raphael, 40–43, 131–32, 206
Longenecker, Richard, 207
Loonstra, Bert, 14, 31, 52–53, 207
Luther, Martin. D., 10, 21, 28, 46, 101, 112, 152, 154, 163, 169, 207

Maccovius, Johannes, 72, 207
Maddox, Mickey, 16, 207
Marsh, George Perkins, 173, 195, 207
Martyr, Justin, 44, 135, 162, 207
Mather, Increase, 11, 155, 207
McCasland, S. V., 207
McCartney, Dan, 207
McKenzie, John L., 207
Mcnamara, Martin, 95, 207, 210–11
Mcneill, John T., 202, 207
Mead, R. T., 207
Metzger, B. M., 207
Mielziner, M., 41, 207

Miller, M. P., 207
Miller, Perry, 2, 207
Miner, Earl K., 167, 169–70, 204, 206–7
Mitchell, Alexander, 207
Mitchell, Fraser, 9, 207
Montefiore, C. G., 208
Moo, Douglas, 21, 208
Moule, C. F. D., 208
Mulder, Martin Jan, 204, 208
Muller, Richard A., xiv, 2–3, 5–8, 13–14, 16–17, 28–32, 36, 45, 48, 51–53, 55, 57–58, 70–74, 83–85, 87, 92, 101, 134, 149–52, 159, 163, 169–71, 208, 210
Mullinger, James B., 208

Neal, Daniel, 2–3, 12, 208
Neil, Stephen, 12, 208
Neusner, Jacob, 54, 208
Newton, Isaac, 113, 208
Nicole, Roger, 208
North, J. D., 127, 208
Numbers, Ronald L., 125–26, 208

Oberman, Heiko A., 133–34, 208
Origen, ix, 20, 22, 28, 36, 44, 133, 166, 209
Owen, John, 2, 11, 17, 84, 86–87, 91, 129, 170, 205, 209, 211

Packer, J. I., 2, 209
Patte, Daniel, 209
Perkins, William, 150, 171, 172, 209
Polman, A. D. R., 22, 76, 209
Poole, Matthew, 13, 74–75, 158, 209
Preus, J. S., 46, 134, 162, 209
Preus, Robert D., 20–21, 133, 163, 209
Poythress, V. S., 209
Puckett, David, 169, 209

Renfrew, C., 113, 209
Richardson, Alan, 209

Ritschl, Otto, 151, 209
Rogers, Jack Bartlett, 14, 50, 209
Rooden, Peter T. Van, 209
Ross, Hugh, 126, 209
Rowley, H. H., 209
Rupp, E. G., 28, 210
Ryken, Leland, 2, 29, 210

Sabourin, Leopold, 210
Sailhamer, John, 210
Schaff, Philip, 4, 210
Schertz, C. E., 8–11, 70–71, 73, 75–76, 85, 89, 103–4, 210
Schper, Abraham, 12, 210
Shires, H. M., 210
Silva, Moises, 22, 27–28, 210
Skinner, Quentin, 3, 15–17, 210
Smalley, Beryl, 21, 210
Smith, Robert W., 210
Sohnius, Georgius, 151, 210
Spicq, Ceslas, 45, 210
Strack, Hermann L., 210
Steinmetz, David C., 16, 201, 208, 210
Strouse, Thomas M., 84, 210
Surberg, Raymond F., 210

Tanner, Kathryn E., 39, 132–33, 210
Tate, J., 41, 211
Tasker, R. V. G., 211
Taylor, Charles, 12, 170, 211
Trueman, Carl R., x, xii, 17, 52, 211
Turrettinus, Franciscus, 211

Van Dixhoorn, Chad, 7, 9, 211

Waal, Van D., ed., 211
Ward, John, 211
Warfield, B. B., 115, 126, 211
Weingreen, Jacob, 211
Weiss, H., 41, 211
Welton, D. M., 8, 211
Whitaker, William, 70, 72–73, 150, 170–71, 211

White, Andrew Dickson, 112, 114–15, 211
Whitfield, Peter, 84, 210, 212
Wilcox, Max, 212
Wood, Charles M., 132, 212
Wright, G. E., 125, 212

Zanchius, Jerome, 4, 163, 212

Subject Index

1 Chronicles, 77
1 Corinthians, 80, 96, 99–101, 103–4, 194
2 Corinthians, 183
1 Samuel, 74
2 Samuel, 23, 26, 74, 154
1 Kings, 23–24, 140
2 Kings, 145
1 John, 70, 107
1 Peter, 183, 194–95
2 Peter, 24, 77, 96
2 Thessalonians, 28
2 Timothy, 95

Abraham, 95, 115, 119, 123, 125, 136, 139, 179, 189–90,
Acts, 50, 121–22, 143, 165, 167, 176, 178, 203, 212
Adam, 65, 80, 94, 112, 115, 124, 144, 166–67, 177, 182, 191–93, 206
Alexandrian school, 21, 44
allegory, allegories, allegorical, ix, 6, 18–21, 33, 39–47, 136, 143, 145, 149, 160, 163–68, 171–73, 195, 199
Amos, 168
Amyraldism, 4
Analogy of Faith (Analogia Fidei), 6, 18, 29, 72, 129, 133, 150–52, 154, 159, 180, 198
Antiochene, 21, 44,
Apocrypha, 38, 137
Apostles' Creed, 135, 138, 141, 148, 151, 155, 159, 197

Augustine, St., 21–22, 27–29, 36, 44, 46, 76, 105, 112, 134–36, 162, 166, 174, 187
authorship
   Dual, 19–22, 26–27, 38, 47, 71, 73, 198–99
   Mosaic, 6, 14, 73–74, 76, 83–84
   Divine, 19–20, 22–23, 25
   Human, 14, 19, 60, 69, 74–75, 78, 109, 197
authority, 18, 20, 24, 28–30, 34, 36, 43, 45, 50, 74–75, 78, 84–85, 90, 92, 97, 100, 130–31, 133–35, 144, 148–50, 159, 163

Belgic Confession, 3
Berakot, 13
Buxtorff, Johannes, 11, 13, 109, 158, 197, 202

cabalism, 105–7, 109, 120
Canons of Dordt, 4
Cappel, Louis, 4, 6, 74, 84, 86–87, 91, 109, 197
Castell, 11, 13, 92, 158
catechism, ix, 3, 150–51
Consensus Ministrii Bremensis Ecclesiae, 3
Chronicles, 13, 24, 59, 75, 77
Chrysostom, John, ix, 28–29, 135
clarity, 4, 17, 27–32, 61, 73, 116, 170, 202
Christ, 1, 10, 16, 34–36, 43, 55, 61, 77, 81–82, 94, 108, 112, 116–17, 122–25, 135, 141,

217

Christ (cont.)
  143, 145–47, 149, 155,
  161–64, 167, 169, 171–73,
  176–79, 181–87, 189–95, 199,
  204, 209–10
Church of England, ix, 3
Cocceius, Johannes, 5–6, 171–72,
  180–81
Cotton, 10–11, 64, 108, 112, 158
criticism, Biblical (historical and
  textual), ix, xi, 7, 10, 12,
  69–74, 77–78, 84, 109, 154,
  197

Daniel, 61, 87, 101, 115, 121, 178–79
Declaration thoruniensis, 4
derash, 40–43, 131, 134, 205
Deuteronomy, 36, 65, 74–76, 79, 82,
  97, 102, 109, 118, 163, 194,
  210–11
dictation theory, 22, 24, 75–76
divine. *See* authorship
dogmatics, 4–6, 13, 30–32, 71–73,
  109, 154

ecclesiastical, 17, 31, 42, 129, 152
ecclesiology, 134
Erastian, 14, 156
evangelical, xi, 39, 152, 182, 201,
  203, 206, 210
exegesis, ix–xi, 1–9, 11, 13, 16–19,
  40–45, 47–48, 53–54, 56,
  59, 64–65, 71, 84, 112, 114,
  130–32, 140, 142, 145, 157,
  160, 162–64, 169, 199, 201,
  203, 206–10
exegetes, xi, 3, 18, 20, 29, 40, 47,
  53–55
exegetical, ix, 1–3, 5, 11, 16–18,
  29, 39, 42–43, 47, 54, 68, 70,
  106–7, 152, 165, 198, 201,
  203–5
Exodus, 25, 56, 59–60, 77–78, 92, 95,
  97, 117–18, 120–21, 123–24,
  140, 145, 162, 177, 184, 186,
  191–92, 194, 202, 211
Ezekiel, 92, 96, 162, 178
Ezra, 74–75, 79, 82–83

figurative, 21, 41–42, 44–46, 166–67,
  171, 188
First Principles, xiv, 20, 36, 166, 209
Flacius, 21, 29, 70, 150, 205
Formula Consensus Helvetica, 4, 85
fundamentalism, 75, 85, 201

Gabler, 5–6
Galatians, 164, 171, 209
Gallican Confession, 3
Genesis, 30, 36, 46, 74, 82, 86,
  97, 102–3, 106, 111, 115,
  123, 126–27, 136, 140, 146,
  163, 169, 178–79, 183, 190,
  194–95, 205, 207
Grammatico(al)-historical, 6, 19, 29,
  39, 72, 73, 149–50, 158–60,
  169, 171, 197

Habakkuk, 117
halakha, 41
Hebrews, 91, 182, 187
Heidelberg, 3, 151
hell, 65, 120, 139, 141, 155, 185
Heptaglot, 13
hermeneutic, x, xi, 1–9, 11–18,
  20–21, 27, 31, 43–44, 47, 49,
  53, 55, 65, 72, 94–95, 111,
  117–18, 129, 132, 134–35,
  142, 152–53, 159, 161, 163,
  165, 169, 171, 194, 197,
  202–9, 212
Holy Spirit (Ghost), 20–27, 29, 32,
  34, 38, 45, 47, 74, 77–78, 80,
  88, 104–5, 107, 113, 117–18,
  121–22, 125, 147, 185, 189,
  196–98
Hosea, 37, 59, 168, 175
human. *See* authorship

incarnation, 66, 185
inspiration, 4, 6, 20, 22–23, 25–26,
    31, 71, 85, 98, 152
intellect(ual), ix–x, 2, 3, 5, 9, 16, 21,
    25–26, 41, 54, 58–60, 68
interpretation, 1–7, 9, 11–12, 14,
    16, 20–21, 27–31, 36, 39, 41,
    43–47, 49, 60, 69, 72, 86, 92,
    94, 109, 117, 122–23, 129,
    132, 134, 145, 147, 150–52,
    154, 163–64, 166, 168–72,
    180, 196, 198
Irish Articles of Religion, 4
Isaiah, 38, 44, 85, 108, 137, 143, 146,
    163, 168, 202

Jeremiah, 37, 75, 77, 146, 175
Jew, 12, 17, 103, 198
Job, 102, 117, 119–20, 140, 192–93
John, 25, 57, 60–62, 70, 92–94, 96,
    123–24, 147, 153–54, 161,
    167, 172, 178, 183, 187–88,
    190, 192–93
John the Baptist, 96, 123, 143, 173,
    183
Jonah, 56, 144, 187
Joshua, 14, 73–75, 119, 123, 145,
    191–92
Judaica, 5, 8, 11–12, 73, 142
Judaism, xi, 17, 19–20, 35, 38,
    40–41, 43, 46, 49, 52–56, 68,
    130–31, 141–43, 148–49,
    152–54, 159, 196–98, 203–4,
    207–8
Jude, 77, 105, 189, 194

Lamentations, 108
language, 3, 5, 10, 12, 15, 22, 26–28,
    30, 38, 47, 53–54, 61, 69–70,
    72–74, 79–81, 84–85, 91–94,
    96–98, 100, 102, 105, 109,
    126, 128, 136, 141, 150, 160,
    188
Leviticus, 183, 211

Lightfoot, John,
literal sense, ix, x, xi, 16–17, 19–21,
    38–47, 72, 129, 134–35, 149,
    157–59, 162–63, 167, 171,
    199, 204–5
literalism, ix, 39, 41–43, 114
logic, 31–32, 41, 48–49, 51–52,
    54–55, 64–67, 134, 160
London Polyglott, 6
Luke, 24–26, 63, 65, 104–5, 124, 145,
    153, 161, 183, 193
LXX, xiii, 89–90, 92, 98, 100–104,
    111, 156, 191

Malachi, 38, 82, 107, 137, 195
Matthew, 21, 37, 63–64, 80, 82, 88,
    96, 120, 137, 140, 145, 148,
    153, 158, 175, 182, 185, 195
Mark, 74, 124, 147, 153–54
Masoretic Text (MT), xiv, 6, 13, 79,
    83–86, 88, 91, 93–98, 101–2.
    104, 106, 110, 197
Micah, 119
Midrash, 10, 12, 43, 87, 142, 198,
    204, 207–8, 210
millenium, 140–41, 156
Mishna, 54, 86, 94, 124, 198, 203
m. Meg, 81, 86
Moses, 3, 20, 59, 61–63, 74–76, 78,
    93, 95, 97, 105, 108, 118–20,
    123–24, 138, 144–45, 165,
    172, 176–77, 185, 191, 193–94
Musculus, 28–29, 149

Nahum, 145
Nehemiah, 80
neo-orthodoxy, 17
Numbers, 78, 95, 108, 118, 176,
    210–11

Obadiah, 77
obscure, 13, 19, 27–29, 32–34, 39,
    47, 62–63, 69, 72, 75, 137,
    142, 165, 172

Obs. Sac., xiv, 180
ODJR, xiv, 50
Old Testament, xi, 6, 10, 18–19, 21–22, 24–26, 35–37, 44–46, 59, 61, 69–70, 76–77, 80–81, 85, 89, 95–96, 98, 102–4, 107–8, 115–24, 128, 134–35, 142, 144, 147, 160–64, 166–67, 169–75, 177–78, 183–96, 199, 201–12
Origen, ix, 20, 22, 28, 36, 44, 133, 166, 209

patristic, ix, 135, 150,
Patrologia Latina, xiv, 134
PG, xiv, 21
Pentateuch, 3, 6, 14, 74–76, 86, 93, 201, 204, 206–7
perspicuity, ix, x, 27–28, 30–31, 35, 43
Peter, 24, 32, 96, 140, 194–95
Peshat, 40–43, 94, 97, 132, 205–6
Pesiq. Rab. Kah., xiv, 166
Philo, 41, 145, 164–65, 167, 205–6
Philologia Sac., xiv, 180
Philology, philological, 22, 71, 73, 87
PL, xiv, 21
Pope(ry), 112, 135, 138, 140–41, 148, 196
Praescr., xiv, 133
Presbyterian, ix, 9, 202,
presupposition, vii, 1, 13, 17–20, 22, 27, 31, 47, 49, 64, 81, 91, 117–18, 137, 139, 142, 201
priest, 55, 175, 185–86, 193
Princ., xiv, 21, 36, 133, 166
prophecy, 24, 36–37, 62, 77, 82, 163, 166, 172–80, 193, 195, 199, 203, 210
Protestant, ix–1, 3–7, 13–14, 17–18, 23, 30–32, 35, 43, 49, 51–53, 68, 70–74, 83–85, 91, 112, 129–30, 141, 149–52, 158–59, 163, 196–98

Protestantism, x, 50, 53, 56, 141, 159
Protestant Orthodoxy, xi, 1, 4–7, 17–18, 30, 52, 68, 70, 73–74, 84, 91, 112, 130, 149, 151, 159, 163, 168, 170, 197
PRRD, xiv, 5–7, 13–14, 28–30, 32, 36, 48, 53, 58, 70–74, 83–85, 87, 91–92, 101, 134, 149–52, 159, 163, 169–71
Psalms, 36, 59–60, 63, 77, 97, 120, 163, 176, 177
psalms, 77, 170, 176–77
Puritan, xi, 1–3, 5, 7, 10–12, 129, 201, 203–8, 210

quadriga, 29, 44

Rabbi, 12, 78
  Eliezer, 187, 204
  Ishmael, 206
  Japhet, 56
  Menasseh Ben Israel, 11
  Nathan, 204
  Simeon, 66
  Yizhak Caro, 55, 202
rabbinic, 9, 10, 14, 41, 43, 55, 71, 86, 98, 106, 109, 131, 143, 198
reason, 17, 34, 40, 42. 47–51, 53–68, 113, 143
redactor, 75, 77–78
Reformation, ix–xiv, 3, 5–7, 9, 16, 21, 27, 30, 35–36, 46, 50, 52–53, 58, 64, 68, 101, 109, 114, 134–35, 142, 149, 154, 170, 201–2, 207–8, 210–11
reformation, 74, 163, 185
Revelation, 60–61, 63, 121–22, 140–41, 155
Rome (Roman Catholic), x, 27, 32, 34, 49, 52, 55, 56, 68, 74, 97, 135, 137–42, 148–49, 152, 154–55, 176, 184, 196–98
Romans, 15, 66, 97, 151

rules, 16–17, 19–20, 22, 27, 44,
    47–48, 51, 57, 64–67, 69, 78,
    88–89, 138, 146, 160–62, 168,
    170, 180–81, 189, 194, 196–98

Sabbath, 15, 63, 80, 94, 115, 123–24,
    144, 155, 178, 182–83, 192
Sabbat, 40, 42, 80
Samaritan, 12, 93, 111
Samuel, 117, 165, 177
Scots Confession, 3
Second Helvetic, 3–4
sensus literalis, xi, 1, 16, 18–20,
    38–40, 42–43, 46–47, 63,
    66, 73, 91, 108, 130–34, 158,
    160–61, 163, 197, 203
Septuagint, xiii, 90, 98–99, 103, 105,
    135
Simon, Richard, 14, 74, 77
Solomon, 33–34, 38, 79, 124,
    191–92, 194
Song of Solomon, 194
SOS Rabbah., xiv, 79,

Talmud, 1–13, 40–41, 79–81, 87–88,
    93, 99, 101, 105, 124, 131,
    142–46, 148, 158, 203, 207,
    210
targum, 13, 81, 86, 92, 94–97, 207,
    210–11
Tertullian, 38, 62, 133, 136
Thirty-Nine Articles, 3
Titus, 161

transubstantiation, 55, 139, 184
type, 41, 163, 166, 169–70, 173–75,
    178–84, 186–91, 193, 195
typology, ix, 2, 18, 20, 161, 163,
    166–67, 169–71, 173–74,
    178–83, 188–92, 195, 203–4,
    206–7

Ussher, James 91, 112–15, 126–27,
    205, 208, 210

Vermigli, Peter Martyr, 29
via media, xi, 17, 20, 68, 109, 130,
    159, 197–98
vowel(s), 6, 13–14, 65, 69, 73, 78,
    83–91, 102, 107, 210
Vulgate, 69, 83, 91–93, 101, 153

Walton, Brian, 6, 12–13, 83, 85, 87,
    91, 158
Westminster Assembly, ix, 7, 10–11,
    14, 113, 152, 154, 156, 158–
    59, 197, 202, 205, 207, 211
Westminster Confession, 4,
Westminster Confession of Faith,
    14, 152
Westminster Divine, 1, 15, 127
Westminster Standard, x
Westminster Theological Journal,
    205, 209, 211
Westminster Theological Seminary,
    x–xii

Scripture Index

OLD TESTAMENT/ HEBREW BIBLE

Genesis
1–11	127
1–3	46
1	106, 123
1:1	123
1:2	146
3:15	178
4:1	82
4:7	86
5	102
5:29	190
6	97, 136
12	179
47:31	103
49	178
49:10	36

Exodus
1:14–15	95
2	145
2:14	124
7:11	95
10	120
12:1	123
17:14–16	118
18	78, 118
18:12–16	118
20:5	25, 60, 121
20:12	162
22:28	97
30	92

Leviticus
16:22	183

Numbers
10:10	78, 118
10:11	78, 118
10:25	108
11:1	108
22:22	95
22:24	95
24:24	176

Deuteronomy
1:6–19	118
17:16	79
29:28	65
29:29	109
33	194
33:2	82, 102
34	74, 76
34:5	97

Joshua
2	192
5	192

1 Samuel
21	77

2 Samuel
19	154
19:29	23, 26, 37, 154

1 Kings
12:24	140
15:14	23–24

2 Kings
2	145

1 Chronicles
16	77

Nehemiah
8:8	80

Job
4:18	140
5:2	140

Psalms
18	77
37	120
37:28	120
69	97
78	120
78:49	120
88	59
88–89	77, 176
96	77
99	177
105	77
105:28	120

Song of Solomon
1:5–6	194

Isaiah
8:2	85
8:19, 20	137
9:7	108
11:4	146
11:6–7	168
53	143
58:7	44

Jeremiah
22:30	146
49:1	77

Ezekiel
8:17	92
11:1	162
36:2	162, 178
36:25	162

Daniel
9:21	179
12	178
12:12, 13	87, 101

Hosea
2:20–23	168
11	175

Amos
9:13–14	168

Jonah
1:16	187
2:5	56

Nahum
1:3	145

Malachi
4:4	107

NEW TESTAMENT

Matthew
1	120
1:5	145
1:8	120
1:22	21
2	175
2:6	21
2:15	37
2:17	21
2:18	37, 175
3:3	21

Matthew (cont.)

4:14	21
5:18	80
6:2	158
12:24	82
15:3	148
16:15	153
17:2	63
27:33	96, 153
27:38	64
28:1	182

Mark

3:17	153
9:1	147
10:10	153
15:6	154
15:25	124

Luke

1:3	25
1:70, 71	161
2:42	124
3:23	193
3:36	104
11:41	153
16:22	65
22:19	183
24:44	63

John

19:1	124
1:4	161
1–14	25
1:5	172
1:29	183
1:51	193
3	25
3:3	25
4:35	167
8:44	94
8:56	190
13:1	93, 153
13:23	92
14:26	147
16:23	147
17:24	57
18:39	154
19:14	192
19:34	187

Acts

8:38	178
11:28	176
13:2	176
17:31	50
21:10	176

Romans

8:23	185
5:9	15
5:17–19	15
9	66
11:10	97
12	151

1 Corinthians

1:21	104
14	96, 99–101, 103
10:4	194
14:2	80

2 Corinthians

5:21	183

Galatians

4:22–24	164

2 Timothy

3:8	95

Titus

1:2	161

Hebrews

4:3	182
9:19	187

1 Peter	
2:24	183
3:19–21	194
3:20–21	195

2 Peter	
2	77
2:15	96
3:15–16	24

1 John	
5:7	70, 107

Jude	
9	189

Revelation	
12:9	63
20:5	156
20:7–8	141

www.ingramcontent.com/pod-product-compliance
Lightning Source LLC
Chambersburg PA
CBHW062020220426
43662CB00010B/1407